DATE DUE

THE SECOND
AMERICAN
REVOLUTION

BOOKS BY GORE VIDAL

NOVELS

Williwaw
In a Yellow Wood
The City and the Pillar
The Season of Comfort
A Search for the King
Dark Green, Bright Red
The Judgment of Paris
Messiah
Julian
Washington, D.C.
Myra Breckinridge
Two Sisters
Burr
Myron
1876
Kalki
Creation

SHORT STORIES

A Thirsty Evil

PLAYS

An Evening with Richard Nixon
Weekend
Romulus
The Best Man
Visit to a Small Planet

ESSAYS

Rocking the Boat
Reflections upon a Sinking Ship
Homage to Daniel Shays
Matters of Fact and of Fiction
The Second American Revolution

THE SECOND AMERICAN REVOLUTION

And Other Essays

(1976-1982)

GORE VIDAL

Random House   New York

Most of the essays have been previously published in the following publica-
tions: *Esquire, Los Angeles Times, The New York Review of Books,* and
Playboy. Grateful acknowledgment is made to the following for permission
to reprint previously published material: *The Nation*: "Some Jews and the
Gays" by Gore Vidal, from *The Nation*, November 14, 1981. Reprinted
by permission. *New Statesman*: "He Dwells with Beauty" by Gore Vidal,
from *New Statesman*, March 17, 1978. Reprinted by permission.

Library of Congress Cataloging in Publication Data
Vidal, Gore, 1925-
The second American revolution and other essays
(1976-1982)
I. Title.
PS3543.I26S28   814'.54   81-48281
ISBN 0-394-52265-6   AACR2

Manufactured in the United States of America

9 8 7 6 5 4 3 2

FIRST EDITION

For Grace Zaring Stone

Contents

THE SECOND
AMERICAN
REVOLUTION

F. Scott Fitzgerald's Case

Francis Scott Fitzgerald was born 1896 in St. Paul, Minnesota; he died 1940 in Hollywood, California, at 1443 North Hayworth Avenue, within walking distance of Schwab's drugstore, then as now a meeting place for those on their way up or down in what is still known in that part of the world as The Industry, elsewhere as the movies.

Between 1920 and 1940, Fitzgerald published four novels, 160 short stories, some fragments of autobiography. He worked on a dozen film scripts. He also wrote several thousand letters, keeping carbon copies of the ones most apt to present posterity with his side of a number of matters that he thought important. Although very little of what Fitzgerald wrote has any great value as literature, his sad life continues to provide not only English Departments but the movies with a Cautionary Tale of the first magnitude. Needless to say, Scott Fitzgerald is now a major academic industry. Currently, there are two new models in the bookstores, each edited by Professor Matthew J. Bruccoli. *The Notebooks of F. Scott Fitzgerald* contains all 2,078 notebook entries while *Correspondence of F. Scott Fitzgerald* includes letters to as well as from Fitzgerald.

A quick re-cap of the Fitzgerald career: in 1920, he published *This Side of Paradise* and married the handsome Zelda Sayre. In 1921, they set out for the territory—in those days, Europe. But the Fitzgeralds' Europe was hardly the Europe of James's "The Passionate Pilgrim." The Fitzgeralds never got around to seeing the sights because, as Jazz Age celebrities, they were the sights. They wanted to have a good time and a good time was had by all for a short time. Then things fell apart. Crash of '29. Zelda's madness. Scott's alcoholism. As Zelda went from one expensive *clinique* to another, money was in short supply. Scott's third and best novel, *The Great Gatsby* (1925), did not make money. Novel number four did not come easily. Back to America in 1931: Baltimore, Wilmington. Fitzgerald made two trips to Hollywood where he wrote movie scripts for money; he made the money but no movies.

The relative failure of *Tender Is the Night* (1934) came at a time when Fitzgerald's short stories no longer commanded the sort of magazine prices that had made the living easy in the Twenties. After a good deal of maneuvering, Fitzgerald wangled a six-month contract as a staff writer for MGM. At $1,000 a week, he was one of the highest paid movie writers. From 1937 to 1940, Fitzgerald wrote movies in order to pay his debts; to pay for Zelda's sanitarium and for his daughter's school; to buy time in which to write a novel. Despite a dying heart, he did pretty much what he set out to do.

In a sense, Fitzgerald's final days are quite as heroic as those of General Grant, as described in *General Grant's Last Stand*, a book that the Scribner's editor, Maxwell Perkins, rather tactlessly sent Fitzgerald after reading the three sad autobiographical sketches in *Esquire* (reprinted, posthumously, by Edmund Wilson in *The Crack-Up*).

"I enjoyed reading *General Grant's Last Stand*," Fitzgerald replied with considerable dignity under the circumstances, "and was conscious of your particular reasons for sending it to me. It is needless to compare the difference in force of character between myself and General Grant, the number of words he could write in a year" (while dying of cancer, dead broke), "and the absolutely virgin field which he exploited with the experiences of a four-year life under the most dramatic of circumstances." It was also needless to mention that despite a failed presidency, a personal bankruptcy, a history of alcoholism, Grant had had such supreme victories as Shiloh, Vicksburg, Appomattox, while Fitzgerald had had only one—*The Great Gatsby*, a small but perfect operation comparable, say, to Grant's investiture of Fort Donelson.

At the time of Fitzgerald's death in 1940, he was already something of a period-piece, a relic of the Jazz Age, of flappers and bathtub gin. The last decade of Fitzgerald's life began with the Depression and ended with World War II; midway through the Thirties, the Spanish Civil War politicized most of the new writers, and many of the old. Predictably, Ernest Hemingway rode out the storm, going triumphantly from the bad play *The Fifth Column* to the bad novel *For Whom the Bell Tolls* (Fitzgerald's comment: "a thoroughly superficial book with all the profundity of *Rebecca*"). Nevertheless, with characteristic panache, the great careerist managed to keep himself atop the heap at whose roomy bottom Fitzgerald had now taken up permanent residence.

But, sufficiently dramatized, failure has its delights, as Fitzgerald demonstrated in those autobiographical pieces which so outraged his old friend, John Dos Passos, who wrote: "Christ, man, how do you find time in the middle of the general conflagration to worry about all that stuff?" But all that stuff was all that Fitzgerald ever had to deal with and he continued to confront his own private conflagration until it consumed him, while eating chocolate on a winter's day just off Sunset Boulevard.

At Princeton, Fitzgerald and Edmund Wilson were friends; they continued to be friends to the end even though Wilson was an intellectual of the most rigorous sort while Fitzgerald was barely literate. Yet they must have had something in common beyond shared youth, time, place, and I suspect that that something was the sort of high romanticism which Fitzgerald personified and Wilson only dreamed of, as he pined for Daisy.

When Wilson put together a volume of Fitzgeraldiana and called it *The Crack-Up*, the dead failed writer was totally, if not permanently, resurrected. Since 1945, there have been hundreds, perhaps thousands of biographies, critical studies, Ph.D. theses written about Fitzgerald. Ironically, the movies which so fascinated and frustrated Fitzgerald have now turned him and Zelda into huge mythic monsters, forever sweeping 'round to *Wiener* waltzes en route to the last reel where they sputter out like a pair of Roman candles on a rainy Fourth of July—disenchanted, beloved infidels.

For Americans, a writer's work is almost always secondary to his life—or life-style, as they say nowadays. This means that the novelist's biographer is very apt to make more, in every sense, out of the life than the writer who lived it. Certainly, Fitzgerald's personal story is a perennially fascinating Cautionary Tale. As for his novels, the two that were popular in his lifetime were minor books whose themes—not to mention titles—appealed enormously to the superstitions and the prejudices of the middle class: *This Side of Paradise* and *The Beautiful and Damned*—if that last title isn't still a lu-lu out on the twice-born circuit where Cleaver and Colson flourish, I will reread the book. But when Fitzgerald finally wrote a distinguished novel, the audience was not interested. What, after all, is the *moral* to Gatsby? Since there seemed to be none, *The Great Gatsby* failed and that was the end of F. Scott Fitzgerald, glamorous best seller of yesteryear, bold chronicler of girls who kissed. It was also to be the beginning of what is now a formidable legend: the "archetypal" writer of whom Cyril Connolly keened (in *The New Yorker*, April 10, 1948) "the young man slain in his glory." Actually, the forty-four-year-old wreck at the bottom of Laurel Canyon was neither young nor in his glory when he dropped dead. But five years later, when Wilson itemized the wreckage, he re-created for a new generation the bright, blond youth, forever glorious, doomed.

Professor Bruccoli's edition of *The Notebooks* comes highly recommended. Mr. James Dickey, the poet and novelist, thinks that "they should be a bible for all writers. But one does not have to be a writer to respond to them—these *Notebooks* make writers of us all." If true, this is indeed a breakthrough. Why go to Bread Loaf when you, too, can earn good money and get tenure by reading a single book? Mr. Budd Schulberg, the novelist, says, "Of all the Notebook masters, beyond Butler, Bennett, even Jules Renaud [*sic*], Fitzgerald emerges—in our judgment—as not only the most thorough and professional but the most entertaining and evocative." This is a stunning assessment. Better than Butler? Better than Jules Renard? Rush to your bookstore! At last, an aphorist superior to the man who wrote in his *cahier*, "I find that when I do not think of myself, I do not think at all."

Professor Bruccoli is understandably thrilled by *The Notebooks* which "were [Fitzgerald's] workshop and chronicle. They were his literary bankroll. They were also his confessional." Edmund Wilson disagrees. In the introduction to *The Crack-Up*, Wilson notes that, even at Princeton, Fitzgerald had been so much an admirer of Butler's *Notebooks* that when he came to fill up his own notebooks it was "as if he were preparing a book to be read as well as a storehouse for his own convenience. . . . Actually, he seems rarely to have used them."

The entries range from idle jottings, proper names, and jokes to extended descriptions and complaints. I fear that I must part company with Wilson, who finds these snippets "extremely good reading." For one thing, many entries are simply cryptic. "Hobey Baker." That's all. Yes, one knows—or some of us know—that Baker was a golden football player at Princeton in Fitzgerald's day. So what? The name itself is just a name and nothing more. As for the longer bits and pieces, they serve only to remind us that even in his best work, Fitzgerald had little wit and less humor. Although in youth he had high spirits (often mistaken in freedom's home for humor) these entries tend toward sadness; certainly, he is filled with self-pity, self-justification, self . . . not love so much as a deep and abiding regard.

In general, Fitzgerald's notes are just notes or reminders. Here are some, presumably numbered by Professor Bruccoli:

12 Sgt. Este
137 Ogden and Jesus
375 Let's all live together.
975 Paul Nelson from School Play Onward
1058 Tie up with Faulkner—Lord Fauntleroy. [If only he had!]
1128 De Sano tearing the chair
1270 Actors the clue to much
1411 Bunny Burgess episode of glass and wife.
1443 The rejection slips
1463 Memory of taking a pee commencement night
1514 Coat off in theatre

I'm not at all sure how these little notes can make writers of us all or even of Fitzgerald. Certainly, they do not entertain or evoke in their present state. One can only hope that Professor Bruccoli will one day make for us a skeleton key to these notes so that we can learn just what it was that Bunny B. did with his wife and the glass. In the meantime, I shall personally develop item 1069: "The scandal of 'English Teaching.'"

There is a section devoted to descriptions of places, something Fitzgerald was very good at in his novels. Number 142 is a nice description of Los Angeles, "a city that had tripled its population in fifteen years," where children play "on the green flanks of the modern boulevard . . . with their knees marked by the red stains of the mercurochrome era, played with toys with a purpose—beams that taught engineering, soldiers that taught manliness, and dolls that taught motherhood. When the dolls were so banged up that they stopped looking like real babies and began to look like dolls, the children developed affection for them." That is sweetly observed. But too many of these descriptions are simply half-baked or strained. The description of a place or mood that is not in some way connected to action is to no point at all.

Those journals and notebooks that are intended to be read must, somehow, deal with real things that are complete in themselves. Montaigne does not write: "Cardinal's house at Lucca," and leave it at that. But then Montaigne was a man constantly thinking about what he had read and observed in the course of a life in the world. Fitzgerald seems not to have read very much outside the Romantic tradition, and though his powers of observation were often keen and precise when it came to the sort of detail that interested him (class differences, remembered light), he had no real life in the world. Early on, he chose to live out a romantic legend that had no reference to anything but himself and Zelda and the child.

As I read *The Notebooks*, I was struck by the lack of literary references (other than a number of quite shrewd comments about Fitzgerald's contemporaries). Although most writers who keep notebooks make random jottings, they also tend to comment on their reading. Fitzgerald keeps an eye out for the competition and that's about it. By the time I got to the section labeled "Epigrams, Wise Cracks and Jokes," I wondered if he had ever read Gide. Whether or not he had read Gide is forever moot. But he had certainly heard of him. "Andre Gide lifted himself by his own jockstrap so to speak—and one would like to see him hoisted on his own pedarasty [*sic*]." Epigram? Wisecrack? Joke?

In these *Notebooks* Fitzgerald makes rather too many nervous references to fairies and pansies. But then his attitudes toward the lesser breeds were very much those of everyone else in those days: "1719 the gibbering dinges on the sidewalks; 1921 Arthur Kober type of Jew without softness . . . trying to realize himself outside of Jewry; 1974 *Native Son*—A well written penny dreadful with the apparent moral that it is good thing for the cause when a feeble minded negro runs amuck."

There are lines from *The Notebooks* which have been much used in biographies of Fitzgerald; even so, they still retain their pathos: "1362 I left my capacity for hoping on the little roads that led to Zelda's sanitarium." But most of the personal entries are simply sad and not very interesting. To hear him tell it, again and again: once upon a time, he was a success and now he's a failure; he was young and now he's middle-aged.

Out of 2,078 entries, I can find only one line worthy of Jules Renard: "In order to bring on the revolution it may be necessary to work inside the communist party." That's funny. Otherwise, Fitzgerald's observations resemble not Jules Renard but, as Mr. Schulberg has noted, Jules Renaud.

One would have thought that Andrew Turnbull's collection of Fitzgerald's letters was all that any reasonable admirer of Fitzgerald would ever need. Fitzgerald was not exactly the sort of letter-writer for whose *pensées* one sprints, as it were, to the mailbox to see if he's remembered to write. When Fitzgerald is not asking for money, he is explaining and complaining. But Professor Matthew J. "research begets research" Bruccoli thinks otherwise. In *Correspondence* he now gives us an altogether too rich display of Fitzgerald's letters complete with the master's astonishing misspellings; fortunately, he has had the good sense, even compassion for the reader, to include a number of interesting letters *to* Fitzgerald. If the marvelous letters of Zelda do not make this project absolutely worthwhile, they at least provide some literary pleasure in the course of a correspondence which, on Fitzgerald's side, is pretty depressing.

Certainly, Fitzgerald had a good deal to gripe about and, to a point, these cries at midnight are poignant. But they are also monotonous. Since Fitzgerald's correspondence is of current interest to a number of American graduate students, the letters deserve preservation but not publication. One can enjoy the letters of Lord Byron and Virginia Woolf without any particular knowledge of their works or even days. But Fitzgerald has not their charm or brutal force. On those rare occasions when he is not staring into the mirror, he can be interesting. "I'd like to put you on to something about Steinbeck," he wrote Wilson a month before he died. "He is a rather cagey cribber. Most of us begin as imitators but it is something else for a man of his years and reputation to steal a whole scene as he did in 'Mice and Men.' I'm sending you a marked

copy of Norris' 'McTeague' to show you what I mean. His debt
to 'The Octupus' is also enormous and his balls, when he uses them,
are usually clipped from Lawrence's 'Kangeroo.' "

Precocious talents mature slowly if at all. Despite youthful
success, there is something "hurried," as Fitzgerald put it, about
his beginnings. Hurried and oddly inauspicious: the soldier who
never fought (at one point he served under Captain Dwight D.
Eisenhower—what did they talk about?) and the athlete who never
competed. Yet, at twenty-one, Fitzgerald wrote Wilson: "God!
How I miss my youth—that's only relative of course but already
lines are beginning to coarsen *in other people* and that's the sure
sign. I don't think you ever realized at Princeton the childlike
simplicity that lay behind all my petty sophistication and my lack
of a real sense of honor." Even before Fitzgerald had a past to
search for, he was on the prowl for lost time, "borne back ceaselessly
into the past."

The most curious aspect of Fitzgerald's early days was his relationship with Monsignor Sigourney Webster Fay at the Newman
School. Fitzgerald was an uncommonly bright and pretty boy and,
from the tone of the letters that Fay wrote him, pederasty was
very much in the air. At one point, in 1917, Fitzgerald was to ac-
company Fay on a mission to Russia in order to bring the Greek
Orthodox Church back to Rome. But the Bolsheviks intervened.
Even so, the whole project has a Corvo-esque dottiness that is
appealing, and one wonders to what extent Fitzgerald understood
the nature of his loving friend whose assistant at the Newman
School, Father William Hemmick ("with his silver-buckled pumps
and cassocks tailored in Paris"), was to end his days in Rome, surrounded by golden ephebes, a practicing fairy, whose apotheosis
was to come that marvelous day when, with all the gravity and
splendor that robes by Lanvin can bestow, Monsignor Hemmick,
in the very teeth, as it were, of the Vicar of Christ on earth, united
in marriage, before the cameras of all the world, Tyrone Power
and Linda Christian. One thing about Scott, he was show-biz from
the start. Fay appears as Father Darcy in *This Side of Paradise*.
Fitzgerald's letters to Fay have vanished. Professor Bruccoli tells us
that "they are believed to have been destroyed by Fay's mother
after his death."

Since many of these letters deal with the personality of Fitzgerald (his drinking, marriage, friendships), it is not entirely idle
to speculate—but pretty idle, even so—on Fitzgerald's sex life.

There are very few youths as handsome as Fitzgerald who go unseduced by men or boys in the sort of schools that he attended. Zelda's occasional accusations that Fitzgerald was homosexual have usually been put down to the fact that she was either off her rocker or, mounted on that rocker, she was eager to wound Fitzgerald, to draw psychic blood. In a position paper which Fitzgerald may or may not have sent Zelda when she was hospitalized, he wrote: "The nearest I ever came to leaving you was when you told me you [thought] that I was a fairy in the Rue Palatine. . . ." The answer to that one is, stay away from the Rue Palatine.

Unfortunately, the street had its fascination for both of them. Zelda was drawn to Madame, her ballet teacher, while Fitzgerald made the acquaintance of a Paris tough (in the Rue Palatine?) and brought him back to America as a butler and "sparring partner." In any case, Zelda managed to so bug her husband on the subject that one day in Paris when he came to take Morley Callaghan's arm, he suddenly let go. "It was like holding on to a cold fish. You thought I was a fairy, didn't you?" In *That Summer in Paris* Callaghan says that he wished that he had been "more consoling, more demonstrative with him that night."

Whatever Fitzgerald's sexual balance, there is no doubt that he was totally absorbed in Zelda. There is little doubt that he was impotent a good deal of the time because anyone who drinks as much as Fitzgerald drank will lose, temporarily at least, the power of erection. In *Papa: A Personal Memoir*, Hemingway's son, an M.D., has made this point about his own hard-drinking father.

"One of the many ironies that inform the career of F. Scott Fitzgerald is that the writer who died 'forgotten' in 1940 is the most fully documented American author of this century." Professor Bruccoli rather smacks his lips in the introduction to the *Correspondence*. "We know more about Fitzgerald than about any of his contemporaries because he preserved the material. . . . The best Fitzgerald scholar of us was F. Scott Fitzgerald." Typing out these words I have a sense of perfect madness. *Scholar* of Fitzgerald? One sees the need for scholars of Dante, Rabelais, Shakespeare. But scholar of a contemporary popular writer who needs no introduction? Isn't this all a bit out of proportion? Are the academic mills now so huge and mindless that any writer of moderate talent and notoriety is grist? All the time wasted in collecting every scrap of paper that Fitzgerald scribbled on might be better spent in trying to understand, say, the nature of that society

which produced the Fitzgerald who wrote those letters. But today's
literary scholars are essentially fact-collectors, scholar-squirrels for
whom every season's May.

That said, one must be grateful to this particular scholar-squirrel
for publishing sixty-two of Zelda's letters to Fitzgerald. Like all
her other writings, the letters are both beautiful and evocative.
After a frantic attempt to become a ballerina, Zelda went clinically
mad. From various sanitariums she did her best to tell Fitzgerald
what going mad is like: "Every day it seems to me that things
are more barren and sterile and hopeless—In Paris, before I realized
that I was sick, there was a new significance to everything: stations
and streets and façades of buildings—colors were infinite; part of
the air, and not restricted by the lines that encompassed them and
lines were free of the masses they held. . . . Then the world became
embryonic in Africa—and there was no need for communication.
The Arabs fermenting in the vastness; the curious quality of their
eyes and the smell of ants; a detachment as if I was on the other
side of a black gauze—a fearless small feeling, and then the end
at Easter. . . ." (This quotation is from Nancy Milford's *Zelda*.) "I
would have liked to dance in New York this fall, but where am
I going to find again these months that dribble into the beets of the
clinic garden?" And "I have been living in vaporous places peopled
with one-dimensional figures and tremulous buildings until I can
no longer tell an optical illusion from a reality . . . that head and
ears incessantly throb and roads disappear. . . . Was it fun in Paris?
Who did you see there and was the Madeleine pink at five o'clock
and did the fountains fall with hollow delicacy into the framing of
space in the Place de la Concorde and did the blue creep out from
behind the Colonades of the rue de Rivoli through the grill of the
Tuileries and was the Louvre gray and metallic in the sun and did
the trees hang brooding over the cafés and were there lights at
night and the click of saucers and the auto horns that play de
Bussey. . . ."

A master of weather and landscape, Zelda was almost as good
with people. She was one of the first to realize that Hemingway
was "phony as a rubber check." When she read *A Farewell to Arms*
in manuscript, she said that the prose sounded "pretty damned
Biblical" while *The Sun Also Rises* was "bullfighting, bull-slinging
and bullshit." Of Edmund Wilson, she wrote: "Bunny's mind is too
speculative. Nothing but futures, of the race, of an idea, of politics,
of birth control. Just constant planning and querulous projecting

and no execution. And he drinks so much that he cares more than he would." No doubt, Fitzgerald was as charmed by the letters as we are. But he also understood her almost as well as he did his lifelong subject, himself. "Her letters," he wrote, "are tragically brilliant on all matters except those of actual importance. How strange to have failed as a social creature—even criminals do not fail that way—they are the law's 'Loyal Opposition' so to speak. But the insane are always mere guests on earth, eternal strangers, carrying around broken dialogues that they cannot read."

Zelda and Scott. In a curious way Zelda and Scott were meant to be perfectly combined in Plato's sense. Since this is not possible for us, each became shadow to the other and despite mutual desire and pursuit, no whole was ever achieved.

In July of 1922, Mr. and Mrs. Fitzgerald were offered the leads in a movie version of *This Side of Paradise*. Andrew Turnbull says that they turned down the offer. In 1927, Mr. and Mrs. Fitzgerald spent two months in Hollywood where he was contracted to write an original screenplay for Constance Talmadge. Although the screenplay was not used, Fitzgerald got his first look at the place where he was to live and die. In 1931, he came back to Hollywood for five weeks' work on *Red-Headed Woman* at MGM. Although Fitzgerald's script was not used, he got to know the boy genius Irving Thalberg, whose "tasteful" films (*The Barretts of Wimpole Street*) were much admired in those days. On one occasion (recorded in the story "Crazy Sunday") Fitzgerald held riveted a party at the Thalbergs with a drunken comedy number. Movie stars do not like to be upstaged by mere writers, especially drunk writers. But next day, the hostess, the ever-gracious Norma Shearer, wired Fitzgerald (no doubt after an apologetic *mea culpa* that has not survived), "I thought you were one of the most agreeable persons at our tea." In Hollywood that means you're fired; he was fired.

All Americans born between 1890 and 1945 wanted to be movie stars. On Scott Fitzgerald's first trip to Hollywood, he was given a screen test (where is it?). As early as 1920, Fitzgerald tells how "summoned out to Griffith's studio on Long Island, we trembled in the presence of the familiar faces of the *Birth of a Nation*. . . . The world of the picture actors was like our own in that it was in New York, but not of it." Later, Zelda's passion to become a ballerina was, at its core, nothing except a desire to be A Star. But like so many romantics, then and now, the Fitzgeralds did not want to go through the grim boring business of becoming movie stars. Rather they wanted to live as if they were *inside* a movie. Cut to Antibes. Dissolve to the Ritz in Paris. Fade to black in Hollywood. Each lived long enough and suffered enough to realize that movies of that sort are to be made or seen, not lived. But by then she was in a sanitarium full-time and he was a movie hack.

In "Pasting It Together" (March 1936) Fitzgerald, aged forty, made note of a cultural change that no one else seemed to have noticed.

> I saw that the novel, which at my maturity was the strongest and supplest medium for conveying thought and emotion from one human being to another, was becoming subordinated to a mechanical and communal art that, whether in the hands of Hollywood merchants or Russian idealists, was capable of reflecting only the tritest thought, the most obvious emotion. It was an art in which words were subordinate to images, where personality was worn down to the inevitable low gear of collaboration. As long past as 1930, I had a hunch that the talkies would make even the best-selling novelist as archaic as silent pictures.

Fitzgerald was right. Forty-four years later, it is the film school that attracts the bright young people while the writers' workshop caters to those whose futures will not be literary but academic. Today, certainly, no new novels by anyone commands the sort of world attention that a new film automatically gets. Yet, for reasons obscure to me, novelists still continue to echo Glenway Wescott, who wrote that Fitzgerald's hunch was "a wrong thought indeed for a novelist." I should have thought it was not wrong but inevitable.

A decade later, when I wrote that the film had replaced the novel as the central art form of our civilization, I was attacked for having said that the novel was dead and I was sent reading lists of grand new novels. Obviously, the serious novel or art-novel or whatever one wants to call the novel-as-literature will continue to be written; after all, poetry is flourishing without the patronage of the common reader. But it is also a fact that hardly anyone outside of an institution is ever apt to look at any of these literary artifacts. Worse, if the scholar-squirrel prevails, writers will not be remembered for what they wrote but for the Cautionary Tales that their lives provide. Meanwhile the sharp and the dull watch movies;

discuss movies; dream movies. Films are now shown in the classroom because it is easier to watch Pabst than to read Dreiser. At
least, it *was* easier. There is now some evidence that the current
television-commercial generation is no longer able to watch with
any degree of concentration a two-hour film without breaks. Thus,
Pabst gives way to the thirty-second Oil of Olay spot.

In our epoch, only a few good writers have been so multitalented
or so well situated in time and place that they could use film as
well as prose. Jean Cocteau, Graham Greene. . . . who else? Certainly not Faulkner, Sartre, Isherwood, Huxley. In the heyday of
the Hollywood studios no serious writer ever got a proper grip on
the system. But then few wanted to. They came to town to make
money in order to buy time to write books. But Fitzgerald was
more prescient than many of his contemporaries. He realized that
the novel was being superseded by the film; he also realized that
the film is, in every way, inferior as an art form to the novel—if
indeed such a collective activity as a movie can be regarded as an
art at all. Even so, Fitzgerald was still enough of an artist or romantic egotist to want to create movies. How to go about it?

In those days, the producer was all-powerful and everyone else
was simply a technician to be used by the producer. Naturally,
there were "stars" in each technical category. A super-hack writer
like Ben Hecht could influence the making of a film in a way that,
often, the director-technician could not or, as Fitzgerald put it in
a letter to Matthew Josephson (March 11, 1938),

> In the old days, when movies were a stringing together of the
> high points in the imagination of half a dozen drunken ex-
> newspapermen, it was true that the whole thing was the director.
> He coordinated and gave life to the material—he carried the story
> in his head. There is a great deal of carry-over from those days,
> but the situation of *Three Comrades*, where Frank Borzage had
> little more to do than be a sort of glorified cameraman, is more
> typical of today. A Bob Sherwood picture, for instance, or a
> Johnny Mahin script, could be shot by an assistant director or a
> script girl, and where in the old days an author would have
> jumped at the chance of becoming a director, there are now
> many, like Ben Hecht and the aforesaid Mahin, who hate the
> eternal waiting and monotony of the modern job.

Although Fitzgerald underplays the power of the producer (in
the case of *Three Comrades* the witty and prodigious writer-

director Joe Mankiewicz), he is right about the low opinion everyone had of the director and the importance, relatively speaking, of
the super-hack writers who pre-directed, as it were, each film by
incorporating in their scripts the exact way that the film was to
be shot. This was still pretty much the case when I was a writer
under contract to MGM a dozen years after Fitzgerald's death.
Scott was still remembered, more or less fondly.

"But," as the Wise Hack at the Writers' Table said, "there
wouldn't've been all this revival stuff, if he'd looked like Wallace
Beery." The Wise Hack had only contempt for Edmund Wilson's
labors to restore Fitzgerald's reputation. "The Emperor's tailor," he
snapped. At the Writers' Table we all snapped or riposted or even,
sometimes, like Fitzgerald, shrilled.

When I said that I'd never much liked Fitzgerald's face in the
early photographs but found the later ones touching because he
always looked as if he was trying very hard not to scream, the
Wise Hack said, "No. Not scream, whimper. There was never
such a whiner. God knows why. He had a good time around here.
Joe admired him. Got him a credit. Got his contract renewed.
Whole thing started with Eddie Knopf who was queer for writers.
It was him who talked the studio into taking Fitzgerald, the trick
of the week after all that shit he shoveled in *Esquire* about what a
drunk he was. Then Joe puts him on *Three Comrades* because he
thought he could get some good period stuff out of him. Then
when that didn't work, Joe got old Ted Paramore to help out on
the script. But that didn't work either. First day on the set, Maggie
Sullavan says, 'I can't say these lines,' and so Joe has to rewrite the
whole damned thing. So why should Scott be pissed off? He knew
enough to know that in this business the writer is the woman."

But Scott was pissed off at what Mankiewicz had done to the
script of the only film on which Fitzgerald's name was ever to
appear and for him to get what is known in the trade as a credit
(debit is usually the better word) was a giant step toward big
money, autonomy, freedom or, as Fitzgerald wrote Zelda (Fall
1937), "If I can finish one *excellent* picture to top *Three Comrades*
I think I can bargain for better terms—more rest *and* more money."
To Beatrice Dance he wrote (November 27, 1937), "I've been
working on a script of *Three Comrades*, a book that falls just
short of the 1st rate (by Remarque)—it leans a little on Hemingway and others but tells a lovely tragic story." To the same woman,
a sadder if no wiser Fitzgerald wrote four months later, "*Three*

Comrades, the picture I have just finished, is in production and though it bears my name, my producer could not resist the fascination of a pencil and managed to obliterate most signs of my personality." To his mother-in-law, Fitzgerald wrote in the next month (April 23, 1938): "*Three Comrades* should be released within ten days, and a good third of that is absolutely mine." But a few weeks later he wrote his sister-in-law: "*Three Comrades* is awful. It was *entirely* rewritten by the producer. I'd rather Zelda didn't see it."

But Zelda saw it and thought that a lot of it was very good even though

> there isn't any dramatic continuity—which robs the whole of suspense. I know it's hard to get across a philosophic treatise on the screen, but it would have been better had there been the sense of some inevitable thesis making itself known in spite of the characters—or had there been the sense of characters dominated by some irresistible dynamic purpose. It drifts; and the dynamics are scattered and sporadic rather than cumulative or sustained.

Even in the loony bin, Zelda was a better critic than the ineffable Frank Nugent of *The New York Times* (who loved the picture) or Fitzgerald, who had written a so-so first draft of a film that was to be altered not only during a collaboration with one Ted (*The Bitter Tea of General Yen*) Paramore but, finally, redone by the producer Joe Mankiewicz.

Fitzgerald's first-draft screenplay was completed September 1, 1937. Edited by the ubiquitous Professor Bruccoli, Fitzgerald's screenplay was published in 1978, along with the various letters that Fitzgerald wrote but did not always send to Mankiewicz and the heads of the studio as well as the position paper that he did give to his collaborator Paramore. In an afterword, Professor Bruccoli gives a short history of the film's production; he also compares the penultimate screenplay with Fitzgerald's first draft.

Now I have always been suspicious of the traditional Cautionary Tale of Fitzgerald's fragile genius, broken on the rack of commerce by "an ignorant and vulgar gent" (Fitzgerald in a letter to Beatrice Dance, four months after the picture's release). Inspired and excited by Professor Brucccoli's researches, I have now turned scholar-squirrel myself. I have penetrated the so-called "vault" at MGM where I was allowed to read not only a copy of the actual shooting script of *Three Comrades* (dated February 2, 1938) but also the revisions that Mankiewicz made during the course of the filming. I also know the answer to the question that has so puzzled my fellow squirrels: did Mankiewicz ever receive Fitzgerald's letter of protest, dated January 20, 1938? He. . . . But let us not get ahead of our story.

On November 5, 1937, the first Fitzgerald-Paramore script was handed in. There was a story conference: one can imagine what it was like. Mankiewicz talking rapidly, eyes opening wide for emphasis while the faded Fitzgerald thought about the last drink—and the next drink; and Paramore did whatever it is that Paramores did or do. Subsequently, two more revised scripts were handed in by Fitzgerald-Paramore. Then between their last script, dated December 21, and the script of January 21, *something happened*.

On January 20, the day before the penultimate script was mimeographed, Fitzgerald wrote Mankiewicz a furious letter in which he attacked the radical changes that Mankiewicz had made in the script. Although Mankiewicz is on record as saying that "Scott Fitzgerald really wrote very bad spoken dialogue," I don't think that this is true. But we shall never know for certain because little of his dialogue ever made it to the screen. In the case of *Three Comrades*, Fitzgerald thought that "37 pages mine about 1/3." I'd say it was rather less.

In Fitzgerald's original script the boy-girl dialogues are charming and, curiously enough, far less wordy than the final version's. Fitzgerald's lack of humor might not have been so noticeable in an anti-Nazi tear-jerker were it not for the fact that Mankiewicz is one of the few genuine wits ever to come out of Hollywood. Where Fitzgerald's dialogue tended to be too sweet, Mankiewicz's dialogue was often pretty sour; the combination was not entirely happy. In any case, Fitzgerald never did get the point to Mankiewicz's jokes.

Fitzgerald's original script was overlong and somewhat confusing. In an excess of conscientiousness, he had studied so many old movies that there was hardly a cliché that he overlooked. When the hero telephones the heroine's sanitarium "CUT TO: QUICK TRAVELING SHOT OF A LINE OF TELEPHONE POLES IN WINTER—The line goes up a snowy mountain. CUT TO:" . . . Mel Brooks cutting the line.

Remarque's story of three German World War I buddies who go into the car-repair business during the rise of the Nazis was plainly not congenial to Fitzgerald's talents but since he needed the money, he did what all good writers who write for hire instinctively do: he pulled the narrative in his own direction. He made the German girl Pat (a rich girl now poor) into a Fitzgerald heroine and he made the boy Bobby (Erich in the final script) into a Fitzgerald hero. Once again, Scott and Zelda light up if not the sky the first-draft screenplay. Erich now has an unacknowledged drinking problem—hardly a page goes by that he doesn't think of bottles of rum or ask for a double whisky (not the usual tipple of your average Weimar Republic worker-lad). Erich's two comrades and the cleaning woman also, as they say in the script, "prosit" quite a lot.

When Pat is dying of tuberculosis in a sanitarium, Fitzgerald has a field day and much of the dialogue is charming. But even in Culver City, Fitzgerald could not escape the shadow of his monstrous friend Hemingway. "*Pat (as if to herself)*: It's raining. It's been raining too long. At night sometimes when I wake, I imagine we're quite buried under all the rain." Fans of *A Farewell to Arms* will recall the soon-to-be-dying Catherine's speech as "All right. I'm afraid of the rain because sometimes I see me dead in it." Told that this is all nonsense, Catherine agrees: " 'It's all nonsense. It's only nonsense. I'm not afraid of the rain. I'm not afraid of the rain. Oh, oh, God, I wish I wasn't.' She was crying. I comforted her and she stopped crying. But outside it kept on raining." There was a lot of rain in those days. Luckily most of it was outside.

Fitzgerald was not entirely at ease with the talk of young men in the car-repair business. He was also hampered by Hollywood's insistence that an English-speaking film about Germans in Germany should be loaded with *achs* and *auf Wiedersehens* and *Herrs*. Mankiewicz also maintains the silliness: the one *auf Wiedersehen* in the script is his. Since profanity was not allowed in those chaste days, Fitzgerald has the lower orders accuse one another of being "twerps," "squirts," "greasepots," when today he would doubtless have used the more succinct if somewhat bleak epithet for all seasons and occasions "ass-hole." Fitzgerald also loaded the script with such epithets as "Holy Cats!" and "Great Snakes!" Wisely, Mankiewicz replaced Scott's cats and snakes with emotion-charged ellipses.

Now for Fitzgerald's January 20 letter. According to Professor Bruccoli, "Mankiewicz has stated that he never received this letter, which survives in a carbon copy in Fitzgerald's papers. Since there is no closing on the letter, it is possible that Fitzgerald did not send

it." But Fitzgerald sent the letter; *and Mankiewicz read the letter.*
Proof?

In Fitzgerald's script the boy and the dying girl are on a balcony,
gazing out over what is supposed to be Thomas Mann's magic
mountain but is actually Sonja Henie's winter wonderland. *"Pat:
Is that the road home? Erich:* Yes. *Pat:* How far is it? *Erich:*
About five hundred miles. In May you'll be starting back along
that road. *Pat:* In May. My God, in May!" Fitzgerald left it at
that—and why not? The dialogue comes straight from Remarque's
novel.

Mankiewicz kept the dialogue. But then he moved the couple
off the balcony and into Pat's bedroom at the sanitarium. Daringly,
they sit on the bed for a really serious chat. After Pat's "(*unbeliev-
ingly*): In May. My God, in May!" Mankiewicz adds: "(*a pause
then she turns to him*): But we're not saying what we should be
saying this first time together. (*he looks at her puzzled*) All these
months I'd figured out what you would say and I would say—
word for word. Do you want to hear? (*he nods, smiling*) We'd be
sitting here on the foot of this bed like this, hand in hand, and
you'd ask, what time is it and I'd say that doesn't matter now. We
love each other beyond time and place now. And you'd say, that's
right. God's in this room with us, lightning's in this room, and the
sea and the sky and the mountains are in this room with us. And
you'd kiss me on the forehead and I'd say, how cool your lips are,
don't move away—(*he kisses her on the forehead*). And you'd say,
ought I to be in this room now? Aren't we breaking the rules? And
I'd say must I start now—not breaking them—(*he looks into her
eyes, unsmiling*) because I can't let you go and then you'd say hello,
Pat, and I'd say, Erich, hello, and suddenly it would all be so real it
would stab my heart and—*Erich:* But—darling—" They embrace
"fiercely" and the camera sails out the window en route to the
magic mountain and Settembrini and Naphta in the distance.

After Fitzgerald read this scene, he wrote Mankiewicz that
Pat's big speech is "utter drool out of *True Romances* . . . God
and 'cool lips,' whatever they are, and lightning and elephantine
play on words. The audience's feeling will be 'Oh, go on and die.' "

Now if there is ever any way of making nervous the sardonic
Mankiewicz it is to call him corny. Like Billy Wilder, he does not
go in for scenes out of *True Romances*. Between January 20 and
February 2 Mankiewicz rewrote the scene. He cut out "God" and
"cool lips" and "lightning." Here is Pat's aria revised: "Well, we'd

be laying here on the foot of this bed just like this, and I'd ask, is that the road home? And you'd say yes, it's six hundred kilometers. And I'd say, that doesn't matter now. We love each other beyond time and place now. You'd say, that's right—and you'd kiss me."*
And five months later there was not, as they used to say, a dry seat in any cinema of the republic when Margaret Sullavan husked those words to Robert Taylor.

What Fitzgerald had not realized was that dialogue must be precisely cut in quality to the player's talents and in length to the player's salary. Margaret Sullavan was a star whose deathbed scenes were one of the great joys of the Golden Age of the movies. Sullavan never simply kicked the bucket. She made speeches, as she lay dying; and she was so incredibly noble that she made you feel like an absolute twerp for continuing to live out your petty life after she'd ridden on ahead, to the accompaniment of the third movement of Brahms's First Symphony.

Fitzgerald's death scene went like this: Pat is all in a heap beside her bed, as Erich enters. "*Erich*: Pat—oh, Pat. (*He raises her, supports her. Pat's head wobbles on her shoulders*) Help—somebody! *Pat: (very low)* It's all right—it's hard to die—but I'm quite full of love—like a bee is full of honey when it comes back to the hive in the evening." On this grammatical error, "her eyes close in death." Joe will fix that line, I thought, as I put to one side Scott's version and picked up the shooting script. But, no, Mankiewicz's final words for Pat are: "It's all right for me to die, darling—and it's not hard—when I'm so full of love." Joe, I say to myself, tensing, make her say "as." But, alas, Miss Sullavan dies "like a bee is full of honey when it comes home in the evening." At least Mankiewicz got rid of Fitzgerald's hive.

In the novel, Remarque killed Pat more realistically—she doesn't talk all that much. But then she had already made her great speech a few pages earlier on why it's OK to be dying because she has Erich's love: "Now it's hard; but to make up, I'm quite full of love, *as* a bee is full of honey when it comes back to the hive in the evening. (Emphasis added by me.) Curiously enough, *there is no rain in the book*. But then the *Föhn* is blowing.

Mankiewicz's main contribution to this tear-jerker was an anti-Nazi subplot which the Breen office objected to. They wanted the

German thugs to be communists. When Mankiewicz threatened to quit, the Breen office backed down; and the film was politically daring for its time. Mankiewicz also added a certain wit to the girl's part, annoying Fitzgerald. He thought that Mankiewicz had made Pat "a sentimental girl from Brooklyn"—a mildly anti-Semitic swipe which was off the mark: Mankiewicz's jokes were usually rather good and as much in character as anything else in the film. Incidentally, for those who subscribe to the *auteur* theory, Frank Borzage was in no way involved with the actual creation of the film that he humbly directed.

Professor Bruccoli tells us that "after MGM dropped his option in 1939, Fitzgerald freelanced at other studios before starting *The Last Tycoon*—which, in its unfinished state, is the best Hollywood novel ever written. In 1977 Hollywood turned *The Last Tycoon* into the worst movie ever made." Well, I am sure that Professor Bruccoli does not regard himself as a literary or film critic. He is a scholar-squirrel and the nuts that he gathers from past Mays are great fun to crack. To say that *The Last Tycoon* is the best Hollywood novel is like saying *Edwin Drood* is the best mystery novel ever written. Since *The Last Tycoon* is a fragment and nothing more, it's not the best anything. *The Day of the Locust*, *The Slide Area*, the crudely written but well-observed *What Makes Sammy Run?* are far more interesting "Hollywood novels" than the fragment Fitzgerald left behind, while to say that *The Last Tycoon* is the worst film Hollywood ever made is silly squirrel-talk. At the risk of betraying an interest, I would propose not the worst film *ever* made (critics are not allowed to use the sort of hyperbole that scholar-squirrels may indulge in) but a film that was certainly much worse than *The Last Tycoon* (and based on, dare I say? a rather better work), *Myra Breckinridge*.

Recently, I ran into the Wise Hack. He was buying the trade papers at the newsstand in the Beverly Hills Hotel. He is very old but still well turned out (blue cashmere blazer, highly polished ox-blood loafers with tassels); he owns a shopping center in down-town Encino; he has emphysema. Although he still keeps up with the latest movie deals, he seldom goes to the movies. "Too many cars," he says vaguely.

When I mentioned Fitzgerald, he sighed. "At least Ketti made some money out of him." It took me a moment to realize that he was referring to Ketti Frings who had written, in 1958, a successful stage version of *Look Homeward, Angel*.

"Did you hear the latest Polish joke?" The Wise Hack's little eyes gleamed behind thick glasses. "This Polish star, she comes to Hollywood to make a picture and she," the Wise Hack wheezed with delight, *"she fucks the writer!"*

Poor Scott: "He had come a long way to this blue lawn, and his dream must have seemed so close that he could hardly fail to grasp it. He did not know that it was already behind him, somewhere back in that vast obscurity beyond the city, where the dark fields of the republic rolled on under the night." *Habent sua fata libelli.* Writers have their scholar-squirrels.

The New York Review of Books
May 1, 1980

Edmund Wilson:
This Critic and This Gin
and These Shoes

On February 2, 1821, gin-drinker Lord Byron wrote in his Ravenna Journal: "I have been considering what can be the reason why I always wake at a certain hour in the morning, and always in very bad spirits—I may say, in actual despair and despondency, in all respects—even of that which pleased me overnight. . . . In England, five years ago, I had the same kind of hypochondria, but accompanied with so violent a thirst that I have drank as many as fifteen bottles of soda-water in one night, after going to bed, and been still thirsty. . . . What is it?—liver?"

In Edmund Wilson's journal, published as *Upstate*, he wrote, in 1955: "One evening (August 13, Saturday) I drank a whole bottle of champagne and what was left of a bottle of old Grand-Dad and started on a bottle of red wine—I was eating Limburger cheese and gingersnaps. This began about five in the afternoon—I fell asleep in my chair, but woke up when Beverly came, thinking it was the next morning. I decided to skip supper; and felt queasy for the next twenty-four hours." The sixty-year-old Wilson does not ask, what is it? as Byron did. Wilson knows. "This kind of life," he writes, rather demurely, "in the long run, does, however, get rather unhealthy."

About the time that Wilson was munching on those gingersnaps and Limburger cheese, washed down with fiery waters, I received a letter from Upton Sinclair (whom I had never met), asking me about something. Then, obsessively, from left field, as it were, Sinclair denounced John Barleycorn. In the course of a long life, practically every writer Sinclair had known had died of drink, starting with his friend Jack London. Needless to say, this was not the sort of unsolicited letter that one likes to read while starting on one's fifteenth bottle of soda water, or to be precise and up-to-date, Coca-Cola, Georgia's sole gift to a nation whose first century was recently described in a book titled, eponymously, *The Alcoholic Republic* . . . of letters, I remember adding to myself when I first saw the book.

In this century, it would be safe to say that a significant percent of American writers are to a greater or lesser degree alcoholics and why this should be the case I leave to the medicine men. Alcoholism ended the careers of Hemingway, Fitzgerald, and Faulkner, to name three fashionable novelists of our mid-century. Out of charity toward the descendants and keepers of the still flickering flames of once glorious literary figures, I shall name no other names. Heavy drinking stopped Hemingway from writing anything of value in his later years; killed Fitzgerald at forty-four; turned the William Faulkner of *As I Lay Dying* into a fable.

Meanwhile, the contemporary of these three blasted stars, Edmund Wilson, outlived and outworked them all; he also outdrank them. Well into his seventies, Wilson would totter into the Princeton Club and order a half dozen martinis, to be prepared not sequentially but simultaneously—six shining glasses in a bright row, down which Wilson would work, all the while talking and thinking at a rapid pace. To the end of a long life, he kept on making the only thing he thought worth making: sense, a quality almost entirely lacking in American literature where stupidity—if sufficiently sincere and authentic—is deeply revered, and easily achieved. Although this *was* a rather unhealthy life in the long run, Wilson had a very long run indeed. But then, he was perfect proof of the proposition that the more the mind is used and fed the less apt it is to devour itself. When he died, at seventy-seven, he was busy stuffing his head with irregular Hungarian verbs. Plainly, he had a brain to match his liver.

Edmund Wilson was the last of a leisurely educated generation who were not obliged, if they were intellectually minded, to join the hicks and hacks of Academe. Wilson supported himself almost entirely by literary journalism, something not possible today if only because, for all practical purposes, literary journalism of the sort that he practiced no longer exists. Instead, book-chat is now dominated either by academic bureaucrats, crudely pursuing bureaucratic careers, or by journalists whose "leprous jealousy" (Flaubert's pretty phrase) has made mephitic the air of our alcoholic literary republic. But then, Flaubert thought that "critics write criticism because they are unable to be artists, just as a man unfit to bear arms becomes a police spy." Wilson would have challenged this romantic notion. Certainly, he would have made the point that to write essays is as much an aspect of the literary artist's temperament as the ability to evoke an alien sensibility on a page while sweating to avoid a double genitive. In any case, Wilson himself wrote stories, plays, novels. He knew how such things were made even if he was not entirely a master of any of these forms.

Of what, then, was Edmund Wilson a master? That is a question in need of an answer, or answers; and there are clues in the book at hand, *The Thirties: From Notebooks and Diaries of the Period.* At the time of Wilson's death, eight years ago, he was editing the notebooks that dealt with the Twenties. He had already finished *Upstate*, a chronicle of his works and days from the early Fifties to 1970. *Upstate* is a highly satisfactory Wilsonian book, filled with sharp personal details, long scholarly asides on those things or people or notions (like New York religions) that had caught his fancy. Although he had planned to rework his earlier records, he soon realized that he might not live long enough to complete them. He then designated, in his will, that Professor Leon Edel edit the remains, with the injunction that the text be published the way he wrote it, except for straightening out "misspellings and faulty punctuations" (but not, apparently, faulty grammar: Wilson often "feels badly"—it *is* liver). With *The Thirties*, Professor Edel had his work cut out for him because, he writes, "It is clear from the condition of the typescript that [Wilson] intended to do much more work on this book." That is understatement.

At the beginning of the Thirties, Wilson completed *Axel's Castle*; at the end, he had finished *To the Finland Station*. He wrote for *The New Republic*, supported, briefly, the American Communist party, visited the Soviet Union, Detroit, Appalachia, Scotsboro,

and tried a season of teaching at the University of Chicago. The
decade, in a sense, was the making of him as critic and triple
thinker. Emotionally, it was shattering: in 1930 he married Margaret Canby; in 1932 she died. He also conducted a wide range of
affairs, many on the raunchy side.

Professor Edel rather flinches at Wilson's "record of his own
copulations" in general and the notes about his marriage in particular (so unlike the home life of our own dear Master): "some
readers may be startled by this intimate candid record of a marriage." But Professor Edel is quick to remind us that this is all part
of "the notebooks of a chronicler, a way of tidying the mind for
his craft of criticism. . . . He tries, rather, to be a camera, for this
is what he finds most comfortable." Well, yes and no.

In 1930 Edmund Wilson was thirty-five. He was a member of
the minor Eastern gentry, a Princeton graduate, a World War I
overseas noncombatant. In the Twenties, he had lived the life of the
roaring boy but unlike the other lads that light-footed it over the
greensward, he never stopped reading and writing and thinking.
Thanks, in large part, to the Christers who had managed to prohibit
the legal sale of spirits, alcohol was as much a curse to that generation as Gin Lane had been to the poor of eighteenth-century London. I suspect that a great deal of the grimness of this volume is a
result of hangover and its concomitant despairs. At the same time,
it is the record of an astonishing constitution: Wilson would write
while he was drinking—something I should not have thought possible for anyone, even his doomed friend Scott Fitzgerald.

From thirty-five to forty-five men go from relative youth to
middle age. The transit is often rocky. As a man's life settles into a
rut, in mindless rut the man is apt to go. Certainly, this was true of
Wilson, as readers of *Memoirs of Hecate County* might have suspected and as readers of *The Thirties* will now know for certain.
During the so-called "ignoble" decade, despite constant drinking,
Wilson was sexually very active. He enjoyed trade in the form of
the Slavic Anna, a working-class woman whose proletarian ways
fascinated him. He had sex with a number of those women who
used to hang about writers, as well as with ladies at the edge of the
great world. He bedded no Oriane but he knew at least one
Guermantes *before* her translation to the aristocracy.

Although Wilson's bedmates are sometimes masked by initials, he
enjoys writing detailed descriptions of what Professor Edel calls his
"copulations." These descriptions are mechanistic, to say the least.

Since they are not connected with character, they are about as erotic as a *Popular Mechanics* blueprint of the sort that is said to appeal to the growing boy. I am not sure just why Wilson felt that he should write so much about cock and cunt except that in those days it was a very daring thing to do, as Henry Miller had discovered when his books were burned and as Wilson was to discover when his own novel, *Memoirs of Hecate County*, was banned.

In literature, sexual revelation is a matter of tact and occasion. Whether or not such candor is of interest to a reader depends a good deal on the revealer's attitude. James Boswell is enchanting to read on sex because he is by self, as well as by sex, enchanted and possessed. The author of *My Secret Life* (if for real) is engaging because he is only interested in getting laid as often as possible in as many different ways and combinations. We also don't know what he looks like—an important aid to masturbation. Frank Harris (not for real) has the exuberance of a natural liar and so moves the reader toward fiction.

The list now starts to get short. The recently published (in English) letters of Flaubert are interesting because he has interesting things to say about what he sees and does in the brothels and baths of North Africa. Also, tactfully, mercifully, he never tells us what he feels or Feels. The sex that Flaubert has with women and men, with boys and girls, is fascinating to read about (even though we know exactly how *he* looks). This is due, partly, to the fact that his experiences are, literally, exotic as well as erotic and, partly, to that famous tone of voice. Today one is never quite certain why memoirists are so eager to tell us what they do in bed. Unless the autobiographer has a case to be argued, I suspect that future readers will skip those sexual details that our writers have so generously shared with us in order to get to the gossip and the jokes.

In Wilson's notebooks, he liked to describe sex in the same way that he liked "doing" landscapes. "It is certainly very hard," he concedes, "to write about sex in English without making it unattractive. *Come* is a horrible word to apply to something ecstatic." Finally, he did neither sex scenes nor landscapes very well. But in sexual matters, he has no real case to make, unlike, let us say, the committed homosexualist who thinks, incorrectly, that candor will so rend the veil that light will be shed upon what the society considers an abominable act and in a blaze of clarity and charity all will be forgiven. This is naïve, as Wilson himself demonstrates in these pages. He was very much an American of his time and class and the notebooks are filled with innumerable references to "fairies" that range from derisive to nervous; yet Wilson also admits to occasional homosexual reveries which he thought "were a way of living in the grip of the vise, getting away into a different world where those values that pressed me did not function."

Nevertheless, it is disquieting to find Wilson, in the Thirties (having admired Proust and Gide), quite unable to accept the fact that a fairy could be a major artist. In *Axel's Castle*, he has great trouble admitting, or not admitting, the sexual source of Proust's jealousy.

On the other hand, he made a curious and admirable exception in the case of Thornton Wilder.

During the Twenties and Thirties, Wilder was one of the most celebrated and successful American novelists. He was also one of the few first-rate writers the United States has produced. Fortunately for Wilder's early reputation, he was able to keep his private life relatively secret. As a result, he was very much a hero in book-chat land. In *The Twenties* Wilson describes a meeting with Wilder. He was startled to find Wilder "a person of such positive and even peppery opinions." Wilson had not read any of Wilder's novels because he thought that "they must be rather on the fragile and precious side" (what else can a fairy write?). As it turned out, each had been reading the new installment of Proust's novel and Wilson was delighted to find that Wilder thought Saint Loup's homosexuality unjustified. Over the years, Wilson was to review Wilder seriously and well. When Wilder was the victim of a celebrated Marxist attack, Wilson came to Wilder's defense—not to mention literature's. But the word was out and Thornton Wilder's reputation never recovered; to this day, he is a literary nonperson. Nevertheless, it is to Wilson's credit that he was able to overcome his horror of fairydom in order to do justice to a remarkable contemporary.

Of a certain Victorian Englishman it was said that no lady's shoe, unescorted, was safe in his company. It could be said of Edmund Wilson that, like Cecil B. De Mille, "he never met a woman's foot he didn't like." Is there any reader of Wilson's novel *I Thought of Daisy* who does not recall Wilson's description of a girl's feet as being like "moist cream cheeses"? But Wilson's podophilia did not stop there: he could have made a fortune in women's footwear. From *The Thirties*: ". . . shoes, blue with silver straps, that arched her insteps very high . . . ," "Katy's little green socks and untied gray moccasins . . . ," "young Scotch girl M.P. [with] large feet bulging out of black shoes . . . ," ". . . silver open-work shoes that disclosed her reddened toenails, such a combination as only she could wear. . . ." In *The Thirties*, I counted twenty-four references to shoes and feet; each, let me quickly say, belonging to a woman. When it came to shoes, Wilson was sternly heterosexual —not for him the stud's boot or the little lad's Ked. But, to be absolutely precise, there is one very odd reference. Wilson is struck by the number of Chicago men who wear spats. Reverie: "Excuse me, sir. But a hook is loose on your left spat. As chance would have it, I have with me a spats-hook. If you'll allow me, sir. . . ." Whenever Wilson strikes the Florsheim note, he is in rut.

As a lover, Wilson is proud of his "large pink prong." (Surely, Anaïs Nin said it was "short and puce"—or was that Henry Miller's thumb?) In action, "My penis went in and out so beautifully sensitively, caressing (me) each time so sweet-smoothly (silkily). . . ." Yet he refers, clinically, to his "all too fat and debauched face" not to mention belly. He was a stubby little man who drank a lot. But his sexual energy matched his intellectual energy; so much for Freud's theory of sublimation.

The section called "The Death of Margaret" is fascinating, and quite unlike anything else he was ever to write. He started scribbling in a notebook aboard an airliner in 1932, en route to California where his wife of two years had just died of a fall. A compulsive writer, Wilson felt, instinctively, that by a close running description of what he saw from the plane window and in the air terminals he could get control of the fact of death and loss, or at least neutralize the shock in the act of recreation. He writes a good many impressionistic pages of the trip before he gets to Margaret. Some very odd items: "—touching fellow passenger's thigh, moving over to keep away from it, did he move, too?— shutting eyes and homosexual fantasies, losing in vivid reality from Provincetown, gray, abstract, unreal sexual stimulus—also thought about coming back with Jean Gorman on train as situation that promises possibilities; but couldn't stomach it—young man too big, not my type—" Then impressions of his time together with Margaret: "I felt for the first time how she'd given me all my self-confidence, the courage that I hadn't had before to say what I thought. . . ."

In Santa Barbara, he stays with her family. "At Mrs. Waterman's house [Margaret's mother], when I began to cry, she said, I've never broken down. . . ." "Second night: homosexual wet dream, figures still rather dim, a boy. Third night: nightmare—the trolls were in the dark part of the cellar. . . ." Finally, the inevitable epitaph; "After she was dead, I loved her." That is the story of every life—and death. For the next decade, Wilson dreams of Margaret and writes down the dreams. In these dreams he usually knows that she is dead but, somehow, they can overcome this obstacle. They don't; even in dreams. Eurydice always stays put: It is the blight man was born for.

During the Thirties, Wilson's interests were more political than literary. The Depression, the New Deal, the Soviet experiment absorbed him. Wilson is at his most attractive and, I should think, characteristic when he describes going to Russia. He wanted to think well of communism, and, to a point, he was enthralled by the "classless" society and by the way that one man, Lenin, "has stamped his thought and his language on a whole people." This is not the treason but the very nature of the true clerk: the word as absolute can be motor to behavior and to governance. Gradually, Wilson is disillusioned about Stalin and the state he was making.

But what is fascinating to read today is not Wilson's account of what he saw and did but the way that he goes about taking on a subject, a language, a world. This is what sets him apart from all other American critics. He has to get to the root of things. He will learn Hebrew to unravel the Dead Sea scrolls. Read a thousand windy texts to figure out the Civil War. Learn Russian to get past the barrier of Constance Garnett's prose. He was the perfect autodidact. He wanted to know it all. Or, as he wrote, after he had a nervous breakdown in the Thirties, "I usually know exactly what I want to do, and it has only been when I could not make up my mind that I have really gone to pieces."

Early in *The Thirties*, Wilson is a fellow traveler of the American communists' *faute de mieux*. He can see no other way out of the Depression than an overthrow of the form of capitalism that had caused it. Before the election of 1932, he wrote: "Hoover stands frankly for the interests of the class who live on profits as against the wage-earning classes. Franklin Roosevelt, though he speaks as a Democrat in the name of the small businessmen and farmers and is likely to be elected by them in the expectation that he can do something for them, can hardly be imagined effecting any very drastic changes in the system which has allowed him to get into office. Whatever amiable gestures he may make, he will be

largely controlled by the profit-squeezing class just as Hoover is."
This is prescient. Apropos the fireside chats: "Roosevelt's unsatisfactory way of emphasizing his sentences, fairyish, or as if there
weren't real conviction behind him—in spite of his clearness and
neatness—but regular radio announcers, I noticed later, did the
same thing. (The remoteness of the speaker from his audience.)"
It is a pity that Wilson, who was on the fringes of the New
Deal, never got to know the president. "Roosevelt is reported to
have answered when someone had said to him that he would
either be the best president the country had ever had or the
most hated: No—that he would either be the most popular or
the last."

Wilson often traveled to Washington in the Thirties and he had
a sense of the place (derived from Henry Adams?) that makes him
sound like one of us cliff-dwellers: "Washington is really a hollow
shell which holds the liberalism of the New Deal as easily as the
crooks and thugs of the Harding Administration—no trouble to
clean it out every night and put something else in the past Administration's place."

Wilson goes to see one Martha Blair—"a rather appealing mouth
and slim arms, though pale thyroid eyes: pink flowered print dress,
with sleeves that gave a glimpse of her upper arms . . . she com-
plained of the small town character of Washington—if you said
you had another engagement, people asked you what it was—
when she had said she was going to Virginia for the weekend they
had asked her where in Virginia." It is odd to see this old formidable
"socialite" of my childhood (she was then in her early thirties) as
viewed from a totally different angle. Martha Blair kept company
in those days with Arthur Krock of *The New York Times*. They
were known as Martha'n'Artha. Wilson thinks they were married
in 1934. I don't. At about that time, I remember there was a great
row between my mother and her husband over whether or not the
unmarried couple Martha and Arthur could stay overnight at our
house in Virginia—where she was so often headed. My mother
won that round. They were often at Merrywood, and Arthur
Krock was the first Jew that I ever met. Anti-Semitism was in full
boisterous American flower in the Thirties, and Wilson's record
of conversations and attitudes haunt a survivor in much the same
way that the background of a Thirties movie will reverse time,
making it possible to see again a *People's Drug* store (golden letter-
ing), straw hats, squared-off cars, and the actual light that encom-

passed one as a child, the very same light that all those who are now dead saw then.

Wilson notes, rather perfunctorily, friends and contemporaries. Scott Fitzgerald makes his usual appearances, and in his usual state. Once again we get the Hemingway-Wilson-Fitzgerald evening. "When Scott was lying in the corner on the floor, Hemingway said, Scott thinks that his penis is too small. (John Bishop had told me this and said that Scott was in the habit of making this assertion to anybody he met—to the lady who sat next to him at dinner and who might be meeting him for the first time.) I explained to him, Hemingway continued, that it only seemed to him small because he looked at it from above. You have to look at it in the mirror. (I did not understand this.)" I have never understood what Hemingway meant either. For one thing, Fitzgerald had obviously studied his diminutive part in a mirror. Even so, he would still be looking down at it unless, like a boy that I went to school with, he could so bend himself as to have an eye to eye, as it were, exchange with the Great American (Male) Obsession.

"Scott Fitzgerald at this time [1934] had the habit of insulting people, and then saying, if the victim came back at him: 'Can't take it, huh?' (I learned years later from Morley Callaghan that this was a habit of Hemingway's, from whom Scott had undoubtedly acquired it.)" There is altogether too little about Wilson's friend Dawn Powell, one of the wittiest of our novelists, and the most resolutely overlooked. But then American society, literary or lay, tends to be humorless. What other culture could have produced someone like Hemingway and *not* seen the joke?

Wilson's glimpses of people are always to the point. But they are brief. He is far more interested in writing descriptions of landscapes. I cannot think where the terrible habit began. Since Fitzgerald did the same thing in his notebooks, I suppose someone at Princeton (Professor Gauss? Project for a scholar-squirrel) must have told them that a writer must constantly describe things as a form of finger-exercise. The result is not unlike those watercolors Victorian girls were encouraged to turn out. Just as Wilson is about to tell us something quite interesting about e. e. cummings, he feels that he must devote a page or two to the deeply boring waterfront at Provincetown. A backdrop with no action in front of it is to no point at all.

There were trolls in the cellar of Wilson's psyche, and they tended to come upstairs "When I was suffering from the bad nerves of a hangover. . . ." There is also an echo of Mrs. Dalloway's vastation in the following passage: "Getting out of an elevator in some office building—I must have been nervously exhausted—I saw a man in a darkened hall—he was in his shirt sleeves with open neck, had evidently been working around the building—his eyes were wide open, and there seemed to be no expression on his face: he looked, not like an ape, but like some kind of primitive man— and his staring face, as I stared at him, appalled me: humanity was still an animal, still glaring out of its dark caves, not yet having mastered the world, not even comprehending what he saw. I was frightened—at him, at us all. *The horrible look of the human race.*"

As a critic, Wilson was not always at his best when it came to the design or pattern of a text—what used to be called aesthetics. He liked data, language. He did not have much sympathy for the New Critics with their emphasis on text *qua* text. After all, nothing human exists in limbo; nothing human is without connection. Wilson's particular genius lay in his ability to make rather more connections than any other critic of his time. As Diderot said of Voltaire: "He knows a great deal and our young poets are ignorant. The work of Voltaire is full of things; their works are empty."

But Wilson was quite aware that "things" in themselves are not enough. Professor Edel quotes from Wilson's Princeton lecture: "no matter how thoroughly and searchingly we may have scrutinized works of literature from the historical and biographical point of view . . . we must be able to tell the good from the bad, the first-rate from the second-rate. We shall not otherwise write literary criticism at all."

We do not, of course, write literary criticism at all now. Academe has won the battle in which Wilson fought so fiercely on the other side. Ambitious English teachers (sic!) now invent systems that have nothing to do with literature or life but everything to do with those games that must be played in order for them to rise in the academic bureaucracy. Their works are empty indeed. But then, their works are not meant to be full. They are to be taught, not read. The long dialogue has broken down. Fortunately, as Flaubert pointed out, the worst thing about the present is the future. One day there will be no. . . . But I have been asked not to give the game away. Meanwhile, I shall drop a single hint: Only construct!

The New York Review of Books
SEPTEMBER 25, 1980

Christopher Isherwood's Kind

In 1954 I had lunch with Christopher Isherwood at MGM. He told me that he had just written a film for Lana Turner. The subject? Diane de Poitiers. When I laughed, he shook his head. "Lana can do it," he said grimly. Later, as we walked about the lot and I told him that I hoped to get a job as a writer at the studio since I could no longer live on my royalties as a novelist (and would not teach), Christopher gave me as melancholy a look as those bright—even harsh—blue eyes can affect. "Don't," he said with great intensity, posing against the train beneath whose wheels Greta Garbo as Anna Karenina made her last dive, "become a hack like me." But we both knew that this was play-acting. Like his friend Aldous Huxley (like William Faulkner and many others), he had been able to write to order for movies while never ceasing to do his own work in his own way. Those whom Hollywood destroyed were never worth saving. Not only has Isherwood written successfully for the camera, he has been, notoriously, in his true art, *the* camera.

"I am a camera." With those four words at the beginning of the novel *Goodbye to Berlin* (1939), Christopher Isherwood became famous. Because of those four words he has been written of (and sometimes written off) as a naturalistic writer, a recorder of surfaces, a film director *manqué*. Although it is true that, up to a point, Isherwood often appears to be recording perhaps too impartially the lights, the shadows, the lions that come within the area of his vision, he is never without surprises; in the course of what looks to be an undemanding narrative, the author will suddenly produce a Polaroid shot of the reader reading, an alarming effect achieved by the sly use of the second person pronoun. You never know quite where *you* stand in relation to an Isherwood work.

During the half century that Christopher Isherwood has been more or less at the center of Anglo-American literature, he has been much scrutinized by friends, acquaintances, purveyors of bookchat. As memoirs of the Twenties, Thirties, Forties now accumulate, Isherwood keeps cropping up as a principal figure, and if he does not always seem in character, it is because he is not an easy character to fix upon the page. Also, he has so beautifully invented himself in the Berlin stories, *Lions and Shadows, Down There on a Visit*, and now *Christopher and His Kind*, that anyone who wants to snap yet again this lion's shadow has his work cut out for him. After all, nothing is harder to reflect than a mirror.

To date the best developed portrait of Isherwood occurs in Stephen Spender's autobiography *World Within World* (1951). Like Isherwood, Spender was a part of that upper-middle-class generation which came of age just after World War I. For the lucky few able to go to the right schools and universities, postwar England was still a small and self-contained society where everyone knew everyone else. In fact, English society was simply an extension of school. But something disagreeable had happened at school just before the Isherwoods and Spenders came on stage. World War I had killed off the better part of a generation of graduates, and among the graduated dead was Isherwood's father. There was a long shadow over the young . . . of dead fathers, brothers; also of dead or dying attitudes. Rebellion was in the air. New things were promised.

In every generation there are certain figures who are who they are at an early age: stars *in ovo*. People want to know them; imitate them; destroy them. Isherwood was such a creature and Stephen Spender fell under his spell even before they met.

At nineteen Spender was an undergraduate at Oxford; another undergraduate was the twenty-one-year-old W. H. Auden. Isherwood himself (three years Auden's senior) was already out in the world; he had got himself sent down from Cambridge by sending up a written examination. He had deliberately broken out of the safe, cozy university world, and the brilliant but cautious Auden revered him. Spender writes how, "according to Auden, [Isherwood] held no opinions whatever about anything. He was wholly and simply interested in people. He did not like or dislike them, judge them favorably or unfavorably. He simply regarded them as material for his Work. At the same time, he was the Critic in whom Auden had absolute trust. If Isherwood disliked a poem, Auden destroyed it without demur."

Auden was not above torturing the young Spender: "Auden withheld the privilege of meeting Isherwood from me." Writing twenty years later, Spender cannot resist adding, "Isherwood was not famous at this time. He had published one novel, *All the Conspirators*, for which he had received an advance of £30 from his publishers, and which had been not very favorably reviewed." But Isherwood was already a legend, as Spender concedes, and worldly success has nothing to do with legends. Eventually Auden brought them together. Spender was not disappointed:

> He simplified all the problems which entangled me, merely by describing his own life and his own attitudes towards these things. . . . Isherwood had a peculiarity of being attractively disgusted and amiably bitter. . . . But there was a positive as well as negative side to his beliefs. He spoke of being Cured and Saved with as much intensity as any Salvationist.

In Isherwood's earliest memoir, *Lions and Shadows* (1938), we are given Isherwood's first view of Spender, a sort of reverse-angle shot (and known to Spender when he wrote *World Within World*): "[Spender] burst in upon us, blushing, sniggering loudly, contriving to trip over the edge of the carpet—an immensely tall, shambling boy of nineteen, with a great scarlet poppy-face, wild frizzy hair, and eyes the violent color of bluebells." The camera turns, catching it all. "In an instant, without introductions, we were all laughing and talking at the top of our voices. . . . He inhabited a world of self-created and absorbing drama, into which each new acquaintance was immediately conscripted to play a part. [Spender] illuminated you" (the second person now starts to take hold: the film's *voice-over* has begun its aural seduction) "like an expressionist producer, with the crudest and most eccentric of spot-lights: you were transfigured, became grandiose, sinister, brilliantly ridiculous or impossibly beautiful, in accordance with his arbitrary, prearranged conception of your role." *You, spot-light, producer. . . .*

In *The Whispering Gallery*, the publisher and critic John Lehmann describes his first meeting with Spender in 1930 and how he "talked a great deal about Auden, who shared (and indeed had inspired) so many of his views, and also about a certain young novelist Christopher Isherwood, who, he told me, had settled in Berlin in stark poverty and was an even greater rebel against the England we lived in than he was. . . ." When Lehmann went to work for Leonard and Virginia Woolf at the Hogarth Press, he got them to publish Isherwood's second novel, *The Memorial.*

Lehmann noted that the generation's Novelist was

> much shorter than myself, he nevertheless had a power of dominating which small people of outstanding intelligence or imaginative equipment often possess. One of my favorite private fancies has always been that the most ruthless war that underlies our civilized existence . . . is the war between the tall and the short.

Even so, "It was impossible not to be drawn to him. . . . And yet for some months after our first meeting . . . our relations remained rather formal: perhaps it was the sense of alarm that seemed to hang in the air when his smile was switched off, a suspicion he seemed to radiate that one might after all be in league with the 'enemy,' a phrase which covered everything he had, with a pure hatred, cut himself off from in English life. . . ."

In 1931 a cold transatlantic eye was turned upon both Isherwood and Spender. The twenty-year-old Paul Bowles presented himself to Isherwood in Berlin. "When I came to Isherwood," Bowles records in *Without Stopping*, "he said he would take me himself to Spender." Bowles did not approve of Spender's looking and acting the part of a poet: "Whether Spender wrote poetry or not seemed relatively unimportant; that at all costs the fact should not be evident was what should have mattered to him." Bowles acknowledges that this primness reflected the attitudes of his Puritan family and background. "I soon found that Isherwood with Spender was a very different person from Isherwood by himself."

But then the camera and its director are bound to alter according to light, weather, cast. "Together they were overwhelmingly British, two members of a secret society constantly making references to esoteric data not available to outsiders." This strikes me as an accurate and poignant description of the difference between American and English writers. The English tend to play off (and with) one another; while the Americans are, if not Waldenized solitaries, Darwinized predators constantly preying upon one another. I think it significant that when the excellent American writer Paul Bowles came to write *his* autobiography, he chose a prose style not unlike that of Julius Caesar's report on how he laid waste Gaul.

"At all our meetings I felt that I was being treated with good-humored condescension. They accepted Aaron [Copland], but they did not accept me because they considered me too young and uninteresting; I never learnt the reason, if there was one, for this exclusion by common consent." Bowles describes a British girl he met with Isherwood. She was called Jean Ross "(When Christopher wrote about her later, he called her Sally Bowles)."

In *Christopher and His Kind*, Isherwood sets up the by now obligatory reverse-angle shot: "(Sally Bowles's second name was chosen for her by Christopher because he liked the sound of it and also the looks of its owner, a twenty-year-old American whom he met in Berlin in 1931. The American thought Christopher treated him with 'good-humored condescension'; Christopher thought the American aloof. . . .)" Apparently, there was a near-miss in Berlin.

Christopher and His Kind describes Isherwood's life from 1929 to 1939. The narrative (based on diaries and written, generally, in the third person) takes up where *Lions and Shadows* ends with "twenty-four-year-old Christopher's departure from England on March 14, 1929, to visit Berlin for the first time in his life." The book ends a decade later when Isherwood emigrates to the United States. Of *Lions and Shadows*, Isherwood says that it describes his "life between the ages of seventeen and twenty-four. It is not truly autobiographical, however. The author conceals important facts about himself . . . and gives his characters fictitious names." But "The book I am now going to write will be as frank and factual as I can make it, especially as far as I myself am concerned." He means to be sexually candid; and he is. He is also that rarest of creatures, the objective narcissist; he sees himself altogether plain and does not hesitate to record for us the lines that the face in the mirror has accumulated, the odd shadow that flaws character.

I have just read the two memoirs in sequence and it is odd how little Isherwood has changed in a half century. The style is much the same throughout. The shift from first to third person does not much alter the way he has of looking at things and it is, of course, the *precise* way in which Isherwood perceives the concrete world that makes all the difference. He is particularly good at noting a physical appearance that suggests, through his selection of nouns, verbs, a psychic description. This is from *Lions and Shadows*:

> [Chalmers] had grown a small moustache and looked exactly my idea of a young Montmartre poet, more French than the French. Now he caught sight of us, and greeted me with a slight wave of the hand, so very typical of him, tentative, diffident, semi-ironical, like a parody of itself. Chalmers expressed himself habitually in fragments of gestures, abortive movements, half-spoken sentences. . . .

Then the same sharp eye is turned upon the narrator:

> Descending the staircase to the dining-room, I was Christopher Isherwood no longer, but a satanically proud, icy, impenetrable demon; an all-knowing, all-pardoning savior of mankind; a martyr-evangelist of the tea-table, from which the most atrocious drawing-room tortures could wring no more than a polite proffer of the buttered scones.

This particular *auteur du cinéma* seldom shoots a scene without placing somewhere on the set a mirror that will record the *auteur* in the act of filming.

At the time of the publication of *Lions and Shadows* in 1938, Isherwood was thirty-four years old. He had published three novels: *All the Conspirators, The Memorial, Mr. Norris Changes Trains*. With Auden he had written the plays *The Dog Beneath the Skin* and *The Ascent of F6*. Finally, most important of all, the finest of his creations had made a first appearance in *Mr. Norris Changes Trains*; with no great fuss or apparent strain, Isherwood had invented Isherwood. The Isherwood of the Berlin stories is a somewhat anodyne and enigmatic narrator. He is looking carefully at life. He does not commit himself to much of anything. Yet what might have been a limitation in a narrator, the author, rather mysteriously, made a virtue of.

Spender describes Isherwood in Berlin as occasionally "depressive, silent or petulant. Sometimes he would sit in a room with Sally Bowles or Mr. Norris without saying a word, as though refusing to bring his characters to life." But they were very much *his* characters. He lived "surrounded by the models for his creations, like one of those portraits of a writer by a bad painter, in which the writer is depicted meditating in his chair whilst the characters of his novels radiate round him under a glowing cloud of dirty varnish. . . ." Isherwood had rejected not only the familiar, cozy world of Cambridge and London's literary life but also the world of self-conscious aestheticism. He chose to live as a proletarian in Berlin where, Spender tells us, "He was comparatively poor and almost unrecognized. His novel, *All the Conspirators*, had been remaindered," Spender notes yet again. Nevertheless, Spender realized that Isherwood

> was more than a young rebel passing through a phase of revolt against parents, conventional morality, and orthodox religion. . . . He was on the side of the forces which make a work of art, even more than he was interested in art itself. . . . . His hatred of institutions of learning and even of the reputation attached to some past work of art, was really hatred of the fact that they came between people and their direct unprejudiced approach to one another.

In *Lions and Shadows* Isherwood writes of school, of friendships, of wanting to be . . . well, Isherwood, a character not yet entirely formed. Auden appears fairly late in the book though early in Isherwood's life: they were together at preparatory school. Younger than Isherwood, Auden wanted "to become a mining engineer. . . . I remember him chiefly for his naughtiness, his insolence, his smirking tantalizing air of knowing disreputable and exciting secrets." Auden was on to sex and the others were not.

Auden and Isherwood did not meet again for seven years. "Just before Christmas, 1925, a mutual acquaintance brought him in to tea. I found him very little changed." Auden "told me that he wrote poetry nowadays: he was deliberately a little over-casual in making this announcement. I was very much surprised, even rather disconcerted." But then, inevitably, the Poet and the Novelist of the age formed an alliance. The Poet had further surprises for the Novelist. Auden's "own attitude to sex, in its simplicity and utter lack of inhibition, fairly took my breath away. He was no Don Juan: he didn't run around hunting for his pleasures. But he took what came to him with a matter-of-factness and an appetite as hearty as that which he showed when sitting down to dinner."

Art and sex: the two themes intertwine in Isherwood's memoirs but in the first volume we do not know what the sex was all about: the reticences of the Thirties forbade candor. Now in *Christopher and His Kind*, Isherwood has filled in the blanks; he is explicit about both sex and love. Not only did the Poet and the Novelist of that era lust for boys, there is some evidence that each might have echoed Marlowe's mighty line: I have found that those who do not like tobacco and boys are fools.

"The book I am now going to write will be as frank and factual as I can make it, especially as far as I myself am concerned." Then the writer shifts to the third person: "At school, Christopher had fallen in love with many boys and been yearningly romantic about them. At college he had at last managed to get into bed with one. This was due entirely to the initiative of his partner, who, when Christopher became scared and started to raise objections, locked the door and sat down firmly on Christopher's lap." For an American twenty-two years younger than Christopher, the late development of the English of that epoch is astonishing. In Washington, D.C., puberty arrived at ten, eleven, twelve, and sex was riotous and inventive between consenting paeds. Yet Tennessee Williams (fourteen years my senior) reports in his *Memoirs* that neither homo- nor heterosexuality began for him until his late twenties. On the other hand, he did not go to a monosexual school as I did, as Isherwood and his kind did.

Isherwood tells us that "other experiences followed, all of them enjoyable but none entirely satisfying. This was because Christopher was suffering from an inhibition, then not unusual among upper-class homosexuals; he couldn't relax sexually with a member of his own class or nation. He needed a working-class foreigner." Germany was the answer. "To Christopher, Berlin meant Boys." Auden promptly introduced him to the Cosy Corner, a hangout for proletarian youths, and Christopher took up with a blond named Bubi, "the first presentable candidate who appeared to claim the leading role in Christopher's love myth."

John Lehmann's recently published "novel" *In the Purely Pagan*

Sense overlaps with Isherwood's memoirs not only in time and place but in a similar sexual preoccupation. "I was obsessed," writes Lehmann's narrator, "by the desire to make love with boys of an entirely different class and background. . . ." This desire for differentness is not unusual: misalliance has almost always been the name of the game hetero or homo or bi. But I suspect that the upper-middle-class man's desire for youths of the lower class derives, mainly, from fear of his own class. Between strongly willed males of the Isherwood-Auden sort, a sexual commitment could lead to a psychic defeat for one of the partners.

The recently published memoirs of Isherwood's contemporary Peter Quennell (*The Marble Foot*) describe how an upper-class *heterosexual* English writer was constantly betrayed by women of his own class. Apparently, Quennell is much too tender, too romantic, too . . . well, feminine to avoid victimization by the ladies. A beautiful irony never to be understood by United Statesmen given to the joys of the sexual majority is that a homosexualist like Isherwood cannot with any ease enjoy a satisfactory sexual relationship with a woman because he himself is so entirely masculine that the woman presents no challenge, no masculine hardness, no exciting *agon*. It is the heterosexual Don Juan (intellectual division) who is the fragile, easily wounded figure, given to tears. Isherwood is a good deal less "feminine" (in the pre-women's lib sense of the word) than Peter Quennell, say, or Cyril Connolly or our own paralyzingly butch Ernest Hemingway.

Isherwood describes his experiments with heterosexuality: "She was five or six years older than [Christopher], easygoing, stylish, humorous. . . . He was surprised and amused to find how easily he could relate his usual holds and movements to his unusual partner. He felt curiosity and the fun of playing a new game. He also felt a lust which was largely narcissistic. . . ." Then: "He asked himself: Do I now want to go to bed with more women and girls? Of course not, as long as I can have boys. Why do I prefer boys? Because of their shape and their voices and their smell and the way they move. And boys can be romantic. I can put them into my myth and fall in love with them. Girls can be absolutely beautiful but never romantic. In fact, their utter lack of romance is what I find most likeable about them." There is a clear-eyed normality (if not great accuracy) about all this.

Then Isherwood moves from the personal to the general and notes the lunatic pressure that society exerts on everyone to be

heterosexual, to deny at all costs a contrary nature. Since heterosexual relations proved to be easy for Isherwood, he could have
joined the majority. But he was stopped by Isherwood the rebel,
the Protestant saint who declared with the fury of a Martin Luther:
"even if my nature were like theirs, I should still have to fight them,
in one way or another. If boys didn't exist, I should have to invent
them." Isherwood's war on what he has called, so aptly, "the
heterosexual dictatorship" has been unremitting and admirable.

In Berlin Isherwood settled down with a working-class boy
named Heinz and most of *Christopher and His Kind* has to do with
their life together during the time when Hitler came to power
and the free and easy Berlin that had attracted Isherwood turned
ugly. With Heinz (whose papers were not in order), Isherwood
moved restlessly about Europe: Copenhagen, Amsterdam, the
Canary Islands, Brussels. In the end Heinz was trapped in Germany,
and forced to serve in World War II. Miraculously, he survived.
After the war, Isherwood met Heinz and his wife—as pleasant an
end as one can imagine to any idyll of that neo-Wagnerian age.

Meanwhile, Isherwood the writer was developing. It is during
this period that the Berlin stories were written; also, *Lions and
Shadows*. Also, the collaboration with Auden on the last of the
verse plays. Finally, there is the inevitable fall into the movies . . .
something that was bound to happen. In *Lions and Shadows* Isherwood describes how "I had always been fascinated by films. . . .
I was a born film fan. . . . The reason for this had, I think, very
little to do with 'Art' at all; I was, and still am, endlessly interested
in the outward appearance of people—their facial expressions, their
gestures, their walk, their nervous tricks. . . . The cinema puts
people under a microscope: you can stare at them, you can examine
them as though they were insects."

Isherwood was invited to write a screenplay for the director
"Berthold Viertel [who] appears as Friedrich Bergmann in the
novelette called *Prater Violet*, which was published twelve years
later." Isherwood and the colorful Viertel hit it off and together
worked on a film called *Little Friend*. From that time on the best
prose writer in English has supported himself by writing movies.
In fact, the first Isherwood work that I encountered was not a
novel but a film that he wrote called *Rage in Heaven*: at sixteen I
thought it splendid. "The moon!" intoned the nutty Robert Mont-
gomery. "It's staring at me, like a great Eye." Ingrid Bergman
shuddered. So did I.

It is hard now for the young who are interested in literature (a tiny minority compared to the young who are interested in that flattest and easiest and laziest of art forms: the movies) to realize that Isherwood was once considered "a hope of English fiction" by Cyril Connolly, and a master by those of us who grew up in World War II. I think the relative neglect of Isherwood's work is, partly, the result of his expatriation. With Auden, he emigrated to the United States just before the war began, and there was a good deal of bitter feeling at the time (they were clumsily parodied by the unspeakable Evelyn Waugh in *Put Out More Flags*). Ultimately, Auden's reputation was hardly affected. But then poets are licensed to be mad, bad, and dangerous to read, while prose writers are expected to be, if not responsible, predictable.

In America Isherwood was drawn first to the Quakers; then to Vedanta. Lately, he has become a militant spokesman of Gay Liberation. If his defense of Christopher's kind is sometimes shrill . . . well, there is a good deal to be shrill about in a society so deeply and so mindlessly homophobic. In any case, none of Isherwood's moral preoccupations is apt to endear him to a literary establishment that is, variously, academic, Jewish/Christian, middle-class, and heterosexual. Yet he has written some of his best books in the United States, including the memoir at hand and the novels *A Single Man* and *A Meeting by the River*. Best of all, he still views the world aslant despite long residence in Santa Monica, a somber place where even fag households resemble those hetero couples photographed in *Better Homes and Gardens*, serving up intricate brunches 'neath the hazel Pacific sky.

What strikes me as most remarkable in Isherwood's career has not been so much the unremitting will to be his own man as the constant clarity of a prose style that shows no sign of slackness even though the author is, astonishingly, in his seventies. There is a good deal to be said about the way that Isherwood writes, particularly at a time when prose is worse than ever in the United States, and showing signs of etiolation in England. There is no excess in an Isherwood sentence. The verbs are strong. Nouns precise. Adjectives few. The third person startles and seduces, while the first person is a good guide and never coy.

Is the Isherwood manner perhaps *too* easy? Cyril Connolly feared that it might be when he wrote in *Enemies of Promise* (1938): "[Isherwood] is persuasive because he is so insinuatingly bland and anonymous, nothing rouses him, nothing shocks him. While secretly despising us he could not at the same time be more tolerant. . . . Now for this a price has to be paid; Herr Issyvoo" (Connolly is contemplating Isherwood's Berlin stories) "is not a dumb ox, for he is not condemned to the solidarity with his characters and with their background to which Hemingway is bound by his conception of art, but he is much less subtle, intelligent and articulate than he might be." Isherwood answered Connolly: "In conversation, Isherwood . . . expressed his belief in construction as the way out of the difficulty. The writer must conform to the language which is understood by the greatest number of people, to the vernacular, but his talent as a novelist will appear in the exactness of his observation, the justice of his situations and in the construction of his book."

Isherwood has maintained this aesthetic throughout a long career. When he turned his back on what Connolly termed Mandarin writing, he showed considerable courage. But the later Isherwood is even better than the early cameraman because he is no longer the anonymous, neutral narrator. He can be shocked; he can be angry.

In *Christopher and His Kind*, Isherwood wonders what attitude to take toward the coming war with Germany. "Suppose, Christopher now said to himself, I have a Nazi Army at my mercy. I can blow it up by pressing a button. The men in the army are notorious for torturing and murdering civilians—all except one of them, Heinz. Will I press the button? No—wait: Suppose I know that Heinz himself, out of cowardice or moral infection, has become as bad as they are and takes part in all their crimes? Will I press that button, even so? Christopher's answer, given without the slightest hesitation, was: Of course not." That is the voice of humanism in a bad time, and one can only hope that thanks to Christopher's life and work, his true kind will increase even as they refuse, so wisely, to multiply.

On Prettiness

In the fifteenth century the adjective "pretty" joined the English language (derived from the Old Teutonic noun *pratti* or *pratta*, meaning trick or wile). At first everyone thought the world of pretty. To be a pretty fellow was to be clever, apt, skillful; a pretty soldier was gallant and brave; a pretty thing was ingenious and artful. It was not until the sixteenth century that something started to go wrong with the idea of prettiness. Although women and children could still take pleasure in being called pretty, a pretty man had degenerated into a fop with a tendency to slyness. Pretty objects continued to be admired until 1875 when the phrase "pretty-pretty" was coined. That did it. For the truly clever, apt, and skillful, the adjective pretty could only be used in the pejorative sense, as I discovered thirty years ago while being shown around King's College by E. M. Forster. As we approached the celebrated chapel (magnificent, superb, a bit much), I said, "Pretty." Forster thought I meant the chapel when, actually, I was referring to a youthful couple in the damp middle distance. A ruthless moralist, Forster publicized my use of the dread word. Told in Fitzrovia and published in the streets of Dacca, the daughters of the Philistines rejoiced; the daughters of the uncircumcised triumphed. For a time, my mighty shield was vilely cast away.

In the last thirty years the adjective pretty has been pretty much abandoned, while the notion of beauty has become so complex that only the dullest of the daughters of the uncircumcised dares use it. Santayana was the last aesthetician to describe beauty without self-consciousness; and that was in 1896. As a result, we now live in a relativist's world where one man's beauty is another man's beast. This means that physical ugliness tends to be highly prized on the ground that it would be not only cruel, but provocative for, let us say, a popular performer to look better than the plainest member of the audience. This is democracy at its most endearing; and only a beauty or a Beaton would have it otherwise.

Sir Cecil Beaton's latest volume of diaries has now been published in the seventy-fourth year of a life devoted to the idea of beauty in people, clothes, décor, landscape, and manners. To the extent that Sir Cecil falls short of beauty in his life and work, he is merely pretty. But that is not such a bad thing. Quite the contrary. Sir Cecil . . . no, I think we had better call him Beaton, in honor of his own creation as opposed to the Queen's. Beaton is the oldest if not the last of a long line of minor artists who have given a good deal of pleasure to a good many people. He is a celebrated photographer. Unfortunately, I cannot judge his pictures because all photographs tend to look alike to me in their busy flatness. For half a century photography has been the "art form" of the untalented. Obviously some pictures are more satisfactory than others, but where is credit due? To the designer of the camera? to the finger on the button? to the law of averages? I was pleased to note in Beaton's pages that Picasso thought the same.

It is as a designer for the theatre that Beaton is at his best. But then clothes and sets are in the round, not flat upon the page. Beaton is absolutely stage-struck, and so wonderfully striking in his stage effects. There is no sense of strain in his theatre work except, perhaps, when he acts. Years ago I saw him in a play by (I think) Wilde. Like an elegant lizard just fed twenty milligrams of Valium, Beaton moved slowly about the stage. The tongue flicked; the lips moved; no word was audible.

Now we have Beaton's written words; and they are most vivid: contents of diaries kept from 1963 to 1974. The mood is often grim. He does not like getting old. He has also not learned that, after fifty, you must never look into a mirror whose little tricks you

don't already know in advance. The same goes for eyes. At the
Rothschild place in Mouton, he takes a good look at himself in a
strange mirror. He is rewarded for his recklessness:

> I was really an alarming sight—wild white hair on end, most of
> the pate quite bald: chins sagging with a scraggly tissued neck:
> pale weak eyes without their former warmth. But this could not
> be me!

More somber details are noted. Finally, "How could I make the
effort to dress myself up in picturesque clothes and try to be attractive to a group of highly critical people?" I am sure that he
managed.

The Parting Years is a haphazard collection of pages taken at
what seems to be random from a number of diaries. No attempt
has been made to link one thing to another. He arrives in New
York to design a production of *La Traviata*. Alfred Lunt is the
director. It is all very exciting. But, for the reader, the curtain
never goes up. How did the production go? Who sang? There are
numerous odd lacunae:

> Oliver Lyttleton, whose desire to amuse has increased with the
> years to the extent that he is a real bore, made one funny joke.
> The evening was a great success.

But what was the joke? On second thoughts, perhaps that is Beaton's strategy. In *Orlando*, Virginia Woolf never allowed us to hear
the brilliant dialogue of Alexander Pope.

Beaton is a good travel-writer. He has a sharp eye for those
horrors of travel that delight the sedentary reader far more than
set descriptions of beautiful or even pretty places. South America
in general and Poland in particular do not get high marks. The
first is too steep; the second too flat. But Beaton is quite as strict
with things English. The cathedrals get a thorough going-over.
"Exeter Cathedral, more squat than Salisbury, but original and
successful, with a frieze of carvings on the façade." Next term if
Exeter C. joins *wholeheartedly* in house-games there is no reason
why that squatness can't be trimmed down. On the other hand,
poor "Wells Cathedral did not look its best. It has a certain character but is not really impressive as a creative expression of de-
votion." Wells C. might do better at a different school.

Beaton is too much the stoic to strike too often the valetudinarian note. But when he does, the effect is chilling. He looks at himself with the same cold eye that he turns upon slovenly Wells Cathedral.

> I don't really feel that I am ever going to come into my own, to justify myself and my existence by some last great gesture. I am likewise certain that nothing I have done is likely to live long after me.

This is no doubt true. Yet one cannot help but admire a man in his seventies who still makes a living by his wits in the world of theatre and fashion where Americans with hearts of stone and egos of brass dominate ("I put up with Americans willingly only when I am on business bent").

Beaton never ceases to be interested in seeing new places, meeting new talent. He checks out The Rolling Stones at the beginning of their fame. He takes up the town's new artist, David Hockney. Meanwhile, he continues to make the rounds of the old from Picasso to Coward. He almost always has something shrewd to say —except of famous hostesses. They get elaborate bread-and-butter-letter eulogies best left unpublished. Beaton is most generous with the young. But then, it is always easier to prefer the young to one's contemporaries. Witness:

> *April 11, 1966:* So Evelyn Waugh is in his coffin. Died of snobbery. Did not wish to be considered a man of letters; it did not satisfy him to be thought a master of letters: it did not satisfy him to be thought a master of English prose. He wanted to be a duke . . .

Beaton and Waugh had known each other at school. Each was a social climber; and each was on to the other. Yet Beaton appears to have got a good deal of pleasure out of his nimble run up the ladder, as opposed to Waugh, who huffed and puffed and "would suddenly seem to be possessed by a devil and do thoroughly fiendish things." It is a pity that there is no present-day writer able to do for this pretty couple what Max Beerbohm did for a similar pair in "Hilary Maltby and Stephen Braxton."

As might be expected, the book is full of obituaries. Outliving contemporaries is always a joy, up to a point. Beaton usually gets the point. Of the Duke of Windsor, he "had never shown any affection for or interest in me." Beaton also notes that the Duke "was inclined to be silly." That is putting it mildly. The Duke's stupidity was of a perfection seldom encountered outside institutions. Of James Pope-Hennessy, he "had 'quality,' was intelligent, and intellectual and serious and yet good company." Beaton is a bit wary of intellectuals. He is better at describing figures like Chanel. He is also good on performers, noting the odd but illuminating detail. Alan Bates

> has invented an original sense of humor. It takes a while to realize what he is up to. . . . He has grown his hair very shaggily long. This is obviously to compensate for the width of the neck which has now become almost inhumanly large.

Much of *The Parting Years* will be mysterious to those not intimately acquainted with the theatre and High Bohemia. Even those who have some knowledge of the terrain will get lost from time to time. First names appear without last names. And last names without first names. It is often hard to figure out just who is who. There is one most intriguing encounter, set in New York. I quote the scene in its entirety. "Truman came back with me to the hotel. We talked over whiskies and sodas until I realized that by English time it was 7.30 in the morning." That's all. What, one wonders, did Beaton and the former president have to say to one another? News of the Queen? Of course. But that wouldn't go on until 1:30 a.m. (Eastern Standard Time). Lady Juliet Duff's failing health? Yes. But one illness is much like another. Music? That must be it. The thirty-third president loved to play the piano. They talked of Horowitz. Of young Van Cliburn who played at Potsdam for Truman and ("Uncle Joe") Stalin. But then, surely, Truman must have mentioned President Johnson. *What did he say?* For once, Beaton is too discreet, unlike his earlier diaries.

I was in Switzerland when Beaton's revelations about his "affair" with Greta Garbo were published in a German magazine. The only comment that I heard her make was glum: "And people think that I am pair-annoyed." But it is the nature of the dandy to flaunt brilliant plumes. In this, Beaton resembles the kingfisher, a bird that flies

so quickly that by the time one says "Look!" they have gone.
This most brilliant metallic bird is said to have such an unpleasant
smell for other birds that it is solitary and safe.

The Greek word for kingfisher is "halcyon"—born of the sea. For
two weeks at the winter solstice the kingfisher's nest is supposed
to float on a tranquil sea until the eggs are hatched. Twice Beaton
uses the word "halcyon" to describe days in summer. But halcyon
can refer only to calm and peaceful winter days, of the sort that
this bright kingfisher deserves for the pleasure that he has given to
all those who for so many years have watched ("Look!") his swift,
pretty flight.

New Statesman
MARCH 17, 1978

The Oz Books

"I have just seen a number of landscapes by an American painter of some repute," wrote John Ruskin in 1856; "and the ugliness of them is Wonderful. I see that they are true studies and that the ugliness of the country must be unfathomable." This was not kind. But then the English of that day had no great liking for the citizens of the Great Republic. Twenty-four years earlier Mrs. Trollope had commented without warmth on the manners and the domestic arrangements of United Statesmen (or persons, as we must now, androgynously, describe ourselves). Twelve years earlier Charles Dickens had published *Martin Chuzzlewit*. Dickens had found the American countryside raw. The cities ramshackle. The people gasping, boastful, even—yes, dishonest. This was not at all kind. But then how could these British travelers have known that in a century's time the barbarous republic beyond the western sea would not once but twice pull from the flames of war (or "conflagration" as they say in Hollywood) England's chestnuts?

In 1856 the United States was a provincial backwater. The eruption of energy that was to fuel the future empire did not begin until four years later when the Civil War broke out. By war's end the United States was a great industrial power with satanic cities every bit as ugly and infernal as Birmingham and Manchester, with a vast flat interior that was peculiarly susceptible to those drastic changes in weather (and so fortune) that make farming an exciting occupation, with a somewhat thin civilization that has not to this day quite got off the ground in the sense that Europe's nation-states were able to do in those dark confused centuries that followed on the death of Charlemagne, and Christendom.

Yet during 1856 a number of interesting things happened in the United States. Mrs. Carl Schurz opened the first kindergarten at Watertown, Wisconsin. In Chelsea, Massachusetts, the Universalist Church observed, for the first time anywhere, Children's Day. In New York City the big theatrical hit of the season was a pantomime (from London) called *Planche, or Lively Fairies*. The year's most successful book of poems was J. G. Whittier's *The Panorama and Other Poems*, a volume that included "The Barefoot Boy." People were unexpectedly interested in the care, education, and comfort of children. It is somehow both fitting and satisfying that on May 15 of the first American Children's Year Lyman Frank Baum was born.

Like most Americans my age (with access to books), I spent a good deal of my youth in Baum's Land of Oz. I have a precise, tactile memory of the first Oz book that came into my hands. It was the original 1910 edition of *The Emerald City*. I still remember the look and the feel of those dark blue covers, the evocative smell of dust and old ink. I also remember that I could not stop reading and rereading the book. But "reading" is not the right word. In some mysterious way, I was translating myself to Oz, a place which I was to inhabit for many years while, simultaneously, visiting other fictional worlds as well as maintaining my cover in that dangerous one known as "real." With *The Emerald City*, I became addicted to reading.

By the time I was fourteen, I had read Baum's fourteen Oz books as well as the nineteen Oz books written after his death in 1919 by a young Philadelphia writer named Ruth Plumly Thompson. I remember puzzling over the strange legend that appeared on the cover of each of the books that she wrote: "by Ruth Plumly Thompson founded on and continuing the famous Oz stories by L. Frank Baum." It took me years to figure out what that phrase meant.

To a child a book is a book. The writer's name is an irrelevant decoration, unlike the title, which prepares one for delight. Even so, I used, idly, to wonder who or what L. Frank Baum was. Baum looked to my eye like Barnum, as in Barnum & Bailey's circus. Was it the same person? or the circus itself? But then, who or what was Bailey? Ruth Plumly Thompson (who was always founded-on and inexorably continuing) seemed to me to be a sort of train. The plum in Plumly registered, of course. Circus. And plums. Founded on and continuing. I never thought to ask anyone about either writer. And no one thought to tell me. But then, in the 1930s very little had been written about either Baum or Thompson.

Recently I was sent an academic dissertation. Certain aspects of Baum's *The Land of Oz* had reoccurred in a book of mine. Was this conscious or not? (It was not.) But I was intrigued. I reread *The Land of Oz*. Yes, I could see Baum's influence. I then reread *The Emerald City of Oz*. I have now reread all of L. Frank Baum's Oz books. I have also read a good deal of what has been written about him in recent years. Although Baum's books were dismissed as trash by at least two generations of librarians and literary historians, the land of Oz has managed to fascinate each new generation and, lately, Baum himself has become an OK subject, if not for the literary critic, for the social historian.

Even so, it is odd that Baum has received so little acknowledgment from those who owe him the most—writers. After all, those books (films, television, too, alas) first encountered in childhood do more to shape the imagination and its style than all the later calculated readings of acknowledged masters. Scientists are often more candid in their admiration (our attempts to find life elsewhere in the universe is known as Operation Ozma). Lack of proper acknowledgment perhaps explains the extent to which Baum has been ignored by literary historians, by English departments, by. . . . As I write these words, a sense of dread. Is is possible that Baum's survival is due to the fact that he is *not* taught? That he is not, officially, Literature? If so, one must be careful not to murder Oz with exegesis.

In search of L. Frank Baum and the genesis of Oz, I have read every sort of study of him from *To Please a Child* by his son Frank Joslyn Baum and Russell P. MacFall to the meticulous introductions of Martin Gardner for the Dover reproductions of the original Oz editions (as well as Gardner's book with R. B. Nye, *The Wizard of Oz & Who He Was*) to issues of the *Baum Bugle* (a newsletter put out by Oz enthusiasts since 1957) to the recent and charming *Oz Scrapbook* as well as to what looks to be a Ph.D. thesis got up as a book called *Wonderful Wizard, Marvelous Land* (1974) by Raylyn Moore.

The introduction to Moore's book is written by the admirable Ray Bradbury in an uncharacteristically overwrought style. Yet prose far to one side, Bradbury makes some good points: "Let us consider two authors" (the other is Edgar Rice Burroughs) "whose works were burned in our American society during the past seventy years. Librarians and teachers did the burning very subtly by not buying. And not buying is as good as burning. Yet, the authors survived."

The hostility of librarians to the Oz books is in itself something of a phenomenon. The books are always popular with children. But many librarians will not stock them. According to the chairman of the Miami Public Library, magic is out: "Kids don't like that fanciful stuff anymore. They want books about missiles and atomic submarines." Less militaristic librarians have made the practical point that if you buy one volume of a popular series you will have to get the whole lot and there are, after all, forty Oz books.

Bradbury seems to think that the Oz books are disdained because they are considered "mediocre" by literary snobs (the same people who do not take seriously Science Fiction?). But I think that he is wrong. After all, since most American English teachers, librarians, and literary historians are not intellectuals, how would any of them know whether or not a book was well or ill written? More to the point, not many would care. Essentially, our educators are Puritans who want to uphold the Puritan work ethic. This is done by bringing up American children in such a way that they will take their place in society as diligent workers and unprotesting consumers. Any sort of literature that encourages a child to contemplate alternative worlds might incite him, later in life, to make changes in the iron Puritan order that has brought us, along with missiles and atomic submarines, the assembly line at Detroit where workers are systematically dehumanized.

It is significant that one of the most brutal attacks on the Oz books was made in 1957 by the director of the Detroit Library System, a Mr. Ralph Ulveling, who found the Oz books to "have a cowardly approach to life." They are also guilty of "negativism." Worst of all, "there is nothing uplifting or elevating about the Baum series." For the Librarian of Detroit, courage and affirmation mean punching the clock and then doing the dull work of a machine while never questioning the system. Our governors not only know what is good for us, they never let up. From monitoring the books that are read in grade school to the brass handshake and the pension (whose fund is always in jeopardy) at the end, they are forever on the job. They have to be because they know that there is no greater danger to their order than a worker whose day-dreams are not of television sets and sex but of differently ordered worlds. Fortunately, the system of government that controls the school system and makes possible the consumer society does not control all of publishing; otherwise, much imaginative writing might exist only in *samizdat*.

Ray Bradbury makes his case for America's two influential imaginative writers, Baum and Edgar Rice Burroughs, creator not only of Tarzan but of John Carter in the Mars series. "John Carter grew to maturity" (in pots?) "two generations of astronomers, geologists, biochemists, and astronauts who cut their teeth on his Barsoomian beasts and Martian fighting men and decided to grow up and grow out away from earth." A decision that would never have been acceptable to our rulers if the Russians had not put Sputnik into orbit, obliging an American president of the time to announce that, all in all, it was probably a good thing for our prestige to go to the moon.

Bradbury then turns to "L. Frank Baum, that faintly old-maidish man who grew boys" (in a greenhouse?) "inward to their most delightful interiors, kept them home, and romanced them with wonders between their ears." Through Bradbury's rich style, a point is emerging: inward to delightful selves. Kept them home. Romanced them. Wonders. Yes, all that is true. And hateful to professional molders of American youth. Boys should be out of the house, competing in games, building model airplanes, beating each other up so that one day they will be obedient soldiers in the endless battle for the free world. Show us a dreaming boy (or girl) at home with a book, and we will show you a potential trouble-maker.

Bradbury compares Baum to Lewis Carroll. This is a mistake. Carroll belongs, in a complex way, not only to our language's high literature but to logic. It is simple-minded and mawkish to say that "Oz is muffins and honey, summer vacations, and all the easy green time in the world" while "Wonderland is cold gruel and arithmetic at six a.m., icy showers, long" (as opposed to narrow?) "schools." Because of this supposed polarity, Bradbury thinks "that Wonder-

land is the darling of the intellectuals." On the subject of Oz, he
is at his best not in this preface but in a good short story called
"The Exiles" (1950).

The text of Raylyn Moore is interesting. She has read what
others have written about Baum. She is perhaps too impressed by
the fact that the hippies (surely they no longer exist this side of
the rainbow) took up Oz in a big way. She also keeps quoting the
author of *The Greening of America* as if he were some sort of
authority. Fortunately, she also quotes from those who have written
interestingly about Baum: Edward Wagenknecht, James Thurber
(in *The New Republic*, 1934), and Henry Littlefield, who demonstrates (in *American Quarterly*, 1964) that *The Wizard of Oz* is a
parable on populism "in which the Tin Woodman is seen as the
eastern industrialist worker (he is discovered by Dorothy in the
eastern land of the Munchkins), the Scarecrow as the farmer, and
the Lion as the politician (William Jennings Bryan), who as a group
approach the Wizard (McKinley) to ask for relief from their
sufferings. Dorothy's magical silver shoes (the proposed silver
standard) traveling along the Yellow Brick Road (gold) are lost
forever in the Deadly Desert when she returns to Kansas (when
Bryan lost the election)." This is certainly elaborate.

Yet Baum in his work and life (as described by those who knew
him) was apolitical. He is known to have marched in a torchlight
parade for Bryan in 1896, the year of McKinley's victory. He also
supported Bryan in 1900. But, politically, that was it. Only once
in the fairy tales have I been able to find a direct political reference.
In *Sea Fairies* there is an octopus who is deeply offended when he
learns that Standard Oil is called an "octopus": " 'Oh, what a disgrace! What a deep, dire, dreadful disgrace!' " But though Baum
was not political in the usual sense, he had very definite ideas about
the way the world should be. I shall come to that.

L. Frank Baum was born at Chittenango in upstate New York,
the son of Benjamin W. Baum, who had become rich in the Penn-
sylvania oil fields. The Baums came from the Palatinate and Frank
Baum's grandparents were German-speaking. Grandfather Baum
was a Methodist lay preacher. Frank's mother was Scots-Irish.
There were eight brothers and sisters. Four died early.

Apparently the Baums enjoyed their wealth. L. Frank Baum
grew up on a large estate called Rose Lawn, near Syracuse. In *Dot
and Tot of Merryland* (1901) Baum describes the house's "wings
and gables and broad verandas," the lawns, flowers, "winding paths

covered with white gravel, which led to all parts of the grounds, looking for all the world like a map." Maps of Oz were later to be important to Baum and to his readers. Oz was . . . no, *is* an oblong country divided into four equal sections whose boundaries converge at the Emerald City, the country's capital as well as geographical center. Each of the four minor countries is a different color: Everything in the north is purple; the south red; the east yellow; the west blue. The effect, exactly, of a certain kind of old-fashioned garden where flower beds are laid out symmetrically and separated from one another by "winding paths covered with white gravel."

At twelve Baum was sent to a military academy which he hated. He escaped by developing a bad heart. Back at Rose Lawn, Baum put out a newspaper on a printing press given him by his father. Later Baum became interested in chicken breeding and acting, two activities not often linked. Happily, the indulgent father could provide Baum not only with eggs but also with a theatrical career. Because Benjamin Baum owned a string of theatres, his son was able to join a touring company at nineteen. Three years later Baum was in New York, with a leading role in Bronson Howard's highly successful play *The Banker's Daughter* (1878). According to contemporary photographs Baum was a handsome young man with gray eyes, straight nose, dark brown hair, and a period mustache that looked to be glued on; he was six feet tall, left-handed; the voice was agreeable and in later years, on the lecture circuit, he was somtimes compared, favorably, to Mark Twain.

The pieces are now falling into place. Weak heart. Dreamy childhood. Gardens of Rose Lawn. Printing press and self-edited newspaper. Chicken breeding. Theatre. At that time the theatre was as close as anyone could come to creating magic. On the rickety stages of a thousand provincial theatre houses, alternative worlds blazed like magic by limelight. In 1882 Baum wrote and played and toured in a musical "comedy" called *Maid of Arran*, a fair success. The same year he married Maud Gage. The marriage was a true success though she was a good deal tougher than he: she spanked the children, he consoled them. Maud's mother was an active suffragette and a friend of Susan B. Anthony. Although the high-minded Puritan Gages were most unlike the easy-going Germanic Baums, relations seem to have been good between Mrs. Gage and her son-in-law, who was pretty much of a failure for the next sixteen years. Baum's theatrical career ended, literally, in flames when the sets and costumes of *Maid of Arran* were burned in a warehouse fire. Suddenly the whole family was downwardly mobile. At twenty-nine Baum went to work as a traveling salesman for a family firm that made axle grease. He also wrote his first book. *The Book of the Hamburgs*, all about chickens.

The lives of Baum and Burroughs are remarkably similar in kind if not in detail. Each knocked about a good deal. Each failed at a number of unsatisfying jobs. Each turned late to writing. Burroughs wrote his first book at thirty-seven; he was thirty-nine when *Tarzan of the Apes* was published. Except for the chicken manual, Baum did not publish until he was forty-one; then at forty-four came *The Wonderful Wizard of Oz*. Forty appears to be the shadow-line in American lives; it must be crossed in style, or else.

Failure has never been much fun in the United States. During the last two decades of the Gilded Age and the first decade of the American Empire, failure must have been uncommonly grim. On every side, enormous fortunes were conspicuously made and spent. To be poor was either a sign of bad character or of bad genes or both. Hard-hearted predestination was in the air. *The Origin of Species* had greatly influenced United Statespersons, and throughout Baum's lifetime Darwin was constantly misread and misquoted in order to support *laissez nous faire*, the Puritan work ethic, and, of course, slavery.

In their twenties and thirties Burroughs and Baum were Darwinian rejects. Burroughs was a railroad dick; Baum operated, first, a failing store in Dakota Territory; then a failing newspaper. During the bad years, Burroughs used to tell himself stories before going to sleep (on the job, too, one would guess). Night after night he would add new episodes to his various serials. Although there is no evidence that Baum indulged in this kind of daydreaming, the best part of his day was the children's bedtime when he would improvise magical stories for them.

Powerless to affect the gray flat everyday world, Burroughs and Baum each escaped into waking dreams. The dreams of Burroughs are those of a fourteen-year-old boy who would like to be physically powerful like Tarzan or magically endowed like John Carter, who was able to defenestrate himself at will from dull earth to thrilling (pre-NASA) Mars. Sex is a powerful drive in all of Burroughs's dreams, though demurely rendered when he wrote them down. The dreams of Baum are somewhat different. They are those of a prepubescent child who likes to be frightened (but not very much) and delighted with puns and jokes in a topsy-turvy magical world where his toys are not only as large as he but able to walk and talk and keep him company. There is no conscious sex in the world of the nine-year-old. Yet there is a concomitant will to power that does express itself, sometimes in unexpected ways.

Since the quotidian did not fulfill the dreams of either Baum or Burroughs, each constructed an alternative world. Most artists do. But it is odd that each should have continued well into middle life to tell himself the sort of stories that most people cease to tell themselves in childhood or early adolescence. It is not usual to be a compulsive storyteller for an audience of one. Yet neither seemed to have had any urgent need to share his private stories with others (I count Baum's children as extensions of himself; there is no record of his inventing stories for anyone else).

Although it is hard to think of Baum as writing political allegories in support of Free Silver, his inventions do reflect the world in which he grew up. When he was a year old, in 1857, the country was swept by a Christian revival whose like we were not to see again until the Carter White House and the better federal prisons started to fill up with evangelical Christians. During Baum's prepubescence the Civil War took place. In his twelfth year Susan B. Anthony started the suffragette movement; and San Francisco fell flat on its hills. In fact, all during the last days of the century, nature was on a rampage and the weather was more than usually abnormal, as the old joke goes.

In 1893, a cyclone destroyed two Kansas towns, killing thirty-one people. I take this disaster to be the one that Baum was to describe seven years later in *The Wizard of Oz*. He himself was marginally associated with one national disaster. On December 6, 1890, Baum wrote a rather edgy "funny" column for his newspaper in Aberdeen, Dakota Territory. He turns inside out the official American line that the Sioux Indians were getting ready to massacre all the whites. Baum pretends to interview an Indian chief who tells him that the Indians are terrified of being massacred by the whites. Two weeks after this story was published, the U.S. Seventh Cavalry slaughtered three hundred Indian men, women, and children at nearby Wounded Knee. Soon afterward, Baum and his family moved to Chicago.

Since no one ever thought to investigate in any detail the sort of books Baum liked to read, we can only guess at influences. He himself mentioned Charles Reade's *The Cloister and the Hearth*, as well as Dickens and Thackeray. When Baum was still a schoolboy, American educators began to emphasize the sciences (the assembly line was on its way) and the traditional humanities gave ground to the inhumanities. Certainly Baum's lifelong interest in science and gadgetry was typical of his time and place.

The overwhelming presence in the Oz books of kings and queens, princes and princesses derives from a line of popular writing that began in 1894 with *The Prisoner of Zenda* and reached a most gorgeous peak with the publication of *Graustark* in 1901. Although Baum was plainly influenced by these books, I suspect that his love of resplendent titles and miniature countries had something to do with his own ancestry. Before Bismarck's invention of the German Empire in 1871, that particular geographical area was decorated—no, gilded with four kingdoms (one of them, Bavaria, contained the home of Baum's ancestors), six grand-duchies, five duchies, seven principalities, and three freetowns. The adjoining Austro-Hungarian Empire was a dual monarchy containing numerous kingdoms, duchies, principalities, not to mention a constant shifting of borders that my own family (perhaps like Baum's) never satisfactorily explained to me.

According to F. J. Baum and MacFall, sixty Utopian novels were published in the United States between 1888 and 1901. The best known was Bellamy's *Looking Backward*, which Baum mildly sent up in the Aberdeen *Saturday Pioneer*. The fact that so many writers were inclined to posit an alternative society to the Gilded Age shows a certain dissatisfaction with the great republic.

Baum is sometimes regarded as a Utopian writer. But I don't think that this is accurate. Utopian writers have political ideas, and Baum seems to have had none at all. Except for a mild parody of the suffragettes, there is little to link political America with magical Oz, whose minuscule countries are governed by hereditary lords. On the other hand, Baum was a social moralist who is said to have been influenced by William Morris's *News from Nowhere*, published in 1891 (not 1892 as R. Moore states). In *The Emerald City*, nearly two decades after the publication of Morris's vision of the good society, Baum writes of Oz in somewhat similar terms: "there were no poor people . . . because there was no such thing as money, and all property of every sort belonged to the Ruler. The people were her children, and she cared for them. Each person was given freely by his neighbors whatever he required for his use, which is as much as anyone may reasonably desire." This is not the sort of society most calculated to appeal to the Librarian of Detroit.

Interestingly enough, there is no reference in the Oz books to a republic of any kind. There are no parliaments or congresses. There are no elections—a most peculiar thing for an American writer to leave out. The various rulers are all feudal except in the last book of the series (*Glinda of Oz*) where Baum introduces us, surprisingly, to a Supreme Dictator. Baum was still at work on the book in March 1919 when Mussolini founded the Fascist Party. Was he, in some way, prescient? Whether or not Baum was predicting fascism, it is significant that he associates the idea of dictatorship with democracy: " 'I'm the Supreme Dictator of all, and I'm elected once a year. This is a democracy, you know, where the people are allowed to vote for their rulers. A good many others would like to be Supreme Dictator, but as I made a law that I am always to count the votes myself, I am always elected.' " If nothing else, the years that Baum lived in Chicago had left their mark on his political thinking. Earlier in the series (*The Emerald City*), there is another elected monarch, the unhappy rabbit King of Bunnyberry. But this election was reminiscent not of Chicago but of the feudal arrangements of the ancient Teutonic kings and their descendants, the Holy Roman emperors.

The authors of *To Please a Child* tell us the genesis of the name Oz. "One evening while the thunder of Admiral George Dewey's guns was still echoing in Manila Bay, Baum was sitting in his Chicago home telling stories to youngsters. The two events brushed each other briefly in the course of manifest destiny and children's literature." I cannot tell if "manifest destiny" is meant ironically. In any case, Baum says that he was telling a story pretty much like *The Wizard of Oz* when one of the children wanted to know where all these adventures took place. Looking about for inspiration, Baum glanced at a copy of the *Chicago Tribune* (dated May 7, 1898) and saw the headlines proclaiming Dewey's victory. Then he noticed a filing cabinet with two drawers: A-N and O-Z. The second label gave its name to Oz. True or not, there is a certain niceness in the way that the militant phase of the American empire was to coincide with Baum's parallel and better world.

Baum had begun to prosper in Chicago. At Mrs. Gage's insistence, he wrote down some of the stories that he had made up for his children. They were published as *Mother Goose in Prose* in 1897; that same year he started a magazine called *The Show*

Window, for window-dressers. The magazine was an unlikely success. Then Baum published *Father Goose, His Book* (1899); he was now established as a popular children's writer. Devoting himself full-time to writing, he produced a half-dozen books in 1899, among them *The Wizard of Oz*.

During the next nineteen years Baum wrote sixty-two books. Most of them were for children and most of them had girl-protagonists. There are many theories why Baum preferred girls to boys as central characters. The simplest is that he had four sons and would have liked a daughter. The most practical is that popular American writing of that day tended to be feminized because women bought the books. The most predictable is the vulgar Freudian line that either Baum secretly wanted to be a girl or, worse, that he suffered from a Dodsonian (even Humbertian) lust for small girls. I suspect that Baum wrote about girls not only because he liked them but because his sort of imagination was not geared to those things that are supposed to divert real boys (competitive games, cowboys and Indians, cops and robbers, murder).

In the preface to *The Wizard of Oz*, L. Frank Baum says that he would like to create *modern* fairy tales by departing from Grimm and Andersen and "all the horrible and blood-curdling incident devised" by such authors "to point a fearsome moral." Baum then makes the disingenuous point that "Modern education includes morality; therefore the modern child seeks only entertainment in its wondertales and gladly dispenses with all disagreeable incident." Yet there is a certain amount of explicit as well as implicit moralizing in the Oz books; there are also "disagreeable incidents," and people do, somehow, die, even though death and illness are not supposed to exist in Oz.

I have reread the Oz books in the order in which they were written. Some things are as I remember. Others strike me as being entirely new. I was struck by the unevenness of style not only from book to book but, sometimes, from page to page. The jaggedness can be explained by the fact that the man who was writing fourteen Oz books was writing forty-eight other books at the same time. Arguably, *The Wizard of Oz* is the best of the lot. After all, the first book is the one in which Oz was invented. Yet, as a child, I preferred *The Emerald City*, *Rinkitink*, and *The Lost Princess* to *The Wizard*. Now I find that all of the books tend to flow together in a single narrative, with occasional bad patches.

In *The Wizard of Oz* Dorothy is about six years old. In the later books she seems to be ten or eleven. Baum locates her swiftly and efficiently in the first sentence of the series. "Dorothy lived in the midst of the great Kansas prairies, with Uncle Henry, who was a farmer, and Aunt Em, who was the farmer's wife." The landscape would have confirmed John Ruskin's dark view of American scenery (he died the year that *The Wizard of Oz* was published).

> When Dorothy stood in the doorway and looked around, she could see nothing but the great gray prairie on every side. Not a tree nor a house broke the broad sweep of flat country that reached the edge of the sky in all directions.

This is the plain American style at its best. Like most of Baum's central characters, Dorothy lacks the regulation father and mother. Some commentators have made, I think, too much of Baum's parentless children. The author's motive seems to me to be not only obvious but sensible. A child separated from loving parents for any length of time is going to be distressed, even in a magic story. But aunts and uncles need not be taken too seriously.

In the first four pages Baum demonstrates the drabness of Dorothy's life; the next two pages are devoted to the cyclone that lifts the house into the air and hurls it to Oz. Newspaper accounts of recent cyclones had obviously impressed Baum. Alone in the house (except for Toto, a Cairn terrier), Dorothy is established as a sensible girl who is not going to worry unduly about events that she cannot control. The house crosses the Deadly Desert and lands on top of the Wicked Witch of the West, who promptly dries up and dies. Right off, Baum breaks his own rule that no one ever dies in Oz. I used to spend a good deal of time worrying about the numerous inconsistencies in the sacred texts. From time to time, Baum himself would try to rationalize errors, but he was far too quick and careless a writer ever to create the absolutely logical mad worlds that Lewis Carroll or E. Nesbit did.

Dorothy is acclaimed by the Munchkins as a good witch who has managed to free them from the Wicked Witch. They advise her to go to the Emerald City and try to see the famous Wizard; he alone would have the power to grant her dearest wish, which is to go home to Kansas. Why she wanted to go back was never clear to me. Or, finally, to Baum: eventually, he moves Dorothy (with aunt and uncle) to Oz.

Along the way to the Emerald City, Dorothy meets a live Scarecrow in search of brains, a Tin Woodman in search of a heart, a Cowardly Lion in search of courage. Each new character furthers the plot. Each is essentially a humor. Each, when he speaks, strikes the same simple, satisfying note.

Together they undergo adventures. In sharp contrast to gray flat Kansas, Oz seems to blaze with color. Yet the Emerald City is a bit of a fraud. Everyone is obliged to wear green glasses in order to make the city appear emerald-green.

The Wizard says that he will help them if they destroy yet another wicked witch. They do. Only to find out that the Wizard is a fake who arrived by balloon from the States, where he had been a magician in a circus. Although a fraud, the Wizard is a good psychologist. He gives the Scarecrow bran for brains, the Tin Woodman a red velvet heart, the Cowardly Lion a special courage syrup. Each has now become what he wanted to be (and was all along). The Wizard's response to their delight is glum: " 'How can I help being a humbug,' he said, 'when all these people make me do things that everybody knows can't be done? It was easy to make the Scarecrow and the Lion and the Woodman happy, because they imagined I could do anything. But it will take more than imagination to carry Dorothy back to Kansas, and I'm sure I don't know how it can be done.' " When the Wizard arranges a balloon to take Dorothy and himself back home, the balloon takes off without Dorothy. Finally, she is sent home through the intervention of magic, and the good witch Glinda.

The style of the first book is straightforward, even formal. There are almost no contractions. Dorothy speaks not at all the way a grown-up might think a child should speak but like a sensible somewhat literal person. There are occasional Germanisms (did Baum's father speak German?): " 'What is that little animal you are so tender of?' " Throughout all the books there is a fascination with jewelry and elaborate costumes. Baum never got over his love of theatre. In this he resembled his favorite author, Charles Reade, of whom *The Dictionary of National Biography* tells us: "At his best Reade was an admirable storyteller, full of resource and capacity to excite terror and pity; but his ambition to excel as a dramatist militated against his success as a novelist, and nearly all his work is disfigured by a striving after theatrical effect."

Baum's passion for the theatre and, later, the movies not only wasted his time but, worse, it had a noticeably bad effect on his prose style. Because *The Wizard of Oz* was the most successful children's book of the 1900 Christmas season (in its first two years of publication, the book sold ninety thousand copies), Baum was immediately inspired to dramatize the story. Much "improved" by other hands, the musical comedy opened in Chicago (June 16, 1902) and was a success. After a year and a half on Broadway, the show toured off and on until 1911. Over the years Baum was to spend a good deal of time trying to make plays and films based on the Oz characters. Except for the first, none was a success.

Since two popular vaudevillians had made quite a splash as the Tin Woodman and the Scarecrow in the musical version of *The Wizard*, Baum decided that a sequel was in order . . . for the stage. But rather than write directly for the theatre, he chose to write a second Oz book, without Dorothy or the Wizard. In an Author's Note to *The Marvelous Land of Oz*, Baum somewhat craftily says that he has been getting all sorts of letters from children asking him "to 'write something more' about the Scarecrow and the Tin Woodman." In 1904 the sequel was published, with a dedication to the two vaudevillians. A subsequent musical comedy called *The Woggle-Bug* was then produced; and failed. That, for the time being, was that. But the idiocies of popular theatre had begun to infect Baum's prose. *The Wizard of Oz* is chastely written. *The Land of Oz* is not. Baum riots in dull wordplay. There are endless bad puns, of the sort favored by popular comedians. There is also that true period horror: the baby-talking ingenue, a character who lasted well into our day in the menacing shapes of Fanny (Baby Snooks) Brice and the early Ginger Rogers. Dorothy, who talked plainly and to the point in *The Wizard*, talks (when she reappears in the third book) with a cuteness hard to bear. Fortunately, Baum's show-biz phase wore off and in later volumes Dorothy's speech improves.

Despite stylistic lapses, *The Land of Oz* is one of the most unusual and interesting books of the series. In fact, it is so unusual that after the Shirley Temple television adaptation of the book in 1960,* PTA circles were in a state of crisis. The problem that knitted then and, I am told, knits even today many a maternal brow is Sexual

---

* In 1939, MGM made a film called *The Wizard of Oz* with Judy Garland. A new book, *The Making of "The Wizard of Oz"* by Aljean Harmetz, describes in altogether too great but fascinating detail the assembling of the movie, which had one and a half producers, ten writers, and four directors. Who then was the "auteur"?

Role. Sexual Role makes the world go round. It is what makes the man go to the office or to the factory where he works hard while the wife fulfills *her* Sexual Role by homemaking and consuming and bringing up boys to be real boys and girls to be real girls, a cycle that must continue unchanged and unquestioned until the last car comes off Detroit's last assembly line and the last all-American sun vanishes behind a terminal dioxin haze.

Certainly the denouement of *The Land of Oz* is troubling for those who have heard of Freud. A boy, Tip, is held in thrall by a wicked witch named Mombi. One day she gets hold of an elixir that makes the inanimate live. Tip uses this magical powder to bring to life a homemade figure with a jack-o'-lantern head: Jack Pumpkinhead, who turns out to be a comic of the Ed Wynn–Simple Simon school. " 'Now that is a very interesting history,' said Jack, well pleased; 'and I understand it perfectly—all but the explanation.' "

Tip and Jack Pumpkinhead escape from Mombi, aboard a brought-to-life sawhorse. They then meet the stars of the show (and a show it is), the Scarecrow and the Tin Woodman. As a central character neither is very effective. In fact, each has a tendency to sententiousness; and there are nowhere near enough jokes. The Scarecrow goes on about his brains; the Tin Woodman about his heart. But then it is the limitation as well as the charm of made-up fairy-tale creatures to embody to the point of absurdity a single quality or humor.

There is one genuinely funny sketch. When the Scarecrow and Jack Pumpkinhead meet, they decide that since each comes from a different country, " 'We must,' " says the Scarecrow, " 'have an interpreter.'

" 'What is an interpreter?' asked Jack.

" 'A person who understands both my language and your own. . . .' " And so on. Well, maybe this is *not* so funny.

The Scarecrow (who had taken the vanished Wizard's place as ruler of Oz) is overthrown by a "revolting" army of girls (great excuse for a leggy chorus). This long and rather heavy satire on the suffragettes was plainly more suitable for a Broadway show than for a children's story. The girl leader, Jinjur, is an unexpectedly engaging character. She belongs to the Bismarckian *Realpolitik* school. She is accused of treason for having usurped the Scarecrow's throne. " 'The throne belongs to whoever is able to take it,' answered Jinjur as she slowly ate another caramel. 'I have

taken it, as you see; so just now I am the Queen, and all who oppose me are guilty of treason. . . .' " This is the old children's game
I-am-the-King-of-the-castle, a.k.a. human history.

Among the new characters met in this story are the Woggle-
Bug, a highly magnified insect who has escaped from a classroom
exhibition and (still magnified) ranges about the countryside. A
parody of an American academic, he is addicted to horrendous puns
on the grounds that " 'a joke derived from a play upon words is
considered among educated people to be eminently proper.' " Anna
livia plurabelle.

There is a struggle between Jinjur and the legitimate forces of
the Scarecrow. The Scarecrow's faction wins and the girls are sent
away to be homemakers and consumers. In passing, the Scarecrow
observes, " 'I am convinced that the only people worthy of consideration in this world are the unusual ones. For the common folks
are like the leaves of a tree, and live and die unnoticed.' " To which
the Tin Woodman replies, " 'Spoken like a philosopher!' " To
which the current editor Martin Gardner responds, with true
democratic wrath, "This despicable view, indeed defended by
many philosophers, had earlier been countered by the Tin Woodman," etc. But the view is not at all despicable. For one thing, it
would be the normal view of an odd magical creature who cannot
die. For another, Baum was simply echoing those neo-Darwinians
who dominated most American thinking for at least a century. It
testifies to Baum's sweetness of character that unlike most writers
of his day he seldom makes fun of the poor or weak or unfortunate.
Also, the Scarecrow's "despicable" remarks can be interpreted as
meaning that although unorthodox dreamers are despised by the
ordinary, their dreams are apt to prevail in the end and become
reality.

Glinda the Good Sorceress is a kindly mother figure to the various children who visit or live in Oz, and it is she who often ties up
the loose ends when the story bogs down. In *The Land of Oz*
Glinda has not a loose end but something on the order of a hang-
man's rope to knot. Apparently the rightful ruler of Oz is Princess
Ozma. As a baby, Ozma was changed by Mombi into the boy Tip.
Now Tip must be restored to his true identity. The PTA went, as
it were, into plenary session. What effect would a book like this
have on a boy's sense of himself as a future man, breadwinner and
father to more of same? Would he want, awful thought, to be a
Girl? Even Baum's Tip is alarmed when told who he is. " 'I!' cried

Tip, in amazement. 'Why I'm no Princess Ozma—I'm not a girl!' "
Glinda tells him that indeed he was—and really is. Tip is understandably grumpy. Finally, he says to Glinda, " 'I might try it for
awhile,—just to see how it seems, you know. But if I don't like
being a girl you must promise to change me into a boy again.' "
Glinda says that this is not in the cards. Glumly, Tip agrees to the
restoration. Tip becomes the beautiful Ozma, who hopes that
" 'none of you will care less for me than you did before. I'm just
the same Tip, you know; only—only—' "

> "Only you're different!" said the Pumpkinhead; and everyone
> thought it was the wisest speech he had ever made.

Essentially, Baum's human protagonists are neither male nor female but children, a separate category in his view if not in that of
our latter-day sexists. Baum's use of sex changes was common to
the popular theatre of his day, which, in turn, derived from the
Elizabethan era when boys played girls whom the plot often required to pretend to be boys. In Baum's *The Enchanted Island of
Yew* a fairy (female) becomes a knight (male) in order to have
adventures. In *The Emerald City* the hideous Phanfasm leader
turns himself into a beautiful woman. When *John Dough and the
Cherub* (1906) was published, the sex of the five-year-old cherub
was never mentioned in the text; the publishers then launched a
national ad campaign: "Is the cherub boy or girl? $500 for the best
answers." In those innocent times Tip's metamorphosis as Ozma
was nothing more than a classic *coup de théâtre* of the sort that
even now requires the boy Peter Pan to be played on stage by a
mature woman.

Today of course any sort of sexual metamorphosis causes distress. Although Raylyn Moore in her plot *précis* of *The Enchanted
Island of Yew* (in her book *Wonderful Wizard, Marvelous Land*)
does make one confusing reference to the protagonist as "he
(she)," she omits entirely the Tip/Ozma transformation, which is
the whole point to *The Land of Oz*, while the plot as given by the
publisher Reilly & Lee says only that "the book ends with an amazing surprise, and from that moment on Ozma is princess of all Oz."
But, surely, for a pre-pube there is not much difference between a
boy and a girl protagonist. After all, the central fact of the pre-
pube's existence is not being male or female but being a child, much
the hardest of all roles to play. During and after puberty, there is

a tendency to want a central character like oneself (my favorite
Oz book was R. P. Thompson's *Speedy in Oz*, whose eleven- or
twelve-year-old hero could have been, I thought, me). Nevertheless, what matters most even to an adolescent is not the gender of
the main character who experiences adventures but the adventures
themselves, and the magic, and the jokes, and the pictures.

Dorothy is a perfectly acceptable central character for a boy to
read about. She asks the right questions. She is not sappy (as Ozma
can sometimes be). She is straight to the point and a bit aggressive.
Yet the Dorothy who returns to the series in the third book, *Ozma
of Oz* (1907), is somewhat different from the original Dorothy.
She is older and her conversation is full of cute contractions that
must have doubled up audiences in Sioux City but were pretty
hard going for at least one child forty years ago.

To get Dorothy back to Oz there is the by now obligatory natural disaster. The book opens with Dorothy and her uncle on board
a ship to Australia. During a storm she is swept overboard. Marius
Bewley has noted that this opening chapter "is so close to Crane's
('The Open Boat') in theme, imagery and technique that it is difficult to imagine, on comparing the two in detail, that the similarity
is wholly, or even largely accidental."*

Dorothy is accompanied by a yellow chicken named Bill. As
they are now in magic country, the chicken talks. Since the chicken
is a hen, Dorothy renames her Billina. The chicken is fussy and
self-absorbed; she is also something of an overachiever: " 'How is
my grammar?' asked the yellow hen anxiously." Rather better than
Dorothy's, whose dialogue is marred by such Baby Snooksisms as
" 'zactly," "auto'biles," " 'lieve," " 'splain."

Dorothy and Billina come ashore in Ev, a magic country on the
other side of the Deadly Desert that separates Oz from the real
world (what separates such magical kingdoms as Ix and Ev from
our realer world is never made plain). In any case, the formula has
now been established. Cyclone or storm at sea or earthquake ends
not in death for child and animal companion but translation to a
magic land. Then, one by one, strange new characters join the travelers. In this story the first addition is Tik-Tok, a clockwork robot
(sixteen years later the word "robot" was coined). He has run
down. They wind him up. Next they meet Princess Languidere.
She is deeply narcissistic, a trait not much admired by Baum (had

* *The New York Review of Books,* December 3, 1964.

he been traumatized by all those actresses and actors he had known on tour?). Instead of changing clothes, hair, makeup, the Princess changes heads from her collection. I found the changing of heads fascinating. And puzzling: since the brains in each head varied, would Languidere still be herself when she put on a new head or would she become someone else? Thus Baum made logicians of his readers.

The Princess is about to add Dorothy's head to her collection when the marines arrive in the form of Ozma and retinue, who have crossed the Deadly Desert on a magic carpet (cheating, I thought at the time; either a desert is impassable or it is not). Dorothy and Ozma meet, and Dorothy, "as soon as she heard the sweet voice of the girlish ruler of Oz knew that she would learn to love her dearly." That sort of thing I tended to skip.

The principal villain of the Oz canon is now encountered: the Nome King (Baum thought the "g" in front of "nome" too difficult for children . . . how did he think they spelled and pronounced "gnaw"?). Roquat of the Rock lived deep beneath the earth, presiding over his legions of hard-working nomes (first cousins to George Macdonald's goblins). I was always happy when Baum took us below ground, and showed us fantastic caverns strewn with precious stones where scurrying nomes did their best to please the bad-tempered Roquat, whose " 'laugh,' " one admirer points out, " 'is worse than another man's frown.' " Ozma and company are transformed into bric-a-brac by Roquat's magic. But Dorothy and Billina outwit Roquat (nomes fear fresh eggs). Ozma and all the other victims of the Nome King are restored to their former selves, and Dorothy is given an opportunity to ham it up:

"Royal Ozma, and you, Queen of Ev, I welcome you and your people back to the land of the living. Billina has saved you from your troubles, and now we will leave this drea'ful place, and return to Ev as soon as poss'ble."

While the child spoke they could all see that she wore the magic belt, and a great cheer went up from all her friends. . . .

Baum knew that nothing so pleases a child as a situation where, for once, the child is in the driver's seat and able to dominate adults. Dorothy's will to power is a continuing force in the series and as a type she is still with us in such popular works as *Peanuts*, where she continues her steely progress toward total dominion in the guise of the relentless Lucy.

Back in the Emerald City, Ozma shows Dorothy her magic picture in which she can see what is happening anywhere in the world. If Dorothy ever wants to visit Oz, all she has to do is make a certain signal and Ozma will transport her from Kansas to Oz. Although this simplified transportation considerably, Baum must have known even then that half the charm of the Oz stories was the scary trip of an ordinary American child from U.S.A. to Oz. As a result, in *Dorothy and the Wizard in Oz* (1908), another natural catastrophe is used to bring Dorothy back to Oz; the long missing Wizard, too. Something like the San Francisco earthquake happens. Accompanied by a dim boy called Zeb and a dull horse called Jim, Dorothy falls deep into the earth. This catastrophe really got to Dorothy and "for a few moments the little girl lost consciousness. Zeb, being a boy, did not faint, but he was badly frightened. . . ." That is Baum's one effort to give some sort of points to a boy. He promptly forgets about Zeb, and Dorothy is back in the saddle, running things. She is aided by the Wizard, who joins them in his balloon.

Deep beneath the earth are magical countries (inspired by Verne's *Journey to the Center of the Earth*, 1864? Did Verne or Baum inspire Burroughs's *Pellucidar*, 1923?). In a country that contains vegetable people, a positively Golden Bough note is sounded by the ruling Prince: " 'One of the most unpleasant things about our vegetable lives [is] that while we are in our full prime we must give way to another, and be covered up in the ground to sprout and grow and give birth to other people.' " But then according to the various biographies, Baum was interested in Hinduism, and the notion of karma.

After a number of adventures Dorothy gestures to Ozma (she certainly took her time about it, I thought) and they are all transported to the Emerald City where the usual party is given for them, carefully described in a small-town newspaper style of the Social-Notes-from-all-over variety. *The Road to Oz* (1909) is the mixture as before. In Kansas, Dorothy meets the Shaggy Man; he is a tramp of the sort that haunted the American countryside after the Civil War when unemployed veterans and men ruined by the depressions of the 1870s took to the road, where they lived and died, no doubt, brutishly. The Shaggy Man asks her for directions. Exasperated by the tramp's slowness to figure out her instructions, she says: " 'You're so stupid. Wait a minute till I run in the house and get my sunbonnet.' " Dorothy is easily "provoked." " 'My, but you're clumsy!' said the little girl." She gives him a "severe look." Then " 'Come on,' she commanded." She then leads him to the wrong, i.e., the magical, road to Oz.

With *The Emerald City of Oz* (1910) Baum is back in form. He has had to face up to the fact that Dorothy's trips from the U.S.A. to Oz are getting not only contrived, but pointless. If she likes Oz so much, why doesn't she settle there? But if she does, what will happen to her uncle and aunt? Fortunately, a banker is about to foreclose the mortgage on Uncle Henry's farm. Dorothy will have to go to work, says Aunt Em, stricken. " 'You might do housework for someone, dear, you are so handy; or perhaps you could be a nursemaid to little children.' " Dorothy is having none of this. "Dorothy smiled. 'Wouldn't it be funny,' she said, 'for me to do housework in Kansas, when I'm a Princess in the Land of Oz?' " The old people buy this one with surprisingly little fuss. It is decided that Dorothy will signal Ozma, and depart for the Emerald City.

Although Baum's powers of invention seldom flagged, he had no great skill at plot-making. Solutions to problems are arrived at either through improbable coincidence or by bringing in, literally, some god (usually Glinda) from the machine to set things right. Since the narratives are swift and the conversations sprightly and the invented characters are both homely and amusing (animated paper dolls, jigsaw puzzles, pastry, cutlery, china, etc.), the stories never lack momentum. Yet there was always a certain danger that the narrative would flatten out into a series of predictable turns.

In *The Emerald City*, Baum sets in motion two simultaneous plots. The Nome King Roquat decides to conquer Oz. Counterpoint to his shenanigans are Dorothy's travels through Oz with her uncle and aunt (Ozma has given them asylum). Once again, the child's situation *vis-à-vis* the adult is reversed.

> "Don't be afraid," she said to them. "You are now in the Land of Oz, where you are to live always, and be comfer'ble an' happy. You'll never have to worry over anything again, 'cause there won't be anything to worry about. And you owe it all to the kindness of my friend Princess Ozma."

And never forget it, one hears her mutter to herself.

But while the innocents are abroad in Oz, dark clouds are gathering. Roquat is on the march. I must say that the Nome King has never been more (to me) attractive as a character than in this book. For one thing, the bad temper is almost permanently out of control. It is even beginning to worry the king himself: " 'To be angry once in a while is really good fun, because it makes others so miserable. But to be angry morning, noon and night, as I am, grows monotonous and prevents my gaining any other pleasure in life.' " Rejecting the offer of the usual anodyne, a "glass of melted silver," Roquat decides to put together an alliance of all the wicked magic figures in order to conquer Oz. He looks among his nomes for an ideal general. He finds him: " 'I hate good people. . . . That is why I am so fond of your Majesty.' " Later the General enlists new allies with the straightforward pitch: " 'Permit me to call your attention to the exquisite joy of making the happy unhappy,' said he at last. 'Consider the pleasure of destroying innocent and harmless people.' " This argument proves irresistible.

The nomes and their allies make a tunnel beneath the Deadly Desert (but surely its Deadliness must go deeper than they could burrow?). Ozma watches all of them on her magic picture. She is moderately alarmed. " 'But I do not wish to fight,' declared Ozma, firmly." She takes an extremely high and moral American line; one that Woodrow Wilson echoed a few years later when he declared that the United States "is too proud to fight" powerful Germany (as opposed to weak Mexico where Wilson had swallowed his pride just long enough for us to launch an invasion). " 'Because the Nome King intends to do evil is no excuse for my doing the same.' " Ozma has deep thoughts on the nature of evil: " 'I must not blame King Roquat too severely, for he is a Nome and his nature is not so gentle as my own.' " Luckily, Ozite cunning carries the day.

Baum's nicest conceit in *The Emerald City* is Rigamarole Town. Or, as a local boy puts it,

> "if you have traveled very much you will have noticed that every town differs from every other town in one way or another and so by observing the methods of the people and the way they live as well as the style of their dwelling places,"

etc. Dorothy and her party are duly impressed by the boy's endless commentary. He is matched almost immediately by a woman who tells them, apropos nothing:

"It is the easiest thing in the world for a person to say 'yes' or 'no' when a question that is asked for the purpose of gaining information or satisfying the curiosity of the one who has given expression to the inquiry has attracted the attention of an individual who may be competent either from personal experience or the experience of others,"

etc. A member of Dorothy's party remarks that if those people wrote books " 'it would take a whole library to say the cow jumped over the moon.' " So it would. And so it does. The Shaggy Man decides that there is a lot to be said for the way that the people of Oz encourage these people to live together in one town "while Uncle Sam lets [them] roam around wild and free, to torture innocent people.' "

Many enthusiasts of the Oz books (among them Ray Bradbury and Russel B. Nye) point with democratic pride to the fact that there is a total absence, according to Mr. Nye, of any "whisper of class consciousness in Oz (as there is in Alice's Wonderland)." Yet Martin Gardner has already noted one example of Baum's "despicable" elitism. Later (*Emerald City*), Baum appears to back away from the view that some people are better or more special than others. "It seems unfortunate that strong people are usually so disagreeable and overbearing that no one cares for them. In fact, to be different from your fellow creatures is always a misfortune." But I don't think that Baum believed a word of this. If he did, he would have been not L. Frank Baum, creator of the special and magical world of Oz, but Horatio Alger, celebrator of pluck and luck, thrift and drift, money. The dreamy boy with the bad heart at a hated military school was as conscious as any Hermann Hesse youth that he was splendidly different from others, and in *The Lost Princess of Oz* Baum reasserts the Scarecrow's position: " 'To be individual, my friends' " (the Cowardly Lion is holding forth), " 'to be different from others, is the only way to become distinguished from the common herd.' "

Inevitably, Baum moved from Chicago to California. Inevitably, he settled in the village of Hollywood in 1909. Inevitably, he made silent films, based on the Oz books. Not so inevitably, he failed for a number of reasons that he could not have foretold. Nevertheless, he put together a half-dozen films that (as far as special effects went) were said to be ahead of their time. By 1913 he had returned, somewhat grimly, to writing Oz books, putting Dorothy firmly on ice until the last book of the series.

The final Oz books are among the most interesting. After a gall bladder operation, Baum took to his bed where the last work was done. Yet Baum's imagination seems to have been more than usually inspired despite physical pain, and the darkness at hand. *The Lost Princess of Oz* (1917) is one of the best of the series. The beginning is splendidly straightforward. "There could be no doubt of the fact: Princess Ozma, the lovely girl ruler of the Fairyland of Oz, was lost. She had completely disappeared." Glinda's magical paraphernalia had also vanished. The search for Ozma involves most of the Oz principals, including Dorothy. The villain Ugu (who had kidnapped and transformed Ozma) is a most satisfactory character. "A curious thing about Ugu the Shoemaker was that he didn't suspect, in the least, that he was wicked. He wanted to be powerful and great and he hoped to make himself master of all the Land of Oz, that he might compel everyone in that fairy country to obey him. His ambition blinded him to the rights of others and he imagined anyone else would act just as he did if anyone else happened to be as clever as himself." That just about says it all.

In *The Tin Woodman* (1918) a boy named Woot is curious to know what happened to the girl that the Tin Woodman had intended to marry when he was flesh and blood. (Enchanted by a witch, he kept hacking off his own limbs; replacements in tin were provided by a magical smith. Eventually, he was all tin, and so no longer a suitable husband for a flesh-and-blood girl; he moved away.) Woot, the Tin Woodman, and the Scarecrow (the last two are rather like an old married couple, chatting in a desultory way about the past) set out to find the girl. To their astonishment, they meet another tin man. He, too, had courted the girl. He, too, had been enchanted by the witch; had chopped himself to bits; had been reconstituted by the same magical smith. The two tin men wonder what has happened to the girl. They also wonder what happened to their original imperishable pieces.

In due course, the Tin Woodman is confronted by his original head. I have never forgotten how amazed I was not only by Baum's startling invention but by the drawing of the Tin Woodman staring into the cupboard where sits his old head. The Tin Woodman is amazed, too. But the original head is simply bored, and snippy. When asked " 'What relation *are* we?' " the head replies, " 'Don't ask me. . . . For my part, I'm not anxious to claim relationship with any common, manufactured article, like you. You may be all right in your class, but your class isn't my class.' " When the Tin Woodman asks the head what it thinks about inside the cupboard, he is told,

> "Nothing. . . . A little reflection will convince you that I have had nothing to think about, except the boards on the inside of the cupboard door, and it didn't take me long to think everything about those boards that could be thought of. Then, of course, I quit thinking."
> "And are you happy?"
> "Happy? What's that?"

There is a further surprise when the Tin Woodman discovers that his old girl friend has married a creature made up of various human parts assembled from him and from the other man of tin. The result is a most divided and unsatisfactory man, and for the child reader a fascinating problem in the nature of identity.

In Baum's last Oz book, *Glinda of Oz* (posthumously published in 1920), magic is pretty much replaced by complex machinery. There is a domed island that can sink beneath the waters of a lake at the mention of a secret word, but though the word is magic, the details of how the island rises and sinks are straight out of *Popular Mechanics.*

Ozma and Dorothy are trapped beneath the water of the lake by yet another narcissistic princess, Coo-eeh-oh. By the time Glinda comes to the rescue, Coo-eeh-oh has been turned into a proud and vapid swan. This book is very much a last roundup (Baum may not have written all of it). Certainly there are some uncharacteristic sermons in favor of the Protestant work ethic: "Dorothy wished in her kindly, innocent heart, that all men and women could be fairies with silver wands, and satisfy all their needs without so much work and worry. . . ." Ozma fields that one as briskly as the Librarian of Detroit could want:

> "No, no, Dorothy, that wouldn't do at all. Instead of happiness your plan would bring weariness. . . . There would be no eager striving to obtain the difficult. . . . There would be nothing to do, you see, and no interest in life and in our fellow creatures."

But Dorothy is not so easily convinced. She notes that Ozma is a magical creature, and *she* is happy. But only, says Ozma, with grinding sweetness, " 'because I can use my fairy powers to make others happy.' " Then Ozma makes the sensible point that although she has magical powers, others like Glinda have even greater powers than she and so " 'there still are things in both nature and in wit for me to marvel at.' "

In Dorothy's last appearance as heroine, she saves the day. She guesses, correctly, that the magic word is the wicked Coo-eeh-oh's name. Incidentally, as far as I know, not a single Oz commentator has noted that Coo-eeh-oh is the traditional cry of the hog-caller. The book ends with a stern admonishment, " 'it is always wise to do one's duty, however unpleasant that duty may seem to be.' "

Although it is unlikely that Baum would have found Ruskin's aesthetics of much interest, he might well have liked his political writings, particularly *Munera Pulveris* and *Fors*. Ruskin's protégé William Morris would have approved of Oz, where

> Everyone worked half the time and played half the time, and the people enjoyed the work as much as they did the play. . . . There were no cruel overseers set to watch them, and no one to rebuke them and find fault with them. So each one was proud to do all he could for his friends and neighbors, and was glad when they would accept the things he produced.

Anticipating the wrath of the Librarian of Detroit, who in 1957 found the Oz books to have a "cowardly approach to life," Baum adds, slyly, "I do not suppose such an arrangement would be practical with us. . . ." Yet Baum has done no more than to revive in his own terms the original Arcadian dream of America. Or, as Marius Bewley noted, "the tension between technology and pastoralism is one of the things that the Oz books are about, whether Baum was aware of it or not." I think that Baum was very much aware of this tension. In Oz he presents the pastoral dream of Jefferson (the slaves have been replaced by magic and good will); and into this Eden he introduces forbidden knowledge in the form of black magic (the machine) which good magic (the values of the pastoral society) must overwhelm.

It is Bewley's view that because "The Ozites are much aware of the scientific nature of magic," Ozma wisely limited the practice of magic. As a result, controlled magic enhances the society just as controlled industrialization could enhance (and perhaps even salvage) a society like ours. Unfortunately, the Nome King has governed the United States for more than a century; and he shows no sign of wanting to abdicate. Meanwhile, the life of the many is definitely nome-ish and the environment has been, perhaps, irreparably damaged. To the extent that Baum makes his readers aware that our country's "practical" arrangements are inferior to those of Oz, he is a truly subversive writer and it is no wonder that the Librarian of Detroit finds him cowardly and negative, because, of course, he is brave and affirmative. But then the United States has always been a Rigamarole land where adjectives tend to mean their opposite, when they mean at all.

Despite the Librarian of Detroit's efforts to suppress magical alternative worlds, the Oz books continue to exert their spell. "You do not educate a man by telling him what he knew not," wrote John Ruskin, "but by making him what he was not." In Ruskin's high sense, Baum was a true educator, and those who read his Oz books are often made what they were not—imaginative, tolerant, alert to wonders, life.

The New York Review of Books
SEPTEMBER 29 AND OCTOBER 13, 1977

Lessing's Science Fiction

Currently, there are two kinds of serious-novel. The first deals
with the Human Condition (often confused, in Manhattan,
with marriage) while the second is a word-structure that deals only
with itself. Although the Human Condition novel can be read—if
not fully appreciated—by any moderately competent reader of the
late Dame Agatha Christie, the second cannot be read at all. The
word-structure novel is intended to be taught, rather like a gnostic
text whose secrets may only be revealed by tenured adepts in sun-
less campus chapels. Last month, a perfect example of the genre
was extravagantly praised on the ground that here, at last, was a
"book" that could not, very simply, be read at all by anyone, ever.

The only thing that the two kinds of serious-novel have in common is the fact that in each case the creator has taken *extraordinary
risks with his talents*. He has driven his art and mind to the fullest
limit of prose; and beyond. He has gambled recklessly with his
gifts; been deer to his own gun; been brave, brave. On the other
hand, the serious-writer's reader's courage has gone entirely unremarked and the slopes of Parnassus are now planted thick with the
shallow graves of those gallant readers who risked their all in du-

bious battle with serious-texts, and failed—their names known only to whatever god makes the syllabus.

Nevertheless, despite the glory of risk-taking and the applause of tens of book-chatterers, today's serious-novelist often betrays a certain edginess whenever he feels obliged to comment publicly on his art. He is apt to admit that the word-structure novel is unsatisfying while the Human Condition novel tends to look more and more like old movies or, worse, like new movies. Needless to say, the fact that hardly anyone outside an institution wants to read a serious-novel has never been a deterrent to our serious-novelists— rather the reverse. They know that silence, cunning, exile all add up to exegesis. But is that enough? I suspect that a crisis is now at hand and that the serious-novel, as we lucky few have known it, may be drawing to a close.

At the risk of poaching on that territory where the buffalo and Leslie Fiedler roam, one might make the case that owing to some sort of perfect misunderstanding about the nature of literature, our ungifted middlebrows have taken over the serious-novel while those highbrows who tend to create an epoch's high literature appear not to be "serious" at all. In any case, the thing is now so muddled that it will be a long time before all this is sorted out. Certainly it will be a long time before anyone can ever again state with George Eliot's serenity and confidence that "Art must be either real and concrete or ideal and eclectic. Both are good and true in their way, but my stories are of the former kind." What, we hear our middlebrows begin to buzz, is real? concrete? ideal? eclectic? *What is art?* Whatever art is, it is not our day's serious-novel, whose texture so closely resembles that gelidity in which great Satan is forever mired at the center of hell's inner ring.

Although Doris Lessing has more in common with George Eliot than she has with any contemporary serious-novelist, she is not always above solemnity, as opposed to mere seriousness. Somewhat solemnly, Lessing tells us in the preface to her new novel *Shikasta* that there may indeed be something wrong with the way that novels are currently being written. She appears not to be drawn to the autonomous word-structure. On the other hand, she is an old-fashioned moralist. This means that she is inclined to take very seriously the quotidian. The deep—as opposed to strip—mining of the truly moral relationship seems to me to be her territory. I say "seems" because I have come to Lessing's work late. I began to read her with *Memoirs of a Survivor*, and now, with *Shikasta*, I have followed her into the realms of science fiction where she is making a continuum all her own somewhere between John Milton and L. Ron Hubbard.

Lessing tells us that, originally, she thought that she might make a single volume out of certain themes from the Old Testament (source of so much of our dreaming and bad behavior) but that she is now launched on a series of fables about interplanetary dominations and powers. "I feel as if I have been set free both to be as experimental as I like, and as traditional." I'm not sure what she means by "experimental" and "traditional." At best, Lessing's prose is solid and slow and a bit flat-footed. She is an entirely "traditional" prose writer. I suspect that she did not want to use the word "imaginative," a taboo word nowadays, and so she wrote "experimental."

In any case, like the splendid *Memoirs of a Survivor*, *Shikasta* is the work of a formidable imagination. Lessing can make up things that appear to be real, which is what storytelling is all about. But she has been sufficiently influenced by serious-writing to feel a need to apologize. "It is by now commonplace to say that novelists everywhere are breaking the bonds of the realistic novel because what we all see around us becomes daily wilder, more fantastic, incredible. . . . The old 'realistic' novel is being changed, too, because of influences from that genre loosely described as space fiction." Actually, I have seen no very vivid sign of this influence and I don't suppose that she has either. But it is not unusual for a writer to regard his own new turning as a highway suddenly perceived by all, and soon to be crowded with other pilgrims en route to the City on the Hill.

If this book has any recent precursor, it is Kurt Vonnegut, Jr. Lessing has praised him elsewhere: "Vonnegut is moral in an old-fashioned way . . . he has made nonsense of the little categories, the unnatural divisions into 'real' literature and the rest, because he is comic and sad at once, because his painful seriousness is never solemn. Vonnegut is unique among us; and these same qualities account for the way a few academics still try to patronize him. . . ."

Lessing is even more influenced by the Old Testament. "It is our habit to dismiss the Old Testament altogether because Jehovah, or Jahve, does not think or behave like a social worker." So much for JC, doer of good and eventual scientist. But Lessing's point is well taken. Because the Old Testament's lurid tales of a furious god form a background to Jesus' "good news," to Mohammed's "recitations," to the Jewish ethical sense, those bloody tales still remain an extraordinary mythic power, last demonstrated in full force by Milton.

In a sense, Lessing's *Shikasta* is a return more to the spirit (not, alas, the language) of Milton than to that of Genesis. But Lessing goes Milton one better, or worse. Milton was a dualist. Lucifer blazes as the son of morning; and the Godhead blazes, too. Their agon is terrific. Although Lessing deals with opposites, she tends to unitarianism. She is filled with the spirit of the Sufis, and if there is one thing that makes me more nervous than a Jungian it is a Sufi. Lessing believes that it is possible "to 'plug in' to an overmind, or Ur-mind, or unconscious, or what you will, and that this accounts for a great many improbabilities and 'coincidences.'" She does indeed plug in; and *Shikasta* is certainly rich with improbabilities and "coincidences." Elsewhere ("In the World, Not of It"), Lessing has expressed her admiration for one Idries Shah, a busy contemporary purveyor of Sufism (from the Arab word *suf*, meaning wool . . . the costume for ascetics).

Idries Shah has been characterized in the pages of *The New York Review of Books* as the author of works that are replete with "constant errors of fact, slovenly and inaccurate translations, even the misspelling of Oriental names and words. In place of scholarship we are asked to accept a muddle of platitudes, irrelevancies, and plain mumbo-jumbo." Lessing very much admires Idries Shah and the woolly ones, and she quotes with approval from Idries Shah's *The Dermis Probe* in which *he* quotes from M. Gauquelin's *The Cosmic Clocks*. "An astonishing parallel to the Sufi insistence on the relatively greater power of subtle communication to affect man, is found in scientific work which shows that all living things, including man, are 'incredibly sensitive to waves of extraordinarily weak energy—when more robust influences are excluded.'" This last quotation within a quotation is the theme of *Shikasta*.

It is Lessing's conceit that a benign and highly advanced galactic civilization, centered on Canopus, is sending out harmonious waves hither and yon, rather like Milton's god before Lucifer got bored. Canopus lives in harmony with another galactic empire named Sirius. Once upon a time warp, the two fought a Great War but now all is serene between the galaxies. I can't come up with the Old Testament parallel on that one. Is Canopus Heaven versus Sirius' Chaos? Anyway, the evil planet Shammat in the galactic empire of Puttiora turns out be our old friend Lucifer or Satan or Lord of the Flies, and the planet Shikasta (that's us) is a battleground between the harmonious vibes of Canopus and the wicked vibes of Shammat, which are constantly bombarding our planet. In the end, Lucifer is hurled howling into that place where he prefers to reign and all is harmony with God's chilluns. Lessing rather lacks negative capability. Where Milton's Lucifer is a joy to contemplate, Lessing's Shammat is a drag whose planetary agents sound like a cross between Tolkien's monster and Sir Lew Grade.

Lessing's narrative devices are very elaborate. Apparently, the Canopian harmonious future resembles nothing so much as an English Department that has somehow made an accommodation to share its "facilities" with the Bureau of Indian Affairs. The book's title page is daunting: "Canopus in Argos: Archives" at the top. Then "Re: Colonised Planet 5" (as I type this, I realize that I've been misreading "Re: Colonised" as recolonised): then "Shikasta"; then "Personal, Psychological, Historical Documents Relating to Visit by JOHOR (George Sherban) Emissary (Grade 9) 87th of the Period of the Last Days." At the bottom of the page, one's eye is suddenly delighted by the homely phrase "Alfred A. Knopf New York 1979." There is not much music in Lessing spheres.

Like the Archangel Michael, Johor travels through Shikasta's time. The planet's first cities were so constructed that transmitters on Canopus could send out benign waves of force; as a result, the local population (trained by kindly giants) were happy and frolicsome. "Canopus was able to feed Shikasta with a rich and vigorous air, which kept everyone safe and healthy, and above all, made them love each other. . . . This supply of finer air had a name. It was called SOWF—the substance-of-we-feeling—I had of course spent time and effort in working out an easily memorable syllable." Of course. But the SOWF is cut off. The cities of the plain are blasted. The Degenerative Disease begins and the race suffers from "grandiosities and pomps," short life spans, bad temper. The Degenerative Disease is Lessing's equivalent for that original sin which befell man when Eve bit on the apple.

There is a certain amount of fun to be had in Johor's tour of human history. He is busy as a bee trying to contain the evil influence of Shammat, and Lessing not only brings us up to date but beyond: the Chinese will occupy Europe fairly soon. Lessing is a master of the eschatological style and *Memoirs of a Survivor* is a masterpiece of that genre. But where the earlier book dealt with a very real London in a most credible terminal state, *Shikasta* is

never quite real enough. At times the plodding style does make
things believable, but then reality slips away . . . too little SOWF,
perhaps. Nevertheless, Lessing is plainly enjoying herself and the
reader can share in that enjoyment a good deal of the time. But,
finally, she lacks the peculiar ability to create alternative worlds.
For instance, she invents for the human dead a limbo she calls Zone
6. This shadowy place is a cross between Homer's Hades and the
Zoroastrian concept of that place where eternal souls hover about,
waiting to be born. Lessing's descriptions of the undead dead are
often very fine, but when one compares her invention with Ursula
Le Guin's somewhat similar land of the dead in the *Earthsea* trilogy, one is aware that Le Guin's darkness is darker, her coldness
colder, her shadows more dense and stranger.

Lessing's affinity for the Old Testament combined with the
woolliness of latter-day Sufism has got her into something of a
philosophical muddle. Without the idea of free will, the human
race is of no interest at all; certainly, without the idea of free will
there can be no literature. To watch Milton's Lucifer serenely
overthrow the controlling intelligence of his writerly creator is an
awesome thing. But nothing like this happens in Lessing's work.
From the moment of creation, Lessing's Shikastans are programmed
by outside forces—sometimes benign, sometimes malign. They
themselves are entirely passive. There is no Prometheus; there is
not even an Eve. The fact that in the course of a very long book
Lessing has not managed to create a character of the slightest interest is the result not so much of any failure in her considerable
art as it is a sign that she has surrendered her mind to SOWF, or to
the woollies, or to the Jealous God.

Obviously, there is a case to be made for predetermination or
predestination or let-us-now-praise B. F. Skinner. Lessing herself
might well argue that the seemingly inexorable DNA code is a
form of genetic programming that could well be equated with
Canopus' intervention and that, in either case, our puny lives are
so many interchangeable tropisms, responding to outside stimuli.
But I think that the human case is more interesting than that. The
fact that no religion has been able to give a satisfactory reason for
the existence of evil has certainly kept human beings on their toes
during the brief respites that we are allowed between those ages of
faith which can always be counted upon to create that we-state
which seems so much to intrigue Lessing and her woollies, a condi-

tion best described by the most sinister of all Latin tags, *e pluribus unum.*

Ultimately, *Shikasta* is not so much a fable of the human will in opposition to a god who has wronged the fire-seeker as it is a fairy tale about good and bad extraterrestrial forces who take some obscure pleasure in manipulating a passive ant-like human race. Needless to say, Doris Lessing is not the first to incline to this "religion." In fact, she has considerable competition from a living prophet whose powerful mind has envisaged a race of god-like Thetans who once lived among us; they, too, overflowed with SOWF; then they went away. But all is not lost. The living prophet has told us their story. At first he wrote a science fiction novel, and bad people scoffed. But he was not dismayed. He knew that he could save us; bring back the wisdom of the Thetans; "clear" us of badness. He created a second holy book, *Dianetics.* Today he is the sole proprietor of the Church of Scientology. Doris Lessing would do well to abandon the woolly Idries Shah in favor of Mr. L. Ron Hubbard, who has already blazed that trail where now she trods—treads?—trods.

The New York Review of Books
DECEMBER 20, 1979

Sciascia's Italy

Since World War II, Italy has managed, with characteristic artistry, to create a society that combines a number of the least appealing aspects of socialism with practically all the vices of capitalism. This was not the work of a day. A wide range of political parties has contributed to the invention of modern Italy, a state whose vast metastasizing bureaucracy is the last living legacy anywhere on earth of the house of Bourbon (Spanish branch). In fact, the allegedly defunct Kingdom of the Two Sicilies has now so entirely engulfed the rest of the peninsula that the separation between Italian state and Italian people is nearly perfect.

Although the Italian treasury loves the personal income tax quite as much as other treasuries, any attempt to collect tax money is thwarted not only by the rich (who resemble their counterparts in the land of the free and the home of the tax accountant), but by nearly everyone else. Only those unfortunate enough to live on fixed incomes (e.g., industrial workers, schoolteachers) are trapped by the withholding tax, Zio Sam's sly invention. Since many Italians are either not on a payroll or, if they are, have a second job, they pay little or no personal tax to a state which is then obliged to raise money through a series of value-added and sales taxes. Needless to say, the treasury is often in deficit, thanks not only to the relative freedom from taxation enjoyed by its numerous entrepreneurs (capitalist Italy) but also to the constant drain on the treasury of the large state-owned money-losing industrial consortia (socialist Italy).

Last year one fourth of the national deficit went to bail out state-controlled industries. As a result, the Communist Party of Italy is perhaps the only Communist Party anywhere on earth that has proposed, somewhat shyly, the return of certain industries to the private sector of the economy. As the former governor of the Bank of Italy, Guido Carli, put it: "The progressive introduction of social-istic elements into our society has not made us a socialist society. Rather, it has whittled down the space in which propulsive economic forces can operate."

The Italians have made the following trade-off with a nation-state which none of them has ever much liked: if the state will not interfere too much in the lives of its citizens (that is, take most of their money in personal taxes), the people are willing to live without a proper postal service, police force, medical care—all the usual amenities of a European industrialized society. But, lately, the trade-off has broken down. Italy suffers from high inflation, growing unemployment, a deficit of some $50 billion. As a result, there are many Italians who do not in the least resemble Ms. Wertmuller's joyous, life-enhancing, singing waiters. Millions of men and women have come to hate the house of Bourbon in whose stifling rooms they are trapped. Therefore, in order to keep from revolution a large part of the population, the government has contrived an astonishing system of pensions and welfare assistance.

In a country with a labor force of 20.5 million people, 13.5 million people are collecting pensions or receiving welfare assistance. Put another way, while the state industries absorb about 5 percent of Italy's GDP or $9.5 billion, the pensioners get 11 percent or $25.2 billion a year.

The shrewd *condottiere* who control Italy realize that the state must, from time to time, placate with milk from her dugs those babes that a malign history has left in her lupine care.

Ten years ago, in the Sicilian town of Caltanissetta, a forty-eight-year-old schoolteacher and clerk in the state granary was given a pension for life. As a result, the part-time writer Leonardo Sciascia became not only a full-time writer but, recently, he has become a political force . . . well, no, not exactly a force (individuals, as such, exert little force in Italy's Byzantine politics) but, rather, a voice of reason in a land where ideology has always tended to take the place of ideas. In the last election, Sciascia stood as a candidate for the Radical Party. The fact that the Radicals nearly quintupled their delegation in the parliament can be attributed, at least in part, to Sciascia's ability to make plain the obvious. After Marco Panella, the Radical Party's unusual leader (one is tired of calling him charismatic), Sciascia is now one of the few literary political figures who is able to illuminate a prospect that cannot be pleasing to anyone, Marxist or Christian Democrat or neither.

Elected to the national parliament last spring, Sciascia opted to go to the European parliament instead. "Sicilians," he muttered, "gravitate either to Rome or to Milan. I like Milan."* Presumably, Strasbourg is an acceptable surrogate for Milan. Actually, Sciascia is unique among Sicilian artists in that he never abandoned Sicily for what Sicilians call "the continent." Like the noble Lampedusa, he has preferred to live and to work in his native Sicily. This means that, directly and indirectly, he has had to contend all his life with the Mafia and the Church, with fascism and communism, with the family, history. During the last quarter century, Sciascia has made out of his curious Sicilian experience a literature that is not quite like anything else ever done by a European—because Sicily is not part of Europe?—and certainly unlike anything done by a North American.

To understand Sciascia, one must understand when and where he was born and grew up and lived. Although this is true of any writer, it is crucial to the understanding of someone who was born in Sicily in 1921 (the year before Mussolini marched on Rome); who grew up under fascism; who experienced the liberation of Sicily by Lucky Luciano, Vito Genovese, and the American army; who has lived long enough to see the consumer society take root in Sicily's stony soil.

Traditionally, Sicily has almost always been occupied by some foreign power. During Sciascia's youth the Sicilians despised fascism because it was not only an alien form of government (what continental government is not alien to the Sicilians?) but a pecu-

---

* This was said in an interview given to *Il Messaggero*. All other quotations—not from his books—are taken from a series of conversations that Sciascia had with the journalist Marcelle Padovani and collected in a volume called *La Sicilia come metafora* (Mondadori, 1979). The un-beautiful English translations are by me.

liarly oppressive alien government. The fascists tried to *change* the
Sicilians. Make them wear uniforms. Conform them to the Duce's
loony pseudo-Roman norm. Although Mussolini himself paid little
attention to the island, he did manage to get upstaged in the piazza
of Piano dei Greci by the capo of the local mafia, one Don Ciccio
Cuccia. Aware that appearance is everything and substance nothing, Mussolini struck back at Don Ciccio (he put him in jail), at
the Mafia in general (he sent down an efficient inspector named
Mori who did the Mafia a good deal of damage post-1924), at Piano
dei Greci (Mussolini changed the name Greci to Albanese . . . more
Roman).

By the time that Sciascia was fourteen years old, Mussolini was
able to announce—almost accurately—that he had broken the back
of the Mafia. Pre-Mori, ten people were murdered a day in Sicily;
post-Mori, only three were murdered a week. Meanwhile, Inspector
Mori was trying to change the hearts and minds of the Sicilians. In
a moment of inspiration, he offered a prize to the best school-boy
essay on how to combat the Mafia. Although there were, predictably, no entries at the time, Sciascia has been trying ever since to
explain to Inspector Mori how best to combat or cope with the
Mafia, with Sicily, with the family, history, life.

"I spent the first twenty years of my life in a society which was
doubly unjust, doubly unfree, doubly irrational. In effect, it was
a non-society Society. La Sicilia, the Sicily that Pirandello gave us
a true and profound picture of. And Fascism. And both in being
Sicilian and living under fascism, I tried to cope by seeking within
myself (and outside myself only in books) the ways and the means.
In solitude. What I want to say is that I know very well that in
those twenty years I ended up acquiring a kind of 'neurosis from
reasoning.' "

Sciascia's early years were spent in the village of Racalmuto,
some twenty-two kilometers from Agrigento. As a clerk's son,
Sciascia was destined to be educated. When he was six, the teacher
assured the class that "the world envied fascism and Mussolini." It
is not clear whether or not the child Sciascia was ever impressed by
the party line, but he certainly disliked the *balilla*, a paramilitary
youth organization to which he was assigned. Fortunately, at the
age of nine, "a distant relative was appointed the local leader of the
balilla." Influence was used and "I was relieved of my obligations"
because "in Sicily the family has its vast ramifications. . . . The

family is the main root of the Mafia, which I know well. But that one time I was the willing beneficiary."

Meanwhile, like most writers-to-be, the young Sciascia read whatever he could. He was particularly attracted to the eighteenth-century writers of the Enlightenment. If he has a precursor, it is Voltaire. Predictably, he preferred Diderot to Rousseau. "Sicilian culture ignored or rejected romanticism until it arrived from France under the name of realism." Later, Sciascia was enchanted —and remains enchanted—by Sicily's modern master, Pirandello. As a boy, "I lived inside Pirandello's world, and Pirandellian drama —identity, the relativeness of things—was my daily dream. I almost thought that I was mad." But, ultimately, "I held fast to reason," as taught by Diderot, Courier, Manzoni.

Although Sciascia is a Pirandellian as well as a man of the Enlightenment, he has a hard clarity, reminiscent of Stendhal. At the age of five, he saw the sea: "I didn't like it, and I still don't like it. Sicilians don't like the sea, even those who live on its shores. For that matter, the majority of Sicilian towns have been built with their backs to the sea, ostentatiously. How could islanders like the sea which is capable only of carrying their men away as emigrants or bringing in invaders?"

Immediately after the war, the revived Mafia and their traditional allies (or clients or patrons) the landowners were separatists. When the government of the new Italian republic offered Sicily regional autonomy, complete with a legislature at Palermo, the Mafia's traditional capital, landowners and mafiosi became fervent Italians and the separatist movement failed. But then, it was doomed in 1945 when the United States refused (unkindly and probably unwisely) to fulfill the dream of innumerable Sicilians by annexing Sicily as an American state. In those innocent days, who knew that before the twentieth century had run its dismal course the Mafia would annex the United States? A marvelous tale still in search of its Pirandello.

Although everyone agreed that Sicily's only hope was industrialization, the Mafia fought industrialization because industry meant labor unions and labor unions (they thought naïvely) are not susceptible to the usual pressures of the honorable society which does and does not exist, rather like the trinity. The first battle between Mafia and industrialization occurred when Sciascia was twenty-three. The communists and socialists held a meeting in the piazza of Villalba. Authority challenged, the local capo ordered his thugs to open fire. Legal proceedings dragged on for ten years, by which time the capo had died a natural death.

What happened at Villalba made a strong impression on Sciascia. Sometimes, in his work, he deals with it directly and realistically; other times, he is oblique and fantastic. But he has never *not*, in a symbolic sense, dealt with this business. Even *Todo Modo* (1974) was an attempt to analyze those forces that opposed one another on a September day in 1944, in a dusty piazza, abruptly loud with guns.

Today the Mafia thrives in Sicily. Gangs still extort money from citrus growers through control of water sources as well as through what once looked to be a permanent veto on refrigeration, a situation that has made Sicilian oranges noncompetitive in Europe. Mafia gangs control dockworkers, the sale of contraband, construction permits, etc. Meanwhile, as Sciascia has described more than once, those continentals who come to Sicily as prosecutors and police inspectors soon learn that the true lover of justice must love death, too. Many of Sciascia's tales have, at their heart, thanatophilia. Lately, he has extended the geographical range of his novels. All Italy is now in the process of being Sicilianized. But then, ever since World War II, Sicilians have been overrepresented in the country's police and judiciary in rather the same way that, post Civil War, American Southerners took control of the Congress and the military and, until recently, had a lock on each. Also, with the influx of Sicilian workers to the northern cities (not to mention to the cities of the United States, Canada, Australia) the Mafia mentality has been exported with a vengeance.

What is the Mafia mentality? What is the Mafia? What is Sicily? When it comes to the exploration of this particular hell, Leonardo Sciascia is the perfect Virgil. As we begin our descent, he reminds us that like most Mediterranean societies Sicily is a matriarchy. The father-god of the conquering Aryans has never had much attraction for Mediterranean peoples. Effigies of the original Great Goddess of the Mediterranean can still be seen all over Sicily; and as the idol simpers at the boy-baby clutched in one hand, the other hand is depicted free to stir the life-giving *minestra*—or wield a knife.

D. H. Lawrence once described an exchange he had with an old woman in a Sicilian church. Why, he wanted to know, was the tortured figure of Jesus always shown in such vivid, such awful detail? Because, said the old woman firmly, he was unkind to his mother.

The sea at the center of the earth is the sea of the mother, and this blood-dark sea is at the heart of Sciascia's latest novel *Candido*: the story of a Sicilian who, during an American air raid in 1943, was born to a mother whom he was to lose in childhood to another culture; thus making it possible for him to begin a journey that would remove him from the orbit of the mother-goddess.

Sciascia has made an interesting distinction between what he calls the "maternal man" (someone like Robert Graves who serves the Great Goddess?) and the "paternal man." Although "I spent my infancy and adolescence surrounded by women, with my aunts and 'mothers' . . . I became a rather 'paternal' man. Many Sicilians are like me: they have hostile relations with their fathers during their youth and then, as if they've just seen themselves in a looking glass, they correct their attitude, realize that they *are* their fathers. They are destined to become them." For Sciascia,

> many wrongs, many tragedies of the South, have come to us from the women, above all when they become mothers. The Mezzogiorno woman has that *terrible* quality. How many crimes of honor has she provoked, instigated or encouraged! Women who are mothers, mothers-in-law. They are capable of the worst kinds of wickedness just in order to make up for the vexations they themselves were subjected to when they were young, as part of a terrifying social conformism. "Ah, yes," they seem to be saying, "you're my son's wife? Well, he's worth his weight in gold!"
>
> These women are elements of violence, of dishonesty, of abuse of power in Southern society, even though some of that ancient power was reduced when the American troops landed in Sicily during the last war. And so it is that Candido (the character in my book) loses his mother at the moment of the arrival in Palermo of U.S. soldiers. If that event dealt a hard blow to the matriarchy, it also introduced "consumerism," a taste for modern gadgets, possessions, a house. . . . From the moment that they began building new housing in Sicily, the sons (and the daughters-in-law) began to leave the old tyrannical hearths of their mothers, thus undermining, in part, the ancient power structure.

After the bombardment, the child is named, "surreally," Candido: neither parent has ever heard of Voltaire. The town is occupied by the American army and Captain John H. (for Hamlet) Dykes becomes, in effect, the mayor. Candido's lawyer-father asks the American to dinner, and Candido's mother falls in love with him. Sourly, surreally, the father comes to believe that Dykes is the blond Candido's father even though the child was conceived nine months before the arrival in Sicily of the Americans. Nevertheless, in the father's mind, Candido is always "the American."

As a result of the April 18, 1948 election (when knowledgeable authorities told me to flee Italy because the Communists would win and there would be—what else?—"a blood bath"), the Christian Democrat Party doubled its vote and Candido's fascist grandfather, the General, was elected to parliament while the General's aide-de-camp, a local nobleman, was also elected, but on the Communist ticket. Nicely, the two ex-fascists work in tandem. Meanwhile, Candido's mother has divorced his father and gone to live with her American lover in Helena, Montana. Candido is left behind.

Sciascia's Candido is a serene, not particularly wide-eyed version of Voltaire's Candide. In fact, this Sicilian avatar is a good deal cleverer than the original. As a boy, "His games—we can try to define them only approximately—were like crossword puzzles which he would play with things. Adults make words cross, but Candido made things cross." One of the things that he makes cross . . . cross the shining river, in fact . . . is his lawyer-father who has assisted in the cover-up of a murder. When Candido overhears a discussion of the murder, he promptly tells his schoolmates the true story. As a result of the boy's candor, the father commits suicide and Candido, now known as "the little monster," goes to live with the General. At no point does Candido feel the slightest guilt. Pondering his father's death, he begins to arrange an image in his mind "of a man who adds up his whole life and arrives at a sum indicating that it would be right for him to put a bullet through his head."

It is now time for Dr. Pangloss to make his entrance, disguised as the Archpriest Lepanto. Highly civilized priests keep recurring in Sciascia's work, although he confesses that "I have never met one."

The Archpriest and the boy spar with each another. "Up to a point, the Archpriest also was convinced that he was a little monster . . . whereas Candido had discovered that the Archpriest had a kind of fixed idea, rather complicated but reducible, more or less, to these terms: all little boys kill their fathers, and some of them, sometimes, kill even Our Father Who is in Heaven." Patiently, Candido sets out to disabuse the Archpriest: "he had not killed his father, and he knew nothing, nor did he want to know anything, about that other Father."

Sciascia's themes now begin to converge. The mother has abandoned the son, a very good thing in the land of the Great Goddess (who would be Attis, who Pan could be?); the father has killed himself because of Candido's truthfulness or candor when he made cross the thing-truth with the thing-*omerta*; now the Heavenly Father, or Aryan sky-god, is found to be, by Candido, simply irrelevant. Plainly, Candido is a monster. He is also free. He becomes even freer when he inherits money and land. But when he cultivates his own land for the good of his tenant farmers, they know despair. When a parish priest is murdered (with the regularity of a Simenon, Sciascia produces his murders), Candido and the Archpriest decide to assist the inspector of police. When, rather cleverly, they apprehend the murderer, everyone is in a rage. They—not the killer—have broken the code. A theologian is called in by the local bishop and an inquiry is held into the Archpriest's behavior. It is decided that he must

> step down as Archpriest: he could not continue to fulfill that office if all the faithful now disapproved of him, even despised him. "And further," the learned theologian said, "not that truth may not be beautiful, but at times it does so much harm that to withhold it is not a fault but a merit."
>
> In handing the theologian his resignation, the Archpriest, now archpriest no longer, said, in a parodying, almost lilting voice, " 'I am the way, the truth, and the life,' but sometimes I am the blind alley, the lie, and death."

With that, the moral education of Candido is complete. On the other hand, that of Dr. Pangloss has just begun. The Archpriest—now Don Antonio—becomes a militant communist. To an extent, Candido goes along with Don Antonio. But he is not one to protest too much. He cannot be a protestant if only because he "was utterly averse to believing that there were any sins other than lying and seeking the pain and humiliation of others."

The political education of Candido—as opposed to moral—begins in early manhood. Like so many educated Italians of that time, he regards communism as a replacement for a church that has not only failed but in the land of the Great Goddess never truly taken hold. Candido likes the writings of Gramsci; finds Marx boring; as for Lenin, "he had come to picture Lenin as a carpenter atop a scaffolding who had worn himself out hitting the same nails on the

head, but all of his efforts had not prevented some nails from being poorly set or going in crooked." (I am not always enchanted
by the translation of Adrienne Foulke.) Although Candido believes
that "to be a Communist was, in a word, almost a fact of nature"
because "capitalism was bearing man toward dissolution," he much
prefers the imaginative writers to the contorted Machiavellianism
of the communist theoreticians: " 'Zola and Gorki, they talk about
things that used to be, and it's as if they were talking about things
that came later. Marx and Lenin talk about things that would
happen, and it's as if they were talking about things that are no
longer.' "

But Candido becomes a member of the Communist Party even
though he is more repelled than not by its sacred texts (excepting,
always, Gramsci). Acting on principle, Candido offers his own
land for a hospital but because of the usual collusion between the
condottiere of the left and the right, another piece of land is bought
by the community and the *condottiere* make their profit. Candido
is thrown out of the Communist Party. In due course, after he is
done out of his fortune by his own family, he goes off with his
cousin Francesca to Turin, "a more and more sullen city. . . . The
North and the South of Italy settled there; they sought crazily to
avoid each other and, at the same time, to strike out at each other;
both were bottled up in making automobiles, a superfluous necessity for all, a necessary superfluity for all." Just before the young
couple move on to Paris, Candido says to Francesca, "Do you know
what our life is, yours and mine? It's a dream dreamed in Sicily.
Perhaps we're still there, and we are dreaming."

In Paris, at the Brasserie Lipp (August 1977), Candido runs into
the long-mislaid mother and her husband, Mr. Dykes. Don Antonio
is also there: he is now as doctrinaire a Communist as he had been
a Roman Catholic. Predictably, the Americans have little to say to
the Sicilians. But Don Antonio does ask former Captain Dykes:
"How did you manage, only a few days after you had arrived in
our town, to choose our worst citizens for public service?" Dykes
is offhand: he had been given a list. Yes, he had suspected that the
people on the list were mafiosi, "But we were fighting a war. . . ."

When Candido's mother, rather halfheartedly, proposes that
Candido visit America, Candido is polite. For a visit, perhaps. " 'But
as for living there, I want to live here. . . . Here you feel that something is about to end and something is about to begin. I'd like to see
what should come to an end come to its end.' Embracing him once

again, his mother thought, He's a monster." Mother and son part, presumably forever.

Rather drunk, Don Antonio has, once again, missed the point to what Candido has been saying. Don Antonio says that "here," meaning France, "something is about to end, and it's beautiful. . . . At home, nothing ends, nothing ever ends." On the way back to his hotel, Don Antonio salutes the statue of Voltaire as "our true father!" But Candido demurs; and the book's last line is: " 'Let's not begin again with the fathers,' he said. He felt himself a child of fortune, and happy." *Margari*, as the Italians say.

I am not sure just what it is that makes Sciascia's novels unique. Where "serious" American writers tend to let the imagination do the work of the imagination, Sciascia prefers to invent for us a world quite as real as any that Dreiser ever dealt with, rendered in a style that is, line by line, as jolting as an exposed electrical wire. I suppose, as a Pirandellian, Sciascia is letting a very real world imagine *him* describing it.

Candido is bracketed by two political events: one of importance to Sciascia, the other to the world as well as Sciascia. From time to time, Italian political parties will propose for election a sympathetic non-party member, preferably a *"technico"* (usually, an economist who has managed to jam the central computer of a major bank) or a *"personaggio,"* a celebrated man like Sciascia. One year before *Candido* was written, pensioner Sciascia was a Communist Party candidate for the Palermo city council. "My 'debut' was solicited by the local [party] leaders as an event destined to have consequences at the local level."

Sciascia accepted the Communist nomination for city councilor with a certain Candide-like innocence. Like most Italians of his generation, he is a man of the left. Unlike most Italians, Sciascia is a social meliorist. As a public man, he has an empirical streak which is bound to strike as mysterious most politically minded Italians. Sciascia has ideas but no ideology in a country where political ideology is everything and political ideas unknown. Sciascia's reasons for going on the city council are straightforward. Grave problems faced Palermo, "in certain quarters there was no water, whole neighborhoods lacked sewers and roads, and the restoration . . . the rehabilitation of the historic center presented all sorts of problems," but "during the eighteen months that I served on the city council, not once did anyone talk about water or any other urgent problems. . . . "

Sciascia was also shocked to find that the council seldom met before nine in the evening; then, around midnight, when people were yawning, a bit of business was done. Finally, Sciascia was wised up,

> off the record, thanks to the benevolence of a socialist councilman who spelled the whole thing out to me in real terms, clearly: thus, I was able to understand how the Communists and the Christian Democrats did business together and I was less than pleased. . . . Aware that my presence in the bosom of the city council was inopportune and useless, and that the possibility of a row between me and the party that had put me there seemed more and more likely, it was obvious that I'd have to quit. I wanted to go without slamming the door, but that wasn't possible.

There was a good deal of fuss when Sciascia quit the council in 1975. But though he may, personally, have found the experience "inopportune and useless," he was able to make good use of it in *Candido*: when Candido tries to give the city land for a hospital, he discovers that nothing can ever be given in a society where everything is bought and sold, preferably twice over.

Sciascia entered Italian political history in the wake of the kidnapping and murder by terrorists of Aldo Moro, the president of the Christian Democrat party. More than anyone else, Moro was responsible for the tentative coming together of left and right in what the Communists like to call the "historic compromise" between Christ and Marx, in what Moro himself used to call, with a positively Eisenhowerian gift for demented metaphor, "the inevitable convergence of parallel lines."

Moro was kidnapped by a mysterious entity known as the Red Brigades. Whoever they were or are, their rhetoric is Marxist. If Italy was shocked by the Moro kidnapping, the intellectuals were traumatized. Since Italy's intellectuals are, almost to a man, Marxists, this was the moment of truth. Moro was the leader of the party that serves the Agnellis, the Pope, and the American (somewhat fractured) hegemony. If the leader of this party is really being tried by a *truly* revolutionary Marxist court, well. . . . Although any communist party is a party of revolution, the Italian party long ago dropped its "to the barricades" rhetoric, preferring to come to power through the ballot box. Until the Moro affair, the Communist Party was prospering. In the previous election they had got well over their usual 30 percent of the vote and it looked as if a coalition government was possible. Christ and Marx were, if not at the altar, getting their prenuptial blood tests. But, suddenly, prenuptial blood tests turned to bloodletting. Why, asked a number of political commentators, are the intellectuals silent?

Eventually, Italy's premier man of letters, Alberto Moravia, admitted to a feeling of "sorrowing extraneousness" while the young Turks at *Lotta Continua* (a radical newspaper of the left) proclaimed: "Neither Red Brigades nor the state." But the real polemic began when it came time to try a number of Red Brigadeers in Turin. So many potential jurors received death threats that sixteen refused to serve. When Eugenio Montale said that he "understood" their fear, Italo Calvino took him to task. "The state," said Calvino, "is all of us." Calvino chose to cling to what Taoists call "the primal unity." So did the Communist Party. Contemptuous of Montale's unease, the Communist leader Giorgio Amendola declared: "Civil courage has never been in great supply among Italian intellectuals."

With that Sciascia went into action. "I intervened," he said later, "because of Calvino's article, in which he expressed embarrassment and concern when Montale said that he 'understood' the sixteen citizens of Turin who refused to be jurors. I felt that I ought to contribute to the debate: I, too, understood the sixteen citizens, just as I understood Montale . . . even I might have declined the honor and the burden of being a juror. What guarantee, I asked, does this state offer when it comes to the protection of those citizens who put themselves at risk by becoming jurors? What guarantee against theft, abuse of power, injustice? None. The impunity that covers crimes committed against the general public and the general good was worthy of a South American regime." As for the Red Brigades: "All my life, everything that I've thought and written makes it clear that I cannot take the side of the Red Brigades."

Sciascia then turned on Amendola. "For him the state must be a sort of mythical and metaphysical entity. . . ." Sciascia's own view of the state is less exalted: a state is a system of well-coordinated services. "But when those services are inadequate or lacking then one must repair them or make something new. If this is not done, then one is defending nothing but corruption and inefficiency under the pretext that one is defending the state." As for Amendola (and, presumably, the Communist Party), he "was simply animated by the desire for an authoritarian state . . . and from a visceral aversion to non-conforming writers."

Ultimately, Sciascia has taken the line that "the Italian Communist Party has become a precise mirror-image of the Christian Democrat Party." Consequently, "one can only make two hypotheses: either the Communist Party has not the capacity to make a valid opposition, and Italians have credited the party with qualities that it never had, or the Italian party is playing the game 'the worse things are the better' or 'to function least is to function best.' . . . These two parties seem to be intertwined and interchangeable not only in their existence today but in their future."

Now, in 1979, Sciascia has moved toward new perceptions if not, necessarily, realities. To the statement, "We cannot *not* be socialist" (the famous paraphrase of Croce's "we cannot *not* be Christians"), he replies that things have changed as "it is plain that, at the level of collective humanity, socialism has known failures even more serious than those of Christianity." For Italian intellectuals of Sciascia's generation, this is a formidable heresy. But he goes even further. Contemplating those who speak of Marxism with a human face, he responds, "I respect their position, but I retain the idea that 'an authentic Marxism' is a utopia within a utopia, a dream, an illusion." Nevertheless, he cannot be anti-communist. This is the dilemma that faces any Italian who takes politics seriously. To the question: what would you like to see happen next? Sciascia replied, perhaps too simply, "The creation of a social democratic party." But then, less simply, he acted upon his own words, and stood for parliament in the Radical Party interest. Like a growing number of Italians, Sciascia finds appealing a party which compensates for its lack of ideology with all sorts of ideas. In the last election, the party tripled its vote.

Although the Radical Party stands for such specific things as liberalized laws on abortion, divorce, drugs, sex, as well as the cleaning up of the environment and the removal of Italy from NATO (something the Communist Party has not mentioned since 1976), the party is constantly being denounced for representing nothing at all. But then, for most Italians, a political party is never a specific program, it is a flag, a liturgy, the sound of a trombone practicing in the night.

"Remember," Sciascia said to Marcelle Padovani, "what Malraux said of Faulkner? 'He has managed to intrude Greek tragedy into the detective story.' It might be said of me that I have brought Pirandellian drama to the detective story!" Often disguised as detective stories, Sciascia's novels are also highly political in a way quite unlike anything that has ever been done in English. While the American writer searches solemnly for his identity, Sciascia is on the trail of a murderer who, invariably, turns out to be not so much a specific character as a social system. That Mafia, which Americans find so exciting and even admirable, is for Sciascia the evil consequence of a long bad history, presided over by The Kindly Ones. Whenever (as in *Il Giorno della Civetta*, 1961)* one of Sciascia's believers in justice confronts the Mafia (which everyone says—in the best Pirandellian manner—does not exist), he is not only defeated, but, worse, he is never understood. Particularly if, like Captain Bellodi from Parma, he regards "the authority vested in him as a surgeon regards the knife: an instrument to be used with care, precision, and certainty; a man convinced that law rests on the idea of justice and that any action taken by the law should be governed by justice." Captain Bellodi was not a success in Sicily.

A decade later, in *Il Contesto*,† Sciascia again concerns himself with justice. But now he has moved toward a kind of surrealism. Sometimes the country he writes about is Italy; sometimes not. A man has gone to prison for a crime that he did not commit. When he gets out of prison, he decides to kill off the country's judges. When Inspector Rogas tries to track down the killer, he himself is murdered. In a splendid dialogue with the country's Chief Justice, Inspector Rogas is told that "the only possible form of justice, of the administration of justice, could be, and will be, the form that in a military war is called decimation. One man answers for humanity. And humanity answers for the one man."

Although moral anarchy is at the basis of this ancient society, Sciascia himself has by no means given up. The epigraphs to *Il Contesto* are very much to the point. First, there is a quotation from Montaigne: "One must do as the animals do, who erase every footprint in front of their lair." Then a response from Rousseau: "O Montaigne! You who pride yourself on your candor and truthfulness, be sincere and truthful, if a philosopher can be so, and tell me whether there exists on earth a country where it is a crime to keep one's given word and to be clement and generous, where the

---

* Published by Knopf in 1964 as *Mafia Vendetta*.
† Published by Harper & Row in 1973 as *Equal Danger*.

good man is despised and the wicked man honored." Sciascia then quotes Anonymous: "O Rousseau!" One has a pretty good idea who this particular Anonymous is.

It is Sciascia's self-appointed task to erase the accumulated footprints (history) in front of the animal's lair (Sicily, Italy, the world). The fact that he cannot undo the remembered past has not prevented him from making works of art or from introducing a healthy skepticism into the sterile and abstract political discourse of his country. No other Italian writer has said, quite so bluntly, that the historic compromise would lead to "a regime in which, finally and enduringly, the two major parties would be joined in a unified management of power to the preclusion of all alternatives and all opposition. Finally, the Italians would be tranquil, irresponsible, no longer forced to think, to evaluate, to choose."

Rather surprisingly, Sciascia seems not to have figured out what the historic compromise ultimately signifies. When he does, he will realize that Italy's two great unloved political parties are simply the flitting shadows of two larger entities. As any Voltairean knows, the Vatican and the Kremlin have more in common than either has with the idea of a free society. Once each realizes that the other is indeed its logical mate, Sciascia will be able to write his last detective story, in which the murder will be done with mirrors. Meanwhile, he continues to give us all sorts of clues; reminds us that criminals are still at large; demonstrates that life goes on *todo modo.*

The New York Review of Books
OCTOBER 25, 1979

V. S. Pritchett as "Critic"

Thirty-three years ago in a preface to *The Living Novel*, V. S. Pritchett described how it was that he came to be the "critic" that he is. I put quotes around the word critic because that is what he himself does when, with characteristic modesty, he tells us how he stopped writing novels and short stories during World War II and turned to criticism. "Without leisure or freedom to write what I wanted, I could at least read what I wanted, and I turned to those most remarkable men and women: the great novelists of the past, those who are called the standard novelists." As he read, he made notes. These notes or reports or reviews were first published in the *New Statesman and Nation*; then collected in *The Living Novel*. Since 1946 he has continued to report regularly on his reading, and *The Myth Makers* is his latest collection of literary essays.

It is interesting to read what Pritchett had to say in 1946 about the impression made on him by "what are called the Standard Novelists [who] have the set air of an officially appointed committee. We had fallen into the error of believing that they were written for critics, for literary historians, for students or for leisured persons of academic tastes; and people who read only the best authors usually let one know it. We had easily forgotten that the masters, great and small, remembered or neglected, were the freshest, the most original, the most importunate and living novelists of their time; that they stood above their contemporaries and survived them, because they were more readable, more entertaining, more suggestive and incomparably more able than the common run of novelist."

There are certain truths so true that they are practically unbelievable.

"We have only to glance," Pritchett continues, "at the second-rate novelists to see how they differ in this sense [of contemporaneity] from the masters. The second-rate are rarely of their time. They are not on the tip of the wave. They are born out of date and out of touch and are rooted not in life but in literary convention."

One thinks of all those busy teachers of English whose spare time is devoted to re-creating yet another version of dead Finnegan and his long-since celebrated wake; or of the *really* ambitious teacher-writer who wants so much for literature to achieve the pure heights of music (an aside, by the way, not a goal of Joyce); or of the would-be master of the two cultures who wants to encompass within a construct of narrative prose all the known laws, let us say, of thermodynamics. Our universities are positively humming with the sound of fools rushing in. The odd angel bleakly hovers; casts no shadow.

During the last third of a century, V. S. Pritchett has continued to be the best English-language critic of . . . well, the *living* novel. How does he do it? And what is it that he does? To begin with, unlike most critics, Pritchett is himself a maker of literature. He is a marvelous short-story writer; if he is less successful as a novelist, it is because, perhaps, he lacks "the novelist's vegetative temperament," as he remarks of Chekhov.

At work on a text, Pritchett is rather like one of those amorphic sea-creatures who float from bright complicated shell to shell. Once at home within the shell, he is able to describe for us in precise detail the secrets of the shell's interior; and he is able to show us, from the maker's own angle, the world the maker saw.

Of Dostoevsky: "Life stories of endless complexity hang shamelessly out of the mouths of his characters, like dogs' tongues, as they run by; the awful gregariousness of his people appears simultaneously with the claustrophobia and the manias of their solitude." Plainly, Pritchett's negative capability is well developed. He has a remarkable affinity for writers entirely different from that tradition of comic irony which has produced most of the best of English literature—including his own—and quite a lot of the bad. It is eerie to observe with what ease Pritchett occupies the shell of a writer who "is a sculptor of molten figures. . . . If anyone took up alienation as a profession it was [Dostoevsky]." Finally, "Dostoevsky's style: it is a talking style in which his own voice and the voices of all his characters are heard creating themselves, as if all were narrators without knowing it."

The first job of a critic is to describe what he has read. This is a lot more difficult than one might suspect. I have often thought that one of the reasons why there have been so few good American literary critics is that those Americans who do read books tend to be obsessed with the personality of the author under review. The politics, sex, class of the author are all-important while the book at hand is simply an excuse to discuss, say, the anti-Semitism of Pound, the homosexuality of Whitman, the social climbing of James. Since the American character is essentially tendentious and sectarian, the American critic must decide in advance whether or not the writer he is writing about is a Good Person; that is, one who accepts implicitly all the going superstitions (a.k.a. values [*sic*]) of the middle class of the day. If the writer is a GP, then what he writes is apt to be good. If he is a BP, forget it.

In the Forties, the New Critics faced up to this national tendency and for a time their concentration on the text *qua* text provided a counterweight. But these paladins of the word have long since faded away, and the character of the United Statesman seems immutable. Or as the founder of *The Nation* put it more than a century ago: "The great mischief has always been that whenever our reviewers deviate from the usual and popular course of panegyric, they start from and end in personality, so that the public mind is almost sure to connect unfavorable criticism with personal animosity." Today, our critics either moralize *ad hominem* or, most chillingly (an "advance" since Godkin's time), pretend that the art of literature is one of the physical sciences and so in desperate need of neologisms, diagrams, laws.

The personality of a writer obviously has some relevance to what he writes, particularly if he is dead and the life has been publicly examined. But it takes great tact to know how to use gossip. Pritchett seldom loses sight of the fact that he is writing about writing, and not about writers at home. In a review of a life of

Tolstoy, he observes, "Like the Lawrences and the Carlyles, the Tolstoys were the professionals of marriage; they knew they were not in it for their good or happiness, that the relationship was an appointed ordeal, an obsession undertaken by dedicated heavy-weights." This is personal; this is relevant . . . at least when discussing a book about the life of a major novelist. Pritchett rarely judges a living writer whose character cannot be known for certain, as opposed to his literary persona, which is fair game.

Pritchett's only American lapse occurs in his discussion of Jean Genet, a writer whose luminous stupidity put Sartre in mind of the saints. Pritchett remarks that the brilliance of Genet's prose is often undone by the "sudden descents into banal reflection and in over-all pretentiousness" while "the lack of charity is an appalling defect and one rebels against the claustrophobia." But then he remarks that "there are scarcely any women in Genet's novels and although this is due to his homosexuality, which is passive and feminine, it has an obvious root in his rage at being abandoned by his mother, who was a prostitute."

We don't know what either "passive" or "feminine" means in this context. As for "obvious root," is it so obvious? And why bad-mouth poor old Mrs. Genet? No guesswork about living writers unless they decide to tell all; in which case, *caveat lector.*

In *The Myth Makers*, Pritchett deals with nineteen writers entirely outside the Anglo-American tradition: seven Russians, five French, five writers of Spanish or Portuguese, Strindberg and Kafka. In other words, Pritchett has removed himself from ancestral ground. Although he is as familiar with French literature as he is with English (in this he very much resembles another Tory critic, the splendid, no longer read George Saintsbury), it must have been a considerable stretch for him to deal with the likes of Eça de Queiroz. If it was, he shows no strain.

Pritchett is at his best with the French; and if it does not take much critical acumen to write intelligently about Flaubert, it does take considerable intelligence to say something new about him ("Flaubert presented the hunger for the future, the course of ardent longings and violent desires that rise from the sensual, the horrible, and the sadistic"), or to illuminate a writer like George Sand, whose "people and landscapes are silhouettes seen in streams of sheet lightning. . . . She was half Literature."

Pritchett has new things to say about the differences between French and English, and how translation to English particularly undoes many of George Sand's effects. "If there is a loss it is because English easily droops into a near-evangelical tune; our language is not made for operatic precisions and we have a limited tradition of authorized hyperbole. Abstractions lose the intellectual formality that has an exact ring in French. . . . She had little sense of humor." This is excellent, and valuable. One thinks of other examples. Although Anaïs Nin was never taken seriously in England, the French eventually came to appreciate her solemn hieratic prose while the Americans, predictably, celebrated her personality. She had little sense of humor.

If there can be said to be a unifying argument to these nineteen essays, it has to do with time and the novel. Pritchett approves Bakhtin's notion that Dostoevsky is "the inventor of a new genre, the polyphonic novel. . . . There is a plurality of voices inner and outer, and they retain 'their unmergedness.' " Pritchett continues with Bakhtin's argument that "the traditional European novel is 'monological,' a thing of the past, and if Dostoevsky's novels seem a chaos compared, say, with *Madame Bovary*, so much the worse for the tradition. Man is not an object but another subject."

In Machado de Assis, Pritchett finds another kind of novel, "constructed by a short-story-teller's mind, for he is a vertical, condensing writer who slices through the upholstery of the realist novel into what is essential. He is a collector of the essences of whole lives and does not labor with chronology, jumping back or forward confidently in time as it pleases him." As for *One Hundred Years of Solitude*, "Márquez seems to be sailing down the blood stream of his people as they innocently build their town in the swamp, lose it in civil wars, go mad in the wild days of the American banana company and finally end up abandoned."

Unexpectedly, Pritchett regards the fabulist Borges as "a master of the quotidian, of conveying a whole history in two or three lines that point to an exact past drama and intensify a future one." Pritchett examines *The Circular Ruins* in which a teacher takes refuge in the ruins of a temple in order "to dream a man." Finally, Borges says of his character (*his* character?), "With relief, with humiliation, with terror, he understood that he too was a mere appearance dreamed by another." Pritchett wonders where this solipsistic conceit comes from. I shall be helpful. Borges got it from Chuang-tze, who wrote at the beginning of the third century B.C. Chuang-tze or "Chou dreamed that he was a butterfly. Then he woke up and found to his astonishment that he was Chou. But it was hard to be sure whether he really was Chou and had only dreamed that he was a butterfly, or was really a butterfly, and was only dreaming that he was Chou."

The most interesting piece in this collection deals with Goncharov, whose *Oblomov* is one of those great novels that are all of a piece and, inexplicably, like nothing else. Since Goncharov wrote only three novels in the course of what must have been a singularly discouraging life (he was State Censor), it is all the more extraordinary that this unique creation should have happened to him. Oblomov, surely dreamed Goncharov. Who else would have bothered? "From what leak in a mind so small and sealed," writes Pritchett, "did the unconscious drip out and produce the character of Oblomov, the sainted figure of nonproductive sloth and inertia; one of those creatures who become larger and larger as we read?" There is no answering this question. "Genius is a spiritual greed," Pritchett remarks apropos Chekhov. But the Censor seems to have been greedier for food than for things of the spirit. Nevertheless, "From Sterne he learned to follow a half-forgotten tune in his head." Then Pritchett notes a difference between East and West in the ways of perceiving events. "If the Western calendared attitude to plot and precise action escaped [Goncharov], he had on his side the Russian sense of the hours of the day running through his scenes and people like a stream or continuous present." One *saw* Madame Bovary at a distance, plain; one *sees* Oblomov close-up, vivid in his sloth.

When Pritchett is obliged to deal with literary biographers and critics, he is generous and tactful. Only once does he express his horror at what the hacks of Academe have done to our language. Professor Victor Brombert's *The Novels of Flaubert: A Study of Themes and Techniques* provides the occasion. Pritchett quotes Professor Brombert at length; he praises things in the professor's book. But Pritchett finds disturbing the fact that the professor does not write well. Although this mild disability would go unremarked (and unnoticed in the land of the tin ear), for Pritchett

> It is depressing to find so good a critic of Flaubert—of all people —scattering academic jargon and archaisms in his prose. The effect is pretentious and may, one hopes, be simply the result of thinking in French and writing in English; but it does match the present academic habit of turning literary criticism into technology. One really cannot write of Flaubert's "direction for

monstrous forms" or of "vertiginous proliferation of forms and gestures"; "dizzying dilation," or "volitation"; "lupanar"—when all one means is "pertaining to a brothel." Philosophers, psychologists, and scientists may, I understand, write of "fragmentations" that suggest "a somnambulist and oneiric state." But who uses the pretentious "obnubilate" when they mean "dim" or "darkened by cloud"? Imaginative writers know better than to put on this kind of learned dog. The duty of the critic is to literature, not to its surrogates. And if I were performing a textual criticism of this critic I would be tempted to build a whole theory on his compulsive repetition of the word "velleities." Words and phrases like these come from the ingenuous and fervent pens of *Bouvard and Pécuchet.*

Literary criticism does not add to its status by opening an intellectual hardware store.

Unfortunately, the hardware store is pretty much all that there is to "literary criticism" in the United States. With a few fairly honorable exceptions, our academics write Brombertese, and they do so proudly. After all, no one has ever told them that it is not English. The fact that America's English departments are manned by the second-rate is no great thing. The second-rate must live, too. But in most civilized countries the second-rate are at least challenged by the first-rate. And score is kept in literary journals. But as McDonald's drives out good food, so these hacks of Academe drive out good prose. At every level in our literary life they flourish. In fact, they have now taken to writing the sort of novels that other tenured hacks can review and teach. Entire issues of "literary journals" are written by them. Meanwhile, in the universities, they are increasing at a positively Malthusian rate; and an entire generation of schoolteachers and book chatterers now believes that an inability to master English is a sign of intellectual grace, and that a writer like Pritchett is not to be taken seriously because he eschews literary velleities for literary criticism. Madame Verdurin has won the day.

Even so, it is good to know that our last critic in English is still at work, writing well—that is, writing as if writing well mattered. It would be nice if Sir Victor lived forever.

The New York Review of Books
JUNE 28, 1979

Thomas Love Peacock: The Novel of Ideas

W hat is a novel for? To be read is the simple answer. But since fewer and fewer people want to read novels (as opposed to what the conglomerate-publishers call "category fiction"), it might be a good idea to take a look at what is being written, and why; at what is being read, and why.

In *Ideas and the Novel* Mary McCarthy notes that since the time of Henry James, the serious novel has dealt in a more and more concentrated—if not refined—way with the moral relations of characters who resemble rather closely the writer and his putative reader. It is not, she says, that people actually write Jamesian novels; rather, "The Jamesian model remains a standard, an archetype, against which contemporary impurities and laxities are measured." In addition, for Americans, sincerity if not authenticity is all-important; and requires a minimum of invention.

During the last fifty years, the main line of the Serious American Novel has been almost exclusively concerned with the doings and feelings, often erotic, of white middle-class Americans, often schoolteachers, as they confront what they take to be life. It should be noted that these problems seldom have much or anything to do with politics, with theories of education, with the nature of the good. It should also be noted that the tone of the Serious Novel is always solemn and often vatic. Irony and wit are unknown while the preferred view of the human estate is standard American, which is to say positive. For some reason, dialogue tends to be minimal and flat.

Virginia Woolf thought that the Victorian novelists "created their characters mainly through dialogue." Then, somehow, "the sense of an audience" was lost. "*Middlemarch* I should say is the transition novel: Mr. Brooke done directly by dialogue: Dorothea indirectly. Hence its great interest—the first modern novel. Henry James of course receded further and further from the spoken word, and finally I think only used dialogue when he wanted a very high light."

Today's Serious Novel is not well lit. The characters do, say, and think ordinary things, as they confront those problems that the serious writer must face in his everyday life. Since the serious novel is written by middle-class, middlebrow whites, political activists, intellectuals, members of the ruling classes, blacks seldom make appearances in these books, except as the odd flasher.

Predictably, despite the reflexive support of old-fashioned editors and book-reviewers, the Serious Novel is of no actual interest to anyone, including the sort of people who write them: they are apt to read Agatha Christie, if they read at all. But then, this is an old story. In 1859, Nathaniel Hawthorne, having just perpetrated that "moonshiny Romance" (his own phrase) *The Marble Faun*, wrote to his publishers: "It is odd enough, moreover, that my own individual taste is for quite another class of works than those which I myself am able to write." Sensible man, he preferred Trollope to himself. Nevertheless, in a sort of void, Serious Novels continue to be published and praised, but they are not much read.

What is a novel for, if it is *not* to be read? Since the rise of modernism a century ago—is there anything quite as old or as little changed as modern literature?—the notion of the artist as saint and martyr, reviled and ignored in his own time, has had a powerful appeal to many writers and teachers. Echoing Stendhal, the ambitious artist will write not for the people of his own day but for the residents of the next century—on the peculiar ground that the sort of reader who preferred Paul de Kock to Stendhal in the nineteenth century and Barbara Cartland to Iris Murdoch in our own will have developed an exquisite sensibility by the year 2080. These innocents seem not to understand that posterity is a permanent darkness where no whistle sounds. It is reasonable to assume that, by and large, what is not read now will not be read, ever. It is also reasonable to assume that practically nothing that is read now will be read later. Finally, it is not too farfetched to imagine a future in which novels are not read at all. But, for the present, if a Serious Novel is not going to be read, it can always be taught—if it is so made as to be more teacherly than readerly. Further, if the serious student keeps on going to school and acquiring degrees, he will find that not only is his life enhanced by the possession of tools with which to crack the code of rich arcane texts but he will also be able to earn a living by teaching others to teach books written to be taught. Admittedly, none of this has much to do with literature but, as a way of life, it is a lot easier than many other—phrase? Service-oriented Fields.

Although there is no reason why the universities should not take over the Serious Novel and manufacture it right on campus, there are signs that the magistri ludi of Academe are now after more glorious game. Suddenly, simultaneously, on many campuses and in many states, a terrible truth has become self-evident. *The true study of English studies is English studies.* If this truth is true, then the novel can be dispensed with. As our teachers begin to compose their so-called "charters," setting forth powerful new theories of English studies, complete with graphs and startling neologisms, the dream of the truly ambitious schoolteacher will be fulfilled and the interpreter-theorist will replace the creator as culture hero.

Meanwhile, in the real world—take the elevator to the mezzanine, and turn left; you can't miss it—what sort of novels are still read, *voluntarily*, by people who will not be graded on what they have read?

Conglomerate-publishers are a good consumer guide, catering, as they do, to a number of different, not always contiguous publics: Gothic stories, spy thrillers, Harlequin romances . . . each genre has its measurable public. Occasionally, books are written which appear to fit a genre but transcend it because they are works of the imagination, dealing with the past or the future; with alternative worlds. Although these books cannot be truly serious because they are not, literally, *true*, there is no serious American novelist who can write as well or as originally (not a recommendation, perhaps) as John Fowles or William Golding, two English writers whose works are often read outside institutions. Yet neither Fowles nor

Golding is taken with any great seriousness by American school-teachers. Fowles is regarded as a sort of Daphne du Maurier with grammar while Golding is known as the author of a book that the young once fancied—and so was taught in the lower grades. For reasons that have to do with the origins of the United States, Americans will never accept any literature that does not plainly support the prejudices and aspirations of a powerful and bigoted middle class which is now supplementing its powerful churches with equally powerful universities where what is said and thought and imagined is homogenized to a degree that teachers and students do not begin to suspect because they have never set foot outside the cage that they were born in. Like the gorilla who was taught to draw, they keep drawing the bars of their cage; and think it the world.

Historical novels and political novels can never be taken seriously because true history and disturbing politics are not acceptable subjects. Works of high imagination cause unease: if it didn't really happen, how can your story be really *sincere* . . . ? The imaginative writer can never be serious unless, like Mr. Thomas Pynchon, he makes it clear that he is writing about Entropy and the Second Law of Thermodynamics and a number of other subjects that he picked up in his freshman year at Cornell. English teachers without science like this sort of thing while physicists are tempted to write excited letters to literary journals. Thus, the Snow-called gap between the two cultures looks to be bridged, while nothing at all has been disturbed in the way that the society obliges us to see ourselves.

One of the great losses to world literature has been the novel of ideas. Or the symposium-novel. Or the dialogue-novel. Or the. . . . One has to search for some sort of hyphenate even to describe what one has in mind. Mary McCarthy calls it the "conversation novel."

From Aristophanes to Petronius to Lucian to Rabelais to Swift to Voltaire to Thomas Love Peacock, there has been a brilliant line of satirical narratives and had it not been for certain events at the beginning of the nineteenth century in England, this useful form might still be with us, assuming that those who have been brought up on sincere simple Serious Novels would appreciate—or even recognize—any play of wit at the expense of dearly held serious superstitions. Where the True is worshiped, truth is alien. But then to be middle class is to be, by definition, frightened of losing one's place. Traditionally, the virtuous member of the middle class is encouraged to cultivate sincerity and its twin, hypocrisy. The sort of harsh truth-telling that one gets in Aristophanes, say, is not possible in a highly organized zoo like the United States where the best cuts are flung to those who never question the zoo's management. The satirist breaks with his origins; looks at things with a cold eye; says what he means, and mocks those who do not know what *they* mean.

It is significant that the only American writer who might have taken his place in the glittering line was, finally, scared off. Since Mark Twain was not about to lose his audience, he told dumb jokes in public while writing, in private, all sorts of earth-shattering notions. Twain thought that if there was a God, He was evil. Twain's poignant invention, Huck, is a boy who wants to get his ass out of the serious, simple, sincere, bigoted world on whose fringe he was born. He is a lovely, true evocation. But he is in flight; can't cope; knows something is wrong. There is a world elsewhere, he suspects; but there are practically no people in it— it is the territory.

Every quarter century, like clockwork, there is a Peacock revival. The great tail feathers unfurl in all their Pavonian splendor, and like-minded folk delight in the display; and that's the end of that for the next twenty-five years. Although it is now too late in history to revive either Peacock or the conversation novel, Marilyn Butler in *Peacock Displayed* has written an admirable book about a valuable writer.

Thomas Love Peacock was born in 1785; he died in 1866. He was well read in Greek, Latin, French, and Italian literature; he was an early and knowledgeable devotee of opera, particularly Mozart, Rossini, Bellini. Since he did not go to school after the age of twelve, he was able to teach himself what he wanted to know, which was a lot. In 1819, he was taken on by the East India Company where he worked until his retirement in 1856. He associated at India House with James and John Stuart Mill; he was a lifelong friend of Jeremy Bentham and of Byron's friend John Cam Hobhouse. For three years, he was close to Shelley; and got him to read the classics. Peacock's wife went mad while his daughter Mary Ellen married a bearded, dyspeptic, cigarette-smoker—three demerits in Peacock's eyes. George Meredith was less than an ideal son-in-law, particularly at table. Some of Mary Ellen's recipes survive. Ingredients for Athenian Eel and Sauce: "Half a pint of good Stock. One tablespoon of Mushroom Ketchup. One mustard-

spoonful of Mustard. One dessert spoonful of Shalot Vinegar. One
dessert spoonful of Anchovy Sauce. One dessert spoonful of Wor-
cester Sauce. Marjoram and Parsley." That was just the sauce.
Meanwhile, cut the eels in pieces. . . . When Mary Ellen deserted
Meredith for the painter Henry Wallis, Meredith's digestive tract
must have known a certain relief. Later he memorialized his father-
in-law as Dr. Middleton in *The Egoist*. Mary Ellen died young.
Despite the deaths of children and a wife's madness, one has the
sense that Peacock's long life was happy; but then he was a true
Epicurean.

Peacock began as a poet in the didactic Augustan style. He was
much interested in politics, as were most of the English writers of
the late eighteenth and early nineteenth centuries. Butler is particularly good in setting Peacock firmly in a world of political faction
and theorizing. By the time Peacock was of age, the American and
French revolutions had happened. The ideas of Rousseau and Paine
were everywhere talked of, and writers wrote in order to change
society. As a result, what was written was considered more important than who wrote it—or even read it. The writer as his own text
was unknown because it was unthinkable, while the writer as
sacred monster was not to emerge until mid-century. Ironically,
Peacock's idealistic friend Shelley was to be Sacred Monster Number Two. Number One was Byron (who figures as Mr. Cypress
in Peacock's *Nightmare Abbey*).

In the first quarter of the century, British intellectual life was
mostly Scottish. The *Edinburgh Review*'s chief critic was Francis
Jeffrey, a liberal Whig who tended to utilitarianism: to what social
end does the work in question contribute? Will it or won't it *do*?
This was Jeffrey's narrow but, obviously, useful approach to literature. Peacock was also a utilitarian; and subscribed to his friend
Bentham's dictum: "the greatest good of the greatest number."
But Peacock regarded the *Edinburgh Review* ("that shallow and
dishonest publication") as much too Whiggish and class-bound.
Peacock seems always to have known that in England the Whig-
versus-Tory debate was essentially hollow because "though there
is no censorship of the press, there is an influence widely diffused
and mighty in its operation that is almost equivalent to it. The
whole scheme of our government is based on influence, and the im-
mense number of genteel persons, who are maintained by the taxes,
gives this influence an extent and complication from which few

persons are free. They shrink from truth, for it shews those dangers which they dare not face." Thus, in our own day, *The New York Times* reflects the will of the administration at Washington which in turn reflects the will of the moneyed interests. Should a contemporary American writer point out this connection, he will either be ignored or, worse, found guilty of Bad Taste, something that middle-class people are taught at birth forever to eschew.

The debate that helped to shape Peacock (and the century) was between Shelley's father-in-law William Godwin and the Reverend Thomas Malthus. The anarchist Godwin believed in progress; thought human nature perfectible. He believed society could be so ordered that the need for any man to work might be reduced to an hour or two a day. Godwin's *Political Justice* and *The Enquirer* inspired Malthus to write *An Essay on the Principle of Population*, published in 1798. Everyone knows Malthus' great proposition: "Population, when unchecked, increases in a geometrical ratio. Subsistence increases only in an arithmetical ratio. A slight acquaintance with numbers will show the immensity of the first power in comparison with the second." This proposition is still being argued, as it was for at least two millennia before Malthus. At the time of Confucius, China was underpopulated; yet all ills were ascribed to overpopulation: "When men were few and things were many," went an already ancient saying, "there was a golden age; but now men are many and things are few and misery is man's lot."

In a series of dialogue-novels, Peacock enlarged upon the debate. *Headlong Hall* appeared in 1816. As Butler notes: "Peacock's satires are all centered on a recent controversy large in its ideological implications but also amusingly rich in personality and detail. For its full effect, the satire requires the reader to be in the know." This explains why the form is not apt to be very popular. At any given moment too few people are in the know about much of anything. As time passes, the urgencies of how best to landscape a park —a debate in *Headlong Hall*—quite fades even though the various points of view from romantic to utilitarian are eternal.

Aristophanes made jokes about people who were sitting in the audience at the theatre of Dionysos. When we do know what's being sent up—Socrates' style, say—the bright savagery is exciting. But who is Glaucon? And what did he steal? Happily, most of Peacock's characters (based on Shelley, Byron, Coleridge, Malthus, et al.) are still well enough known to some readers for the jokes to work. More important, the tone of Peacock's sentences is highly pleasing. He writes a stately, balanced prose that moves, always, toward unexpected judgment or revelation.

Peacock begins a review of Thomas Moore's novel *The Epicurean* with: "This volume will, no doubt, be infinitely acceptable to the ladies 'who make the fortune of new books.' Love, very intense; mystery, somewhat recondite; piety, very profound; and philosophy, sufficiently shallow. . . . In the reign of the emperor Valerian, a young Epicurean philosopher is elected chief of that school in the beginning of his twenty-fourth year, a circumstance, the author says, without precedent, and we conceive without probability."

Melincourt was published in 1817, starring a truly noble savage, a monkey called Sir Oran Haut-ton. Malthus makes an appearance as Mr. Fax. Sir Oran, though he cannot speak, is elected to Parliament. *Nightmare Abbey* (1818) is a take-off on the cult of melancholy affected, in one way, by Byron (Mr. Cypress) and, in another, by Coleridge (Mr. Flosky). Shelley appears as Scythrop, though Butler makes the point that neither Shelley nor Peacock ever admitted to the likeness. Mr. Cypress has quarreled with his wife; he sees only darkness and misery as man's estate. Peacock works in actual lines from *Childe Harold* to mock if not Byron Byronism, while Mr. Flosky's dialogue is filled with metaphysical conceits that even he cannot unravel. Scythrop is not practical.

Peacock's next two works, *Maid Marian* (1818) and *The Misfortunes of Elphin* (1829), are set, respectively, in the late twelfth century and the sixth century. But Robin Hood's England is used to illuminate Peacock's dim view of the Holy Alliance of his own day while sixth-century Wales is used to savage Wellington's current Tory administration. *Crotchet Castle* (1831) is like the early books in form: culture is the theme. One of the characters is Dr. Folliott, a philistine Tory who mocks those who would improve man's lot. Since Dr. Folliott has been thought to be a voice for his creator, serious critics have tended to dismiss Peacock as a crotchety, unserious hedonist whose tastes are antiquarian and whose political views are irrelevant. Butler takes exception to this; she thinks that Folliott's likeness to his creator "cannot in fact survive a close reading." On education, Folliott advances opinions that were not Peacock's:

I hold that there is every variety of natural capacity from the idiot to Newton and Shakespeare; the mass of mankind, midway between these extremes, being blockheads of different degrees; education leaving them pretty nearly as it found them, with this single difference, that it gives a fixed direction to their stupidity, a sort of incurable wry neck to the thing they call their understanding.

I rather suspect that Peacock, in a certain mood, felt exactly as Dr. Folliott did. He also possessed negative capability to a high degree. In this instance, he may well be saying what he thinks at the moment, perfectly aware that he will think its opposite in relation to a different formulation on the order, say, of certain observations in Jefferson's memoirs which he reviewed in 1830. Peacock was absolutely bowled over by the mellifluous old faker's announcement that between "a government without newspapers, or newspapers without a government" he would choose the latter. This is, surely, one of the silliest statements ever made by a politician; yet it is perennially attractive to—yes, journalists. In any case, Jefferson was sufficiently sly to add, immediately, a line that is seldom quoted by those who love the sentiment: "But I should mean that every man should receive those papers, and be capable of reading them." The last phrase nicely cancels all that has gone before. Jefferson was no leveler.

In any case, the endlessly interesting controversy of who should be taught what and how and why is joined in this bright set of dialogues and every position is advanced. We get the Tory view, as published by the Rev. E. W. Grinfield; he thought that the masses need nothing more than to have religion and morals instilled in them: "We inculcate a strong attachment to the constitution, *such as it now is*; we teach them to love and revere our establishments in Church and State, even *with all their real or supposed imperfections*; and we are far more anxious to make them good and contented citizens, than to fit them for noisy patriots, who would perhaps destroy the constitution whilst pretending to correct it." There, in one sentence, is the principle on which American public education is based (*vide* Frances Fitzgerald's *America Revised*).

In opposition to Grinfield is John Stuart Mill:

I thought, that while the higher and richer classes held the power of government, the instruction and improvement of the mass of the people were contrary to the self-interest of those classes, because tending to render the people more powerful for throwing off the yoke; but if the democracy obtained a large, and perhaps the principal share, in the governing power, it would become the interest of the opulent classes to promote their education, in order to ward off really mischievous errors, and especially those which would lead to unjust violations of property.

This has proven to be idealistic. Neither Washington nor Moscow thinks it worthwhile to teach their citizens to address themselves to "real or supposed imperfections" in the system. Rather, to keep the citizens "good and contented" is the perennial aim of powerful governing classes or, as one of Peacock's Tory characters puts it: "Discontent increases with the increase of information."

Five years before Peacock's death at eighty-one, he published the most satisfying of his works (I still don't know what to call them: they are not novels as novels were written then or now, and they are not theatre pieces even though many pages are set up like a play-script), *Gryll Grange*. The subject is everything in general, the uses of the classics in particular. The form is resolutely Pavonian. Each character represents a viewpoint; each makes his argument.

Here is an example of Peacock when he slips into dialogue.

LORD CURRYFIN: Well, then, what say you to the electric telegraph, by which you converse at the distance of thousands of miles? Even across the Atlantic, as no doubt we shall do yet.

MR. GRYLL: Some of us have already heard the Doctor's opinion on the subject.

THE REVEREND DOCTOR OPIMIAN: I have no wish to expedite communication with the Americans. If we could apply the power of electrical repulsion to preserve us from ever hearing anything more of them, I should think that we had for once derived a benefit from science.

MR. GRYLL: Your love for the Americans, Doctor, seems something like that of Cicero's friend Marius for the Greeks. He would not take the nearest road to his villa, because it was called the Greek-road. Perhaps if your nearest way home were called the American-road, you would make a circuit to avoid it.

THE REVEREND DOCTOR OPIMIAN: I am happy to say that I am not put to the test. Magnetism, galvanism, electricity, are "one form of many names." Without magnetism, we should never have discovered America; to which we are indebted for nothing but evil; diseases in the worst form that can afflict humanity, and slavery in the worst form in which slavery can exist. The Old World had the sugarcane and the cotton-plant, though it did not so misuse them. Then, what good have we got from America? What good of any kind, from the whole continent and its islands, from the Esquimaux to Patagonia?

MR. GRYLL: Newfoundland salt fish, Doctor.

THE REVEREND DOCTOR OPIMIAN: That is something, but it does not turn the scale.

MR. GRYLL: If they have given us no good, we have given them none.

THE REVEREND DOCTOR OPIMIAN: We have given them wine and classical literature; but I am afraid Bacchus and Minerva have equally "Scattered their bounty upon barren ground." On the other hand, we have given the red men rum, which has been the chief instrument of their perdition. On the whole, our intercourse with America has been little else than interchange of vices and diseases.

LORD CURRYFIN: Do you count it nothing to have substituted civilized for savage men?

THE REVEREND DOCTOR OPIMIAN: Civilized. The word requires definition. But looking into futurity, it seems to me that the ultimate tendency of the change is to substitute the worse for the better race; the Negro for the Red Indian. The Red Indian will not work for a master. No ill-usage will make him. Herein, he is the noblest specimen of humanity that ever walked the earth. Therefore, the white men exterminate his race. But the time will come, when, by mere force of numbers, the black race will predominate, and exterminate the white.

Mr. Falconer remonstrates that "the white slavery of our [English] factories is not worse than the black slavery of America. We have done so much to amend it, and shall do more. Still much remains to be done." Opimian responds: "And will be done, I hope and believe. The Americans do nothing to amend their system." When Lord Curryfin remarks that he has met many good Americans who think as Doctor Opimian does, the response is serene: "Of that I have no doubt. But I look to public acts and public men."

In the half century between Peacock's first work and his last, the novel was transformed by Dickens and the comedy of character replaced the comedy of ideas. In fact, character—the more prodigious the better—was the novel. In the year of *Gryll Grange* (1860), the novel was about to undergo yet another change with the publication of *The Mill on the Floss*. In the everyday world of George Eliot's characters the play of intelligence is quite unlike

that of Peacock, since the only vivid intelligence in an Eliot novel
is that the author or, as Mary McCarthy writes: ". . . the kind
of questions her characters put to themselves and to each other,
though sometimes lofty, never question basic principles such as the
notion of betterment or the inviolability of the moral law."

Elsewhere in *Ideas and the Novel*, McCarthy contrasts Peacock
with James. Where James managed to exclude almost everything
in the way of ideas from the novel in order to concentrate on getting all the way 'round, as it were (oh, *as it were!*), his made-up
characters, "consider Thomas Love Peacock," she writes. "There
the ordinary stuff of life is swept away to make room for abstract
speculation. That, and just that, is the joke. . . . In hearty, plain-
man style (which is partly a simulation), Peacock treats the brain's
sickly products as the end-result of the general disease of modish-
ness for which the remedy would be prolonged exposure to common, garden reality." But that was written of *Nightmare Abbey*:
common, garden reality flourishes during the debates in *Gryll
Grange*, a book which Butler believes "occupies the same position
in Peacock's oeuvre as *The Clouds* in that of Aristophanes: both
seem less directly political than usual because the author's approach
is oblique and fantastic, almost surreal."

It is fitting that in *Gryll Grange* the characters are composing a
comedy in the Aristophanic manner while the book itself is a variation on Old Comedy. Although the tone of this old man's work is
highly genial, he still strikes with youthful vigor the negative. He
still says no to Romanticism which had, by then, entirely triumphed, and which, not much changed, continues to dominate our
own culture.

In a review of C. O. Müller's *A History of the Literature of Ancient Greece*, Peacock explains the value of the negative: "there is
much justice in the comparison of Lucian and Voltaire. The view
is not only just, it is also eminently liberal. That 'the results of the
efforts of both against false religion and false philosophy were
merely negative'; that they had 'nothing tangible to substitute for
what they destroyed,' is open to observation." Indeed it is. After
all, this is the constant complaint of those who support the crimes
and injustices of the status quo. Peacock proceeds to observe, "To
clear the ground of falsehood is to leave room for the introduction
of truth. Lucian decidedly held that moral certainty, a complete
code of duty founded on reason, existed in the writings of Epicurus; and Voltaire's theism, the belief in a pervading spirit of good,

was clear and consistent throughout. The main object of both was, by sweeping away false dogmas, to teach toleration. Voltaire warred against opinions which sustained themselves by persecution."

Needless to say, there is no more certain way of achieving perfect unpopularity in any society than to speak against the reigning pieties and agreed-upon mendacities. The official line never varies: To be negative is to be bad; to be positive is to be good. In fact, that is even more the rule in our society than it was in Peacock's smaller world where the means to destroy dissent through censorship or ridicule or silence were not as institutionalized as they are now.

Even so, Peacock himself was forced to play a very sly game when he dealt with the Christian dictatorship of England. After giving an admiring account of Epicurus' "favorite dogma of the mortality of the soul," he remarks, "In England, we all believe in the immortality of the soul" because "the truth of the Christian Religion is too clearly established amongst us to admit of dispute." In his novels, he treated Christianity with great caution. What he really thought of a religion that was the negation of all that *he* held positive only came to light posthumously.

In 1862, a year after Mary Ellen's death, he sent to the printers a poem he had written in Greek on Jesus' exuberantly vicious tirade (Matthew 10:34): "Think not that I am come to send peace on earth: I came not to send peace, but a sword." The executors of Peacock's estate suppressed the poem; and only the last lines survive in translation. A pagan appears to be exhorting a crowd to "come now in a body and dash in pieces" this armed enemy, Jesus. "Break in pieces, hurl down him who is a seller of marvels, him who is hostile to the Graces, and him who is abominable to Aphrodite, the hater of the marriage bed, this mischievous wonder-worker, this destroyer of the world, CHRIST." There are times when positive capability must masquerade as negative.

Butler is at her most interesting when she relates Peacock to our own time where "students of literature are taught to think more highly of introspection than of objectivity, to isolate works of art from their social context, and to give them a high and special kind of value." She ascribes this to "the early nineteenth century irrationalist reaction—Romanticism—[which] is a current movement still. . . . In England at the close of the Napoleonic Wars, Romanticism was perceived to encourage indifference to contemporary

politics, or to offer outright aid to illiberal governments. A literature that is concerned with style, and with feeling, rather than
with intellect and reason, may be merely decorative; in relation to
practical affairs, it will almost certainly be passive."

One can understand the emphasis that our universities continue
to place on the necessary separation of literature from ideas. "We
are stunned," writes Butler, "by reiteration into believing that what
the world wants is positive thinking. Peacock makes out a case,
illustrated by Voltaire, for negative thinking, and its attendant vir-
tues of challenge, self-doubt, mutual acceptance, and toleration."
Finally, "Since Coleridge we have been fond of the artist-prophet,
and the art-work which is monologue, or confession, or even opium
dream. Peacock, whose art is based on the dialogue, has waited a
long time for his turn to be heard."

I don't know how these things are being arranged in Butler's
England but the passive yea-sayer who has no ideas at all about
politics, religion, ethics, history is absolutely central to our syllabus
and his only competition is the artist as advertiser of sweet self
alone. The culture would not have it otherwise and so, as McCarthy
puts it, "in the place of ideas, images still rule the roost, and Balzac's distinction between the *roman idée* and the *roman imagé* appears to have been prophetic, though his order of preference is
reversed."

In *Ideas and the Novel,* McCarthy joins in the battle (assuming
that this is not just a skirmish in a byway where the mirror lies
shattered). Although McCarthy takes the Pavonian side, she moves
beyond Peacock's satiric dialogue-novels to those formidable nineteenth-century novelists to whom ideas are essential and, for her,
it is James not Coleridge who is terminus to this line. "When you
think of James in the light of his predecessors," she writes, "you
are suddenly conscious of what is not there: battles, riots, tempests,
sunrises, the sewers of Paris, crime, hunger, the plague, the scaf-
fold, the clergy, but also minute particulars such as you find in
Jane Austen—poor Miss Bates's twice-baked apples."

McCarthy is particularly interesting when she examines Victor
Hugo, a great novelist doomed to be forever unknown to Americans. She examines Hugo's curious way of staying outside his characters whose "emotions are inferred for us by Victor Hugo and
reported in summary form." Hugo deals with ideas on every subject from capital punishment to argot. He is also possessed by an
Idea: "The manifest destiny of France to lead and inspire was

identified by Hugo with his own mission to the nation as seer and epic novelist." McCarthy's survey of this sort of, admittedly, rare master (Tolstoy, Dostoevsky, Manzoni, Balzac, Stendhal, George Eliot) is illuminating, particularly when she discusses "the ambition to get everything in, to make this book *the* Book," a passion still to be found post-James in Proust and Joyce "Though public spirit as an animating force was no longer evident (in fact the reverse) . . . the ambition to produce a single compendious sacred writing survived, and we may even find it today in an author like Pynchon (*Gravity's Rainbow*)."

It is usual in discussion of the novel (what is it for? what is it?) to point to the displacement that occurred when the film took the novel's place at the center of our culture. What James had removed from the novel in the way of vulgar life, film seized upon: "It was not until the invention of the moving-picture," writes McCarthy, "that the novel lost its supremacy as purveyor of irreality to a multitude composed of solitary units." McCarthy goes on to make the point that "unlike the novel, the moving-picture, at least in my belief, cannot be an idea-spreader; its images are too enigmatic, e.g., Eisenstein's baby carriage bouncing down those stairs in *Potemkin*. A film cannot have a spokesman or chorus character to point the moral as in a stage play; that function is assumed by the camera, which is inarticulate. And the absence of spokesmen in the films we remember shows rather eerily that with the cinema, for the first time, humanity has found a narrative medium that is incapable of thought."

If McCarthy's startling insight is true (I *think* it is), the curious invention by the French of the auteur-theory begins to make a degree of sense. Aware that something was missing in films (a unifying intelligence), M. Bazin and his friends decided that the camera's lens was nothing but a surrogate for the director who held it or guided it or aimed it, just as the painter deploys his brush. For M. Bazin *et cie.*, the director is the unifying intelligence who controls the image and makes sense of the piece: he is The Creator. Needless to say, this perfect misapprehension of the way movies were made in Hollywood's Golden Age has been a source of mirth to those who were there.

The movie-goer is passive, unlike the reader; and one does not hear a creator's voice while watching a movie. Yet, curiously enough, the kind of satire that was practiced by Aristophanes might just find its way onto the screen. As I watched *Airplane*, I kept hoping that its three auteurs (bright show-biz kids) would open up the farce. Include President Carter and his dread family; show how each would respond to the near-disaster. Add Reagan, Cronkite, the Polish Pope. But the auteurs stuck to the only thing that show-biz people ever know about—other movies and television commercials. Although the result is highly enjoyable, a chance was missed to send up a whole society in a satire of the Old Comedy sort.

At the end of McCarthy's notes on the novel, she looks about for new ways of salvaging a form that has lost its traditional content. She thinks that it might be possible, simply, to go back in time: "If because of ideas and other unfashionable components your novel is going to seem dated, don't be alarmed—date it." She mentions several recent examples of quasi-historical novels; she also notes that "in the U.S.A., a special license has always been granted to the Jewish novel, which is free to juggle ideas in full public; Bellow, Malamud, Philip Roth still avail themselves of the right, which is never conceded to us goys." With all due respect to three interesting writers, they don't use their "concession" with any more skill than we mindless goys. The reason that they sometimes appear to be dealing in ideas is that they arrived post-James. Jewish writers over forty do—or did—comprise a new, not quite American class, more closely connected with ideological, argumentative Europe (and Talmudic studies) than with those of us whose ancestors killed Indians, pursued the white whale, suffered, in varying degrees, etiolation as a result of overexposure to the Master's lesson. In any case, today's young Jewish writers are every bit as lacking in ideas as the goyim.

McCarthy admires Robert Pirsig's *Zen and the Art of Motorcycle Maintenance*, "an American story of a cross-country trip with philosophical interludes." She believes that "if the novel is to be revitalized, maybe more such emergency strategies will have to be employed to disarm and disorient reviewers and teachers of literature, who, as always, are the reader's main foe." They are not the writer's ally either—unless he conforms to their kitsch romantic notions of what writing ought to be or, more to the point, what it must never be.

Although I suspect that it is far too late for emergency strategies, one final tactic that *might* work is to infiltrate the genre forms. To fill them up, stealthily, with ideas, wit, subversive notions: an Agatha Christie plot with well-cut cardboard characters that dem-

onstrated, among other bright subjects, the rise and fall of mone-
tarism in England would be attractive to all sorts of readers and
highly useful.

In any case, write what you know will always be excellent advice
for those who ought not to write at all. Write what you think,
what you imagine, what you suspect: that is the only way out of
the dead end of the Serious Novel which so many ambitious people
want to write and no one on earth—or even on campus—wants to
read.

The New York Review of Books
December 4, 1980

Who Makes the Movies?

Forty-nine years ago last October Al Jolson not only filled with hideous song the sound track of a film called *The Jazz Singer*, he also spoke. With the words "You ain't heard nothin' yet" (surely the most menacing line in the history of world drama), the age of the screen director came to an end and the age of the screenwriter began.

Until 1927, the director was king, turning out by the mile his "molds of light" (André Bazin's nice phrase). But once the movies talked, the director as creator became secondary to the writer. Even now, except for an occasional director-writer like Ingmar Bergman,* the director tends to be the one interchangeable (if not entirely expendable) element in the making of a film. After all, there are thousands of movie technicians who can do what a

---

* Questions I am advised to anticipate: What about such true *auteurs du cinéma* as Truffaut? Well, *Jules et Jim* was a novel by Henri-Pierre Roché. Did Truffaut adapt the screenplay by himself? No, he worked with Jean Gruault. Did Buñuel create *The Exterminating Angel*? No, it was "suggested" by an unpublished play by José Bergamin. Did Buñuel take it from there? No, he had as co-author Luis Alcorisa. So it goes.

director is supposed to do because, in fact, collectively (and some-times individually) they actually do do his work behind the camera and in the cutter's room. On the other hand, there is no film without a written script.

In the Fifties when I came to MGM as a contract writer and took my place at the Writers' Table in the commissary, the Wise Hack used to tell us newcomers, "The director is the brother-in-law." Apparently the ambitious man became a producer (that's where the power was). The talented man became a writer (that's where the creation was). The pretty man became a star.

Even before Jolson spoke, the director had begun to give way to the producer. Director Lewis Milestone saw the writing on the screen as early as 1923 when "baby producer" Irving Thalberg fired the legendary director Erich von Stroheim from his film *Merry Go Round*. "That," wrote Milestone somberly in *New Theater and Film* (March 1937), "was the beginning of the storm and the end of the reign of the director. . . ." Even as late as 1950 the star Dick Powell assured the film cutter Robert Parrish that "anybody can direct a movie, even I could do it. I'd rather not because it would take too much time. I can make more money acting, selling real estate and playing the market." That was pretty much the way the director was viewed in the Thirties and Forties, the so-called classic age of the talking movie.

Although the essential creator of the classic Hollywood film was the writer, the actual master of the film was the producer, as Scott Fitzgerald recognized when he took as protagonist for his last novel Irving Thalberg. Although Thalberg himself was a lousy movie-maker, he was the head of production at MGM; and in those days MGM was a kind of Vatican where the chief of production was Pope, holding in his fists the golden keys of Schenck. The staff producers were the College of Cardinals. The movie stars were holy and valuable objects to be bought, borrowed, stolen. Like icons, they were moved from sound stage to sound stage, studio to studio, film to film, bringing in their wake good fortune and gold.

With certain exceptions (Alfred Hitchcock, for one), the direc-tors were, at worst, brothers-in-law; at best, bright technicians. All in all, they were a cheery, unpretentious lot, and if anyone had told them that they were *auteurs du cinéma*, few could have coped with the concept, much less the French. They were technicians;

proud commercialities, happy to serve what was optimistically known as The Industry.

This state of affairs lasted until television replaced the movies as America's principal dispenser of mass entertainment. Overnight the producers lost control of what was left of The Industry and, un-expectedly, the icons took charge. Apparently, during all those years when we thought the icons nothing more than beautiful painted images of all our dreams and lusts, they had been not only alive but secretly greedy for power and gold.

"The lunatics are running the asylum," moaned the Wise Hack at the Writers' Table, but soldiered on. Meanwhile, the icons started to produce, direct, even write. For a time, they were able to ignore the fact that with television on the rise, no movie star could outdraw the "$64,000 Question." During this transitional decade, the director was still the brother-in-law. But instead of marrying himself off to a producer, he shacked up, as it were, with an icon. For a time each icon had his or her favorite director and The Industry was soon on the rocks.

Then out of France came the dreadful news: all those brothers-in-law of the classic era were really autonomous and original artists. Apparently each had his own style that impressed itself on every frame of any film he worked on. Proof? Since the director was the same person from film to film, each image of his *oeuvre* must then be stamped with his authorship. The argument was circular but no less overwhelming in its implications. Much quoted was Giraudoux's solemn inanity: "There are no works, there are only *auteurs*."

The often wise André Bazin eventually ridiculed this notion in *La Politique des Auteurs*, but the damage was done in the pages of the magazine he founded, *Cahiers du cinéma*. The fact that, regardless of director, every Warner Brothers film during the classic age had a dark look owing to the Brothers' passion for saving money in electricity and set-dressing cut no ice with ambitious critics on the prowl for high art in a field once thought entirely low.

In 1948, Bazin's disciple Alexandre Astruc wrote the challenging *"La Caméra-stylo."* This manifesto advanced the notion that the director is—or should be—the true and solitary creator of a movie, "penning" his film on celluloid. Astruc thought that *caméra-stylo* could tackle any subject, any genre. . . . I will even go so far as to say that contemporary ideas and philosophies of life are such that only the cinema can do justice to them. Maurice Nadeau wrote in an article in the newspaper *Combat*: "If Descartes lived today, he would write novels." With all due respect to Nadeau, a Descartes of today would already have shut himself up in his bedroom with a 16mm camera and some film, and would be writing his philosophy on film: for his *Discours de la Méthode* would today be of such a kind that only the cinema could express it satisfactorily.

With all due respect to Astruc, the cinema has many charming possibilities but it cannot convey complex ideas through words or even, paradoxically, dialogue in the Socratic sense. *Le Genou de Claire* is about as close as we shall ever come to dialectic in a film and though Rohmer's work has its delights, the ghost of Descartes is not very apt to abandon the marshaling of words on a page for the flickering shadows of talking heads. In any case, the Descartes of Astruc's period did not make a film; he wrote the novel *La Nausée*.

But the would-be camera-writers are not interested in philosophy or history or literature. They want only to acquire for the cinema the prestige of ancient forms without having first to crack the code. "Let's face it," writes Astruc:

> between the pure cinema of the 1920s and filmed theater, there is plenty of room for a different and individual kind of film-making.
>   This of course implies that the scriptwriter directs his own scripts; or rather, that the scriptwriter ceases to exist, for in this kind of film-making the distinction between author and director loses all meaning. Direction is no longer a means of illustrating or presenting a scene, but a true act of writing.

It is curious that despite Astruc's fierce will to eliminate the script-writer (and perhaps literature itself), he is forced to use terms from the art form he would like to supersede. For him the film director uses a *pen* with which he *writes* in order to become—highest praise—an *author*.

As the French theories made their way across the Atlantic, bemused brothers-in-law found themselves being courted by odd-looking French youths with tape recorders. Details of long-forgotten Westerns were recalled and explicated. Every halting word from the *auteur*'s lips was taken down and reverently examined. The despised brothers-in-law of the Thirties were now Artists. With newfound confidence, directors started inking major pacts to meg superstar thesps whom the meggers could control as hyphenates: that is, as director-producers or even as writer-director-producers. Although the icons continued to be worshiped and overpaid, the truly big deals were now made by directors. To them, also, went the glory. For all practical purposes the producer has either vanished from the scene (the "package" is now put together by a "talent" agency) or merged with the director. Meanwhile, the screenwriter continues to be the prime creator of the talking film, and though he is generally paid very well and his name is listed right after that of the director in the movie reviews of *Time*, he is entirely in the shadow of the director just as the director was once in the shadow of the producer and the star.

What do directors actually do? What do screenwriters do? This is difficult to explain to those who have never been involved in the making of a film. It is particularly difficult when French theoreticians add to the confusion by devising false hypotheses (studio director as *auteur* in the Thirties) on which to build irrelevant and misleading theories. Actually, if Astruc and Bazin had wanted to be truly perverse (and almost accurate), they would have declared that the cameraman is the *auteur* of any film. They could then have ranked James Wong Howe with Dante, Braque, and Gandhi. Cameramen do tend to have styles in a way that the best writers do but most directors don't—style as opposed to preoccupation. Gregg Toland's camera work is a vivid fact from film to film, linking *Citizen Kane* to Wyler's *The Best Years of Our Lives* in a way that one cannot link *Citizen Kane* to, say, Welles's *Confidential Report*. Certainly the cameraman is usually more important than the director in the day-to-day making of a film as opposed to the preparation of a film. Once the film is shot the editor becomes the principal interpreter of the writer's invention.

Since there are few reliable accounts of the making of any of the classic talking movies, Pauline Kael's book on the making of *Citizen Kane* is a valuable document. In considerable detail she establishes the primacy in that enterprise of the screenwriter Herman Mankiewicz. The story of how Orson Welles saw to it that Mankiewicz became, officially, the noncreator of his own film is grimly fascinating and highly typical of the way so many director-hustlers acquire for themselves the writer's creation.* Few directors in this area possess the modesty of Kurosawa, who said, recently, "With a very good script, even a second-class director may make a first-class film. But with a bad script even a first-class director cannot make a really first-class film."

A useful if necessarily superficial look at the way movies were written in the classic era can be found in the pages of *Some Time in the Sun*. The author, Mr. Tom Dardis, examines the movie careers of five celebrated writers who took jobs as movie-writers. They are Scott Fitzgerald, Aldous Huxley, William Faulkner, Nathanael West, and James Agee.

Mr. Dardis' approach to his writers and to the movies is that of a deeply serious and highly concerned lowbrow, a type now heavily tenured in American Academe. He writes of "literate" dialogue, "massive" biographies. Magisterially, he misquotes Henry James on the subject of gold. More seriously, *he misquotes Joan Crawford*. She did not say to Fitzgerald, "Work hard, Mr. Fitzgerald, work hard!" when he was preparing a film for her. She said "*Write* hard. . . ." There are many small inaccuracies that set on edge the film buff's teeth. For instance, Mr. Dardis thinks that the hotel on Sunset Boulevard known, gorgeously, as The Garden of Allah is "now demolished and reduced to the status of a large parking lot. . . ." Well, it is not a parking lot. Hollywood has its own peculiar reverence for the past. The Garden of Allah was replaced by a bank that subtly suggests in glass and metal the mock-Saracen façade of the hotel that once housed Scott Fitzgerald. Mr. Dardis also thinks that the hotel was "demolished" during World War II. I stayed there in the late Fifties, right next door to fun-loving, bibulous Errol Flynn.

Errors and starry-eyed vulgarity to one side, Mr. Dardis has done a good deal of interesting research on how films were written and made in those days. For one thing, he catches the ambivalence felt by the writers who had descended (but only temporarily) from literature's Parnassus to the swampy marketplace of the movies. There was a tendency to play Lucifer. One was thought to have sold out. "Better to reign in hell than to serve in heaven," was more

---

* Peter Bogdanovich maintains that Kael's version of the making of *Citizen Kane* is not only inaccurate but highly unfair to Orson Welles, a master whom I revere.

than once quoted—well, paraphrased—at the Writers' Table. We knew we smelled of sulphur. Needless to say, most of the time it was a lot of fun if the booze didn't get you.

For the Parnassian writer the movies were not just a means of making easy money; even under the worst conditions, movies were genuinely interesting to write. Mr. Dardis is at his best when he shows his writers taking seriously their various "assignments." The instinct to do good work is hard to eradicate.

Faulkner was the luckiest (and the most cynical) of Mr. Dardis' five. For one thing, he usually worked with Howard Hawks, a director who might actually qualify as an *auteur*. Hawks was himself a writer and he had a strong sense of how to manipulate those clichés that he could handle best. Together Faulkner and Hawks created a pair of satisfying movies, *To Have and Have Not* and *The Big Sleep*. But who did what? Apparently there is not enough remaining evidence (at least available to Mr. Dardis) to sort out authorship. Also, Faulkner's public line was pretty much: I'm just a hired hand who does what he's told.

Nunnally Johnson (as quoted by Mr. Dardis) found Hawks's professional relationship with Faulkner mysterious. "It may be that he simply wanted his name attached to Faulkner's. Or since Hawks liked to write it was easy to do it with Faulkner, for Bill didn't care much one way or the other. . . . We shall probably never know just how much Bill cared about any of the scripts he worked on with Hawks." Yet it is interesting to note that Johnson takes it entirely for granted that the director wants—and must get—*all* credit for a film.

Problem for the director: how to get a script without its author? Partial solution: of all writers, the one who does not mind anonymity is the one most apt to appeal to an ambitious director. When the studio producer was king, he used to minimize the writer's role by assigning a dozen writers to a script. No director today has the resources of the old studios. But he can hire a writer who doesn't "care much one way or the other." He can also put his name on the screen as co-author (standard procedure in Italy and France). Even the noble Jean Renoir played this game when he came to direct *The Southerner*. Faulkner not only wrote the script, he liked the project. The picture's star Zachary Scott has said that the script was entirely Faulkner's. But then, other hands were engaged and "the whole problem," according to Mr. Dardis, "of who did what was nearly solved by Renoir's giving himself sole credit for the screenplay—the best way possible for an *auteur* director to label his films."

Unlike Faulkner, Scott Fitzgerald cared deeply about movies; he wanted to make a success of movie-writing and, all in all, if Mr. Dardis is to be believed (and for what it may be worth, his account of Fitzgerald's time in the sun tallies with what one used to hear), he had a far better and more healthy time of it in Hollywood than is generally suspected.

Of a methodical nature, Fitzgerald ran a lot of films at the studio. (Unlike Faulkner, who affected to respond only to Mickey Mouse and Pathé News). Fitzgerald made notes. He also did what an ambitious writer must do if he wants to write the sort of movie he himself might want to see: he made friends with the producers. Rather censoriously, Mr. Dardis notes Fitzgerald's "clearly stated intention to work with film producers rather than with film directors, here downgraded to the rank of 'collaborators.' Actually, Fitzgerald seems to have had no use whatsoever for directors as such." But neither did anyone else.

During much of this time Howard Hawks, say, was a low-budget director known for the neatness and efficiency of his work. Not until the French beatified him twenty years later did he appear to anyone as an original artist instead of just another hired technician. It is true that Hawks was allowed to work with writers, but then, he was at Warner Brothers, a frontier outpost facing upon barbarous Burbank. At MGM, the holy capital, writers and directors did not get much chance to work together. It was the producer who worked with the writer, and Scott Fitzgerald was an MGM writer. Even as late as my own years at MGM (1956–1958), the final script was the writer's creation (under the producer's supervision). The writer even pre-empted the director's most important function by describing each camera shot: Long, Medium, Close, and the director was expected faithfully to follow the writer's score.

One of the most successful directors at MGM during this period was George Cukor. In an essay on "The Director" (1938), Cukor reveals the game as it used to be played. "In most cases," he writes, "the director makes his appearance very early in the life story of a motion picture." I am sure that this was often the case with Cukor but the fact that he thinks it necessary to mention "early" participation is significant.

There are times when the whole idea for a film may come from [the director], but in a more usual case he makes his entry when he is summoned by a producer and it is suggested that he should be the director of a proposed story.

Not only was this the most usual way but, very often, the director left the producer's presence with the finished script under his arm. Cukor does describe his own experience working with writers but Cukor was something of a star at the studio. Most directors were "summoned" by the producer and told what to do. It is curious, incidentally, how entirely the idea of the working producer has vanished. He is no longer remembered except as the butt of familiar stories: fragile artist treated cruelly by insensitive cigar-smoking producer—or Fitzgerald savaged yet again by Joe Mankiewicz.

Of Mr. Dardis' five writers, James Agee is, to say the least, the lightest in literary weight. But he was a passionate film-goer and critic. He was a child of the movies just as Huxley was a child of Meredith and Peacock. Given a different temperament, luck, birthdate, Agee might have been the first American cinema *auteur*: a writer who wrote screenplays in such a way that, like the score of a symphony, they needed nothing more than a conductor's interpretation, . . . an interpretation he could have provided himself and perhaps would have provided if he had lived.

Agee's screenplays were remarkably detailed. "All the shots," writes Mr. Dardis, "were set down with extreme precision in a way that no other screenwriter had ever set things down before. . . ." This is exaggerated. Most screenwriters of the classic period wrote highly detailed scripts in order to direct the director but, certainly, the examples Mr. Dardis gives of Agee's screenplays show them to be remarkably visual. Most of us hear stories. He saw them, too. But I am not so sure that what he saw was the reflection of a living reality in his head. As with many of today's young directors, Agee's memory was crowded with memories not of life but of old films. For Agee, rain falling was not a memory of April at Exeter but a scene recalled from Eisenstein. This is particularly noticeable in the adaptation Agee made of Stephen Crane's *The Blue Hotel*, which, Mr. Dardis tells us, no "film director has yet taken on, although it has been televised twice, each time with a different director and cast and with the Agee script cut to the bone, being used only as a guidepost to the story." This is nonsense. In 1954,

CBS hired me to adapt *The Blue Hotel*. I worked directly from Stephen Crane and did not know that James Agee had ever adapted it until I read *Some Time in the Sun*.

At the mention of any director's name, the Wise Hack at the Writers' Table would bark out a percentage, representing how much, in his estimate, a given director would subtract from the potential 100 percent of the script he was directing. The thought that a director might *add* something worthwhile never crossed the good gray Hack's mind. Certainly he would have found hilarious David Thomson's *A Biographical Dictionary of Film*, whose haphazard pages are studded with tributes to directors.

Mr. Thomson has his own pleasantly eccentric pantheon in which writers figure hardly at all. A column is devoted to the dim Micheline Presle but the finest of all screenwriters, Jacques Prévert, is ignored. There is a long silly tribute to Arthur Penn; yet there is no biography of Penn's contemporary at NBC television, Paddy Chayefsky, whose films in the Fifties and early Sixties were far more interesting than anything Penn has done. Possibly Chayefsky was excluded because not only did he write his own films, he would then hire a director rather the way one would employ a plumber—or a cameraman. For a time, Chayefsky was the only American *auteur*, and his pencil was the director. Certainly Chayefsky's early career in films perfectly disproves Nicholas Ray's dictum (approvingly quoted by Mr. Thomson): "If it were all in the script, why make the film?" If it is not all in the script, there is no film to make.

Twenty years ago at the Writers' Table we all agreed with the Wise Hack that William Wyler subtracted no more than 10 percent from a script. Some of the most attractive and sensible of Bazin's pages are devoted to Wyler's work in the Forties. On the other hand, Mr. Thomson does not like him at all (because Wyler lacks those redundant faults that create the illusion of a Style?). Yet whatever was in a script, Wyler rendered faithfully: when he was given a bad script, he would make not only a bad movie, but the script's particular kind of badness would be revealed in a way that could altogether too easily boomerang on the too skillful director. But when the script was good (of its kind, *of its kind!*), *The Letter*, say, or *The Little Foxes*, there was no better interpreter.

At MGM, I worked exclusively with the producer Sam Zimbalist. He was a remarkably good and decent man in a business where such qualities are rare. He was also a producer of the old-fashioned sort. This meant that the script was prepared for him and with him. Once the script was ready, the director was summoned; he would then have the chance to say, yes, he would direct the script or, no, he wouldn't. Few changes were made in the script after the director was assigned. But this was not to be the case in Zimbalist's last film.

For several years MGM had been planning a remake of *Ben-Hur*, the studio's most successful silent film. A Contract Writer wrote a script; it was discarded. Then Zimbalist offered me the job. I said no, and went on suspension. During the next year or two S. N. Behrman and Maxwell Anderson, among others, added many yards of portentous dialogue to a script which kept growing and changing. The result was not happy. By 1958 MGM was going bust. Suddenly the remake of *Ben-Hur* seemed like a last chance to regain the mass audience lost to television. Zimbalist again asked me if I would take on the job. I said that if the studio released me from the remainder of my contract, I would go to Rome for two or three months and rewrite the script. The studio agreed. Meanwhile, Wyler had been signed to direct.

On a chilly March day Wyler, Zimbalist, and I took an overnight flight from New York. On the plane Wyler read for the first time the latest of the many scripts. As we drove together into Rome from the airport, Wyler looked gray and rather frightened. "This is awful," he said, indicating the huge script that I had placed between us on the back seat. "I know," I said. "What are we going to do?"

Wyler groaned: "These Romans. . . . Do you know anything about them?" I said, yes, I had done my reading. Wyler stared at me. "Well," he said, "when a Roman sits down and relaxes, what does he unbuckle?"

That spring I rewrote more than half the script (and Wyler studied every "Roman" film ever made). When I was finished with a scene, I would give it to Zimbalist. We would go over it. Then the scene would be passed on to Wyler. Normally, Wyler is slow and deliberately indecisive; but first-century Jerusalem had been built at enormous expense; the first day of shooting was approaching; the studio was nervous. As a result, I did not often hear Wyler's famous cry, as he would hand you back your script, "If I knew what was wrong with it, I'd fix it myself."

The plot of *Ben-Hur* is, basically, absurd and any attempt to make sense of it would destroy the story's awful integrity. But for a film to be watchable the characters must make some kind of psychological sense. We were stuck with the following: the Jew Ben-Hur and the Roman Messala were friends in childhood. Then they were separated. Now the adult Messala returns to Jerusalem; meets Ben-Hur; asks him to help with the Romanization of Judea. Ben-Hur refuses; there is a quarrel; they part and vengeance is sworn. This one scene is the sole motor that must propel a very long story until Jesus Christ suddenly and pointlessly drifts onto the scene, automatically untying some of the cruder knots in the plot. Wyler and I agreed that a single political quarrel would not turn into a lifelong vendetta.

I thought of a solution, which I delivered into Wyler's good ear. "As boys they were lovers. Now Messala wants to continue the affair. Ben-Hur rejects him. Messala is furious. *Chagrin d'amour*, the classic motivation for murder."

Wyler looked at me as if I had gone mad. "But we can't do *that*! I mean this is Ben-Hur! My God. . . ."

"We won't really do it. We just suggest it. I'll write the scenes so that they will make sense to those who are tuned in. Those who aren't will still feel that Messala's rage is somehow emotionally logical."

I don't think Wyler particularly liked my solution but he agreed that "anything is better than what we've got. So let's try it."

I broke the original scene into two parts. Charlton Heston (Ben-Hur) and Stephen Boyd (Messala) read them for us in Zimbalist's office. Wyler knew his actors. He warned me: "Don't ever tell Chuck what it's all about, or he'll fall apart."* I suspect that Heston does not know to this day what luridness we managed to contrive around him. But Boyd knew: every time he looked at Ben-Hur it was like a starving man getting a glimpse of dinner through a pane of glass. And so, among the thundering hooves and clichés of the last (to date) *Ben-Hur*, there is something odd and authentic in one unstated relationship.

As agreed, I left in early summer and Christopher Fry wrote the rest of the script. Before the picture ended, Zimbalist died of a heart attack. Later, when it came time to credit the writers of the film, Wyler proposed that Fry be given screen credit. Then Fry

---

* Wyler now denies that I ever told him what I was up to. It is possible that these conversations took place with Zimbalist but I doubt it. Anyway, the proof is on the screen.

insisted that I be given credit with him, since I had written the first half of the picture. Wyler was in a quandary. Only Zimbalist (and Fry and myself—two interested parties) knew who had written what, and Zimbalist was dead. The matter was given to the Screenwriters Guild for arbitration and they, mysteriously, awarded the credit to the Contract Writer whose script was separated from ours by at least two other discarded scripts. The film was released in 1959 (not 1959–1960, as my edition of *The Film-goer's Companion* by Leslie Halliwell states) and saved MGM from financial collapse.

I have recorded in some detail this unimportant business to show the near-impossibility of determining how a movie is actually created. Had *Ben-Hur* been taken seriously by, let us say, those French critics who admire *Johnny Guitar*, then Wyler would have been credited with the unusually subtle relationship between Ben-Hur and Messala. No credit would ever have gone to me because my name was not on the screen, nor would credit have gone to the official scriptwriter because, according to the *auteur* theory, every aspect of a film is the creation of the director.

The twenty-year interregnum when the producer was supreme is now a memory. The ascendancy of the movie stars was brief. The directors have now regained their original primacy, and Milestone's storm is only an echo. Today the marquees of movie houses feature the names of directors and journalists ("*A work of art*," J. Crist); the other collaborators are in fine print.

This situation might be more acceptable if the film directors had become true *auteurs*. But most of them are further than ever away from art—not to mention life. The majority are simply technicians. A few have come from the theatre; many began as editors, cameramen, makers of television series, and commercials; in recent years, ominously, a majority have been graduates of film schools. In principle, there is nothing wrong with a profound understanding of the technical means by which an image is impressed upon celluloid. But movies are not just molds of light any more than a novel is just inked-over paper. A movie is a response to reality in a certain way and that way must first be found by a writer. Unfortunately, no contemporary film director can bear to be thought a mere interpreter. He must be sole creator. As a result, he is more often than not a plagiarist, telling stories that are not his.

Over the years a number of writers have become directors, but except for such rare figures as Cocteau and Bergman, the writers who have gone in for directing were generally not much better at writing than they proved to be at directing. Even in commercial terms, for every Joe Mankiewicz or Preston Sturges there are a dozen Xs and Ys, not to mention the depressing Z.

Today's films are more than ever artifacts of light. Cars chase one another mindlessly along irrelevant freeways. Violence seems rooted in a notion about what ought to happen next on the screen to help the images move rather than in any human situation anterior to those images. In fact, the human situation has been eliminated not through any intentional philosophic design but because those who have spent too much time with cameras and machines seldom have much apprehension of that living world without whose presence there is no art.

I suspect that the time has now come to take Astruc seriously . . . after first rearranging his thesis. Astruc's *caméra-stylo* requires that "the script writer ceases to exist. . . . The filmmaker/author writes with his camera as a writer writes with his pen." Good. But let us eliminate not the screenwriter but that technician-hustler— the director (a.k.a. *auteur du cinéma*). Not until he has been re-placed by those who can use a pen to write from life for the screen is there going to be much of anything worth seeing. Nor does it take a genius of a writer to achieve great effects in film. Compared to the works of his nineteenth-century mentors, the writing of Ingmar Bergman is second-rate. But when he writes straight through the page and onto the screen itself his talent is transformed and the result is often first-rate.

As a poet, Jacques Prévert is not in the same literary class as Valéry, but Prévert's films *Les Enfants du Paradis* and *Lumière d'été* are extraordinary achievements. They were also disdained by the French theoreticians of the Forties who knew perfectly well that the directors Carné and Grémillon were inferior to their script-writer; but since the Theory requires that only a director can create a film, any film that is plainly a writer's work cannot be true cinema. This attitude has given rise to some highly comic critical musings. Recently a movie critic could not figure out why there had been such a dramatic change in the quality of the work of the director Joseph Losey after he moved to England. Was it a difference in the culture? the light? the water? Or could it—and the critic faltered—could it be that perhaps Losey's films changed when he . . . when he—oh, dear!—got Harold Pinter to write screenplays for him? The critic promptly dismissed the notion. Mr. Thomson prints no biography of Pinter in his *Dictionary*.

I have never much liked the films of Pier Paolo Pasolini, but I find most interesting the ease with which he turned to film after some twenty years as poet and novelist. He could not have been a film-maker in America because the costs are too high; also, the technician-hustlers are in total charge. But in Italy, during the Fifties, it was possible for an actual *auteur* to use for a pen the camera (having first composed rather than stolen the narrative to be illuminated).

Since the talking movie is closest in form to the novel ("the novel is a narrative that organizes itself in the world, while the cinema is a world that organizes itself into a narrative"—Jean Mitry), it strikes me that the rising literary generation might think of the movies as, peculiarly, their kind of novel, to be created by them in collaboration with technicians but without the interference of The Director, that hustler-plagiarist who has for twenty years dominated and exploited and (occasionally) enhanced an art form still in search of its true authors.

The New York Review of Books
November 25, 1976

Sex Is Politics

"**B**ut surely you do not favor the publishing of pornography?" When you hear someone say do not instead of don't, you know that you are either in court or on television. I was on television, being interviewed by two men—or persons, as they say nowadays. One was a conservative, representing the decent opinion of half a nation. One was a reactionary, representing the decent opinion of half a nation.

"Of course, I favor the publishing of—"

"You *favor* pornography?" The reactionary was distressed, appalled, sickened.

"I said the *publishing* of pornography, yes. . . ."

"But what's the difference? I mean between being in favor of publishing pornography and pornography?"

The conservative was troubled. "Whether or not I personally like or dislike pornography is immaterial." Television is a great leveler. You always end up sounding like the people who ask the questions. "The freedom to publish *anything* is guaranteed by the First Amendment to the Constitution. That is the law. Whether you or I or anyone likes what is published is"—repetition coming

up. I was tired—"is, uh, immaterial. The First Amendment guaran-
tees us the right to say and write and publish what we want. . . ."

Before I could make the usual exemptions for libel and for the
reporting of troop movements during wartime and for that man or
person who falsely yells fire in a crowded theatre (all absolutes are
relative beneath the sun), the conservative struck. "But," he said,
eyes agleam with what looked to be deep feeling but was actually
collyrium, "the founders of the United States"—he paused, reverently; looked at me, sincerely; realized, unhappily, that I was
staring at the lacing to his hairpiece (half the men who appear on
television professionally are bald; why?). Nervously, he touched
his forehead, and continued—"of America intended freedom of
speech only for . . . uh, politics."

"But sex is politics," I began . . . and ended.

I got two blank stares. I might just as well have said that the
Pelagian heresy will never take root in south Amish country.
Neither the conservative nor the reactionary had ever heard anyone say anything like that before and I knew that I could never
explain myself in the seven remaining in-depth minutes of air
time. I was also distracted by that toupee. Mentally, I rearranged it.
Pushed it farther back on his head. Didn't like the result. Tried it
lower down. All the while, we spoke of Important Matters. I said
that I did not think it a good idea for people to molest children.
This was disingenuous. My secret hero is the late King Herod.

Sex is politics.

In the year or two since that encounter on television, I have been
reminded almost daily of the fact that not only is sex politics but
sex both directly and indirectly has been a major issue in this year's
election. The Equal Rights Amendment, abortion, homosexuality
are hot issues that affect not only the political process but the
private lives of millions of people.

The sexual attitudes of any given society are the result of
political decisions. In certain militaristic societies, homosexual relationships were encouraged on the ground that pairs of dedicated
lovers (Thebes' Sacred Legion, the Spartan buddy system) would
fight more vigorously than reluctant draftees. In societies where
it is necessary to force great masses of people to do work that they
don't want to do (building pyramids, working on the Detroit
assembly line), marriage at an early age is encouraged on the
sensible ground that if a married man is fired, his wife and children
are going to starve, too. That grim knowledge makes for docility.

Although our notions about what constitutes correct sexual behavior are usually based on religious texts, those texts are invariably interpreted by the rulers in order to keep control over the ruled. Any sexual or intellectual or recreational or political activity that might decrease the amount of coal mined, the number of pyramids built, the quantity of junk food confected will be proscribed through laws that, in turn, are based on divine revelations handed down by whatever god or gods happen to be in fashion at the moment. Religions are manipulated in order to serve those who govern society and not the other way around. This is a brand-new thought to most Americans, whether once or twice or never bathed in the Blood of the Lamb.

Traditionally, Judaeo-Christianity approved of sex only between men and women who had been married in a religious ceremony. The newlyweds were then instructed to have children who would, in turn, grow up and have more children (the Reverend Malthus worried about this inverted pyramid), who would continue to serve the society as loyal workers and dutiful consumers.

For the married couple, sexual activity outside marriage is still a taboo. Although sexual activity before marriage is equally taboo, it is more or less accepted if the two parties are really and truly serious and sincere and mature . . . in other words, if they are prepared to do their duty by one day getting married in order to bring forth new worker-consumers in obedience to God's law, which tends to resemble with suspicious niceness the will of the society's owners.

Fortunately, nothing human is constant. Today civil marriages outnumber religious marriages; divorce is commonplace; contraception is universally practiced, while abortion is legal for those with money. But our rulers have given ground on these sexual-social issues with great reluctance, and it is no secret that there is a good deal of frustration in the board rooms of the republic.

For one thing, workers are less obedient than they used to be. If fired, they can go on welfare—the Devil's invention. Also, the fact that most jobs men do women can do and do do has endangered the old patriarchal order. A woman who can support herself and her child is a threat to marriage, and marriage is the central institution whereby the owners of the world control those who do the work. Homosexuality also threatens that ancient domination, because men who don't have wives or children to worry about are not as easily dominated as those men who do.

At any given moment in a society's life, there are certain hot buttons that a politician can push in order to get a predictably hot response. A decade ago, if you asked President Nixon what he intended to do about unemployment, he was apt to answer, "Marijuana is a halfway house to something worse." It is good politics to talk against sin—and don't worry about non sequiturs. In fact, it is positively un-American—even Communist—to discuss a real issue such as unemployment or who is stealing all that money at the Pentagon.

To divert the electorate, the unscrupulous American politician will go after those groups not regarded benignly by Old or New Testament. The descendants of Ham are permanently unpopular with white Americans. Unhappily for the hot-button pusher, it is considered bad taste to go after blacks openly. But code phrases may be used. Everyone knows that "welfare chiseler" means nigger, as does "law and order." The first on the ground that the majority of those on welfare are black (actually, they are white); the second because it is generally believed that most urban crimes are committed by blacks against whites (actually they are committed by jobless blacks against other blacks). But poor blacks are not the only target. Many Christers and some Jews don't like poor white people very much, on the old Puritan ground that if you're good, God will make you rich. This is a familiar evangelical Christian line, recently unfurled by born-again millionaire Walter Hoving. When he found himself short $2,400,000 of the amount he needed to buy Bonwit Teller, Mr. Hoving "opened himself up to the Lord," who promptly came through with the money. "It was completely a miracle." Now we know why the rich are always with us. God likes them.

Jews are permanently unpopular with American Christers because they are forever responsible for Jesus' murder, no matter what those idolatrous wine-soaked Roman Catholics at the Second Vatican Council said. It is true that with the establishment of Israel, the Christers now have a grudging admiration for the Jew as bully. Nevertheless, in once-and-twice-born land, it is an article of faith that America's mass media are owned by Jews who mean to overthrow God's country. Consequently, "mass media" is this year's code phrase for get the kikes, while "Save Our Children" means get the fags.

But politics, like sex, often makes for odd alliances. This year, militant Christers in tandem with militant Jews are pushing the sort of hot buttons that they think will strengthen the country's ownership by firming up the family. Apparently, the family can be strengthened only by depriving women of equal status not only in the marketplace but also in relation to their own bodies (Thou shalt not abort). That is why the defeat of the Equal Rights Amendment to the Constitution is of great symbolic importance.

Family Saviors also favor strong laws designed, ostensibly, to curtail pornography but actually intended to deny freedom of speech to those that they dislike.

Now, it is not possible for a governing class to maintain its power if there are not hot buttons to push. A few months ago, the "Give-away of the Panama Canal" issue looked as though it were going to be a very hot button, indeed. It was thought that if, somehow, American manhood could be made to seem at stake in Panama, there was a chance that a sort of subliminal sexual button might be pushed, triggering throughout the land a howl of manly rage, particularly from ladies at church receptions: American manhood has never been an exclusively masculine preserve. But, ultimately, American manhood (so recently kneed by the Viet Cong) did not feel endangered by the partial loss of a fairly dull canal, and so that button jammed.

The issue of Cuban imperialism also seemed warm to the touch. Apparently, Castro's invincible troops are now on the march from one end of Africa to the other. If Somalia falls, Mali falls; if Mali falls. . . . No one cares. Africa is too far away, while Cuba is too small and too near to be dangerous.

In desperation, the nation's ownership has now gone back to the tried-and-true hot buttons: save our children, our fetuses, our ladies' rooms from the godless enemy. As usual, the sex buttons have proved satisfyingly hot.

But what do Americans actually think about sex when no one is pressing a button? Recently, *Time* magazine polled a cross section of the populace. Not surprisingly, 61 percent felt that "it's getting harder and harder to know what's right and what's wrong these days." Most confused were people over 50 and under 25. Meanwhile, 76 percent said that they believed that it was "morally wrong" for a married man to be unfaithful to his wife, while 79 percent thought it wrong for a woman to cheat on her husband.

Sexual relations between teenagers were condemned by 63 percent while 34 percent felt that a young man should be a virgin on his wedding night or afternoon. Nevertheless, what people consider to be morally objectionable does not seem to have much effect on what they actually do: 55 percent of unmarried women and 85 percent of unmarried men admit to having had sex by the age of 19 ... no doubt, while jointly deploring teenage immorality. A worldly 52 percent think it is *not* morally wrong for an unmarried couple to live together.

Forty-seven percent thought that homosexual relations were morally wrong; 43 percent thought that they were all right: 10 percent didn't know. Yet 56 percent "would vote for legislation guaranteeing the civil rights of homosexuals." Although a clear majority thought that fags should be allowed to serve in the Army, run for office, live where they choose, Anita Bryant has done her work sufficiently well to deny them the right to teach school (48 percent against, 44 percent for) or be ministers (47 percent against, 44 percent for).

Pornography continues to be the hottest of buttons: seventy-four percent want the government to crack down on pornographers. Meanwhile, 76 percent think that that old devil permissiveness "has led to a lot of things that are wrong with the country these days."

Finally, 70 percent thought that "there should be no laws, either Federal or state, regulating sexual practice." Either this can be interpreted as a remarkable demonstration of live and let live (an attitude notoriously not shared by the current Supreme Court) or it can be nothing more than the cynical wisdom of our people who know from experience that *any* area the government involves itself in will be hopelessly messed up.

Despite the tolerance of the 70 percent, some 20 percent to 40 percent of the population are moral absolutists, according to the Kinsey Institute's soon-to-be-published *American Sexual Standards*. Fiercely, these zealots condemn promiscuity, adultery, homosexuality, masturbation, long hair and fluoride. Out there in the countryside (and in cities such as St. Paul and Wichita), they are the ones who most promptly respond to the politician who pushes a sex button in order to . . . what? Create an authoritarian society? Keep the workers docile within the confines of immutable marriage? Punish sin? Make money? Money! There is a lot of money out there on the evangelical Christian circuit and much of it is tax-exempt.

In the fall of 1977, the journalist Andrew Kopkind visited Bensenville, Illinois, in the heart of the heart of the country, in order to study those roots of grass that are now not only as high as an elephant's eye but definitely swaying to the right. *Save the Family* is this year's rallying cry. Since hardly anyone ever openly questions the value of the family in human affairs, any group that wants to save this allegedly endangered institution is warmly supported.

But to the zealots of what Kopkind calls the New Right, saving the family means all sorts of things not exactly connected with the nuclear family. Kopkind discovered that Family Saviors support "the death penalty, Laetrile, nuclear power, local police, Panama Canal, saccharin, FBI, CIA, defense budget, public prayer and real-estate growth."

Family Saviors view darkly "busing, welfare, public-employee unions, affirmative action, amnesty, marijuana, communes, gun control, pornography, the 55-mph speed limit, day-care centers, religious ecumenism, sex education, car pools and the Environmental Protection Agency." Kopkind believes that those attitudes are fairly spontaneous. He is probably right—up to a point. To get Americans to vote constantly against their own interests, however, requires manipulation of the highest order, and it starts at birth in these remarkably United States and never ends.

Until recently, it had not occurred to anyone that a profamily movement might be politically attractive. Our demagogues usually concentrate on communism versus Americanism. But Nixon's jaunts to Peking and Moscow diminished communism as an issue. Those trips also served to remind Americans that we are a fragile minority in a world where the majority is Marxist. Although communism is still a button to be pressed, it tends to tepidity.

On the other hand, to accuse your opponent of favoring any of those vicious forces that endanger the family is to do him real harm. In the past 18 months, Family Saviors have been remarkably effective. They have defeated equal-rights ordinances for homosexualists in Dade County, St. Paul, Wichita, Eugene; obliged the House of Representatives to reverse itself on an anti-abortion bill; stalled (for a time) the Equal Rights Amendment, and so on. Sex is the ultimate politics and very soon, one way or another, every politician is going to get—as it were—into the act.

Officially, our attitudes toward sex derive from the Old and New Testaments. Even to this day, Christian fundamentalists like to say that since every single word in the good book is absolutely true, every one of God's injunctions must be absolutely obeyed if we don't want the great plains of the republic to be studded with pillars of salt or worse. Actually, even the most rigorously literal of fundamentalists pick and choose from Biblical texts. The authors of Leviticus proscribe homosexuality—and so do all good Christers. But Leviticus also proscribes rare meat, bacon, shellfish, and the wearing of nylon mixed with wool. If Leviticus were to be obeyed in every instance, the garment trade would collapse.

The authors of the Old and New Testaments created not only a religious anthology but also a political order in which man is woman's eternal master (Jewish men used to pray, "I thank thee, Lord, that thou hast not created me a woman"). The hatred and fear of women that runs through the Old Testament (not to mention in the pages of our justly admired Jewish novelists) suggests that the patriarchal principle so carefully built into the Jewish notion of God must have been at one time opposed to a powerful and perhaps competitive matriarchal system. Whatever the original reasons for the total subordination of woman to man, the result has been an unusually ugly religion that has caused a good deal of suffering not only in its original form but also through its later heresy, Christianity, which in due, and ironic, course was to spin off yet another heresy, communism.

The current wave of Christian religiosity that is flowing across the republic like an oil slick has served as a reminder to women that they must submit to their husbands. This is not easy, as twice-born Anita Bryant admits. She confesses to a tendency to "dump her garbage" all over her husband and master and employee, Bob Green. But she must control herself: "For the husband is the head of the wife, even as Christ is the head of the Church" (Ephesians 5:23). Anita also knows that because of woman's disobedience, the prototypes of the human race were excluded from the Garden of Eden.

Brooding on the Old Testament's dislike of women, Freud theorized that an original patriarchal tribe was for a time replaced by a matriarchal tribe that was then overthrown by the patriarchal Jews: the consequent "re-establishment of the primal father in his historic rights was a great step forward." This speculative nonsense is highly indicative of the way that a mind as shrewd and as original as Freud's could not conceive of a good (virtuous?) society that was not dominated by man the father.

"What do women want?" Freud once asked, plaintively. Well, Sigmund, they want equality with men. But that equality was not acceptable either to the authors of the Old Testament or to Freud himself. Today, almost 3,000 years after Moses came down from Sinai, women are approaching equality with men in the United States. But the war against woman's equality still goes on; at the moment, it is being conducted in the name of The Family.

The New Testament's Christ is a somewhat milder figure than the Jehovah of the Old Testament. Yet one is very much the son of the other, and so, presumably, nothing basic was supposed to change in the relations between the sexes. In fact, at one point, Jesus displays a positively Portnoyesque exasperation with the traditional Jewish mother. "Woman," he says to Mary, "what art thou to me?" Mary's no doubt lengthy answer has not been recorded.

As a Jew, Jesus took seriously the Ten Commandments. But he totally confused the whole business of adultery by saying that even to entertain so much as a Carter-like lust for a woman is the equivalent of actually committing adultery. Jesus also went on record as saying that whores had as good a chance of getting to heaven as IRS men. It is possible that he meant this as a joke. If so, it is the only joke in the New Testament.

To an adulteress, Jesus said, "Neither do I condemn thee," before suggesting that she stop playing around. Jesus had nothing to say about homosexuality, masturbation or the Equal Rights Amendment; but he did think the absolute world of eunuchs (Matthew 19:10–12). Finally, Jesus believed that the world was about to end. "But I tell you of a truth, there are some standing here, who shall not taste of death, till they see the kingdom of God" (Luke 9:27). As far as we can tell, the world did not end in the first century A.D., and all those standing there died without having seen the kingdom.

A few years later, Saint Paul had his vision on the road to Damascus. "Both Jews and gentiles all are under sin," he—what is that best-seller verb?—shrilled. Since Paul was also convinced that the world was about to end, he believed that man must keep himself ritually pure for the day of judgment, and ritual purity required a total abstention from sex. For those who could not remain heroically chaste (to "abide even as I"), Paul rather sourly agreed that "it is better to marry than to burn"—burn with lust, by the way, not hell-fire, as some primitive Christers like to interpret that passage.

Paul also advised married men to live with their wives "as though they had none. . . . For the form of this world is passing away."

Although this world's form did not pass away, Paul's loathing of sexuality did not pass away, either. As a result, anyone brought up in a Christian-dominated society will be taught from birth to regard his natural sexual desires as sinful, or worse.

A state of constant guilt in the citizenry is a good thing for rulers who tend not to take very seriously the religions that they impose on their subjects. Since marriage was the only admissible outlet for the sexual drive, that institution was used as a means of channeling the sexual drive in a way that would make docile the man, while the woman, humanly speaking, existed only as the repository of the sacred sperm (regarded as a manifestation of the Holy Ghost).

Woman was commanded to serve and obey her husband as totally as he, in turn, served and obeyed his temporal, Bible-quoting master. If one had set out deliberately to invent a religion that would effectively enslave a population, one could not have done much better than Judaeo-Christianity.

Curiously enough, Paul is the only Old or New Testament maven to condemn lesbianism, an activity that Queen Victoria did not believe existed and Jesus ignored. But Paul knew better. Why, even as he spoke, Roman ladies were burning "in their lust one toward another . . . !" Whenever Paul gets onto the subject of burning lust, he shows every sign of acute migraine.

Now, what is all this nonsense really about? Why should natural sexual desires be condemned in the name of religion? Paul would have said that since judgment day was scheduled for early next year, you should keep yourself ritually clean and ritual cleanliness amongst the Jews involved not only sexual abstinence but an eschewal of shellfish. But Paul's hatred of the flesh is somewhat hard to understand in the light of Jesus' fairly relaxed attitude. On the other hand, Paul's dislike of homosexuality is a bit easier to understand (though never properly understood by American Christers). It derives from the Old Testament book Leviticus, the so-called Holiness Code.

Homosexual relations between heroes were often celebrated in the ancient world. The oldest of religious texts tells of the love between two men, Gilgamesh and Enkidu. When Enkidu died, Gilgamesh challenged death itself in order to bring his lover back to life. In the *Iliad*, Gilgamesh's rage is echoed by Achilles when *his* lover Patroclus dies before the walls of Troy. So intense was the love between the heroes David and Jonathan that David noted in his obituary of Jonathan, "Thy love to me was wonderful, passing the love of women." Elsewhere in the Old Testament, the love that Ruth felt for Naomi was of a sort that today might well end in the joint ownership of a ceramics kiln at Laguna Beach. Why, then, the extraordinary fuss about homosexuality in Leviticus?

Leviticus was written either during or shortly after the Jewish exile in Babylon (586–538 B.C.). The exile ended when Persia's Great King Cyrus conquered Babylon. Tolerant of all religions, Cyrus let the Jews go home to Jerusalem, where they began to rebuild the temple that had been destroyed in 586. Since it was thought that the disasters of 586 might have been averted had the Jews been a bit more straitlaced in their deportment, Leviticus was drafted. It contained a very stern list of dos and don'ts. Adultery, which had been proscribed by Moses, was now not only proscribed but the adulterers were to be put to death, while "If a man . . . lie with mankind, as he lieth with a woman, both of them have committed an abomination" and must be put to death.

What is all this about? In earlier days, Jonathan and David were much admired. Was their celebrated love for each other an abomination? Obviously not. The clue to the mystery is the word abomination, which derives from the Hebrew word *to'ebah*, meaning idolatrous. At the time of Leviticus (and long before), the Great Goddess was worshiped throughout the Middle East. She had many names: Cybele, Astarte, Diana, Anahita. Since the Jews thought that the Great Goddess was in direct competition with their Great God, they denounced her worshipers as idolatrous, or *to'ebah*, or abominable; and particularly disapproved of the ritual sex associated with her worship. Many of Cybele's admirers castrated themselves for her glory while male and female prostitutes crowded the temple precincts, ready for action.

In Babylon, every respectable woman was obliged to go at least once in a lifetime to the temple and prostitute herself to the first pilgrim who was willing to pay her. According to Herodotus, ill-favored women were obliged to spend an awful lot of time at the temple, trying to turn that reluctant trick which would make them blessed in the eyes of the goddess.

No doubt, many Jews in Babylon were attracted, if not to the goddess' worship, to the sexual games that went on in her temples. Therefore, the authors of Leviticus made it clear that any Jew who went with a male or female temple prostitute was guilty of an idolatrous or abominable act in the eyes of the Great God Jehovah —a notoriously jealous god by his own admission. As a result, the abominations in Leviticus refer *not* to sexual acts as such but to sexual acts associated with the cult of the Great Goddess.

Elsewhere in the Old Testament, Sodom was destroyed not because the inhabitants were homosexualists but because a number of local men wanted to gang-rape a pair of male angels who were guests of the town. That was a violation of the most sacred of ancient taboos: the law of hospitality. Also, gang rape, whether homosexual or heterosexual, is seldom agreeable in the eyes of any deity.

Human beings take a long time to grow up. This fact means that the tribe or the family or the commune is obliged to protect and train the young in those skills that will be needed for him to achieve a physical maturity whose sole purpose seems to be the passing on to a new generation of the sacred DNA code. The nature of life is more life. This is not very inspiring, but it is all that we know for certain that we have. Consequently, our religiopolitical leaders have always glorified the tribe or the family or the state at the expense of the individual. But societies change and when they do, seemingly eternal laws are superseded. Flat earth proves to be a sphere. Last year's wisdom is this year's folly.

In an overpopulated world, the Biblical injunction to be fruitful and multiply is less and less heeded. Thanks to increased automation and incontinent breeding, every industrial society in the world now has more workers than it needs. Meanwhile, housing has become so expensive that it is no longer possible for three generations of a family to live in the same house, the ideal of most Christers and strict Jews. Today the nuclear family consists of a boy for you and a girl for me in a housing development . . . hardly an ideal setting for either children or parents.

At this point, it would seem sensible to evolve a different set of arrangements for the human race. Certainly, fewer families would mean fewer children, and that is a good thing. Those who have a gift for parenthood (an infinitely small minority) ought to be encouraged to have children. Those without the gift ought to be discouraged. People would still live in pairs if that pleased them, but the social pressure to produce babies would be lifted.

Unhappily, the thrust of our society is still Judaeo-Christian. As a result, the single American male and the working woman are second-class citizens. A single man's median income is $11,069, while his married brother's income is $14,268 and his working sister's salary is $9,231. This is calculated discrimination. Plainly, it is better to marry than to be ill-paid.

After tax reform, this year's major political issue is Save the Family. Predictably, the Christers have been gunning for women's libbers and fags, two minorities that appear to endanger the family. Not so predictably, a number of Jews are now joining in the attack. This is odd, to say the least. Traditionally, Jews tend to a live-and-let-live attitude on the sensible ground that whenever things go wrong in any society where Jews are a minority, they will get it in the neck. So why make enemies? Unfortunately, Jewish tolerance has never really extended to homosexuality, that permanent abomination. Fag-baiting by American Jewish journalists has always been not only fashionable but, in a covert way, antigoyim.

Eighteen years ago, the busy journalist Alfred Kazin announced that homosexuality was a dead end for a writer. Apparently, fags couldn't make great literature. Today he is no longer quite so certain. In a recent issue of *Esquire*, Kazin accepted the genius of Gertrude Stein, but he could not resist mocking her lesbianism; he also felt it necessary to tell us that she was "fat, queer-looking," while her lover Alice B. Toklas was equally ugly. Although Kazin can accept—barely—the genius of an occasional fag writer, he detests what he calls "the gay mob." He is distressed that "homosexuality is being politicized and is becoming a social fact and a form of social pressure. Does the increasing impatience on all sides with the family, the oldest human institution, explain the widespread growth or emergence of homosexuality amidst so much anxiety about overpopulation?" This is one of those confused rhetorical questions whose answer is meant to be implicit in the polemical tone.

Actually, there is no such thing as a homosexual person, any more than there is such a thing as a heterosexual person. The words are adjectives describing sexual acts, not people. Those sexual acts are entirely natural; if they were not, no one would perform them. But since Judaism proscribes the abominable, the irrational rage that Kazin and his kind feel toward homosexualists has triggered an opposing rage. Gay militants now assert that there is something called gay sensibility, the outward and visible sign of a new kind of human being. Thus madness begets madness.

I have often thought that the reason no one has yet been able to come up with a good word to describe the homosexualist (sometimes known as gay, fag, queer, etc.) is because he does not exist. The human race is divided into male and female. Many human beings enjoy sexual relations with their own sex; many don't; many respond to both. This plurality is the fact of our nature and not worth fretting about.

Today Americans are in a state of terminal hysteria on the subject of sex in general and of homosexuality in particular because the owners of the country (buttressed by a religion that they have shrewdly adapted to their own ends) regard the family as their last means of control over those who work and consume. For two millennia, women have been treated as chattel, while homosexuality has been made to seem a crime, a vice, an illness.

In the *Symposium*, Plato defined the problem: "In Ionia and other places, and generally in countries which are subject to the barbarians [Plato is referring to the Persians, who were the masters of the Jews at the time Leviticus was written], the custom [homosexuality] is held to be dishonorable; loves of youths share the evil repute in which philosophy and gymnastics are held, because they are inimical to tyranny; the interests of rulers require that their subjects should be poor in spirit and that there should be no strong bond of friendship or society among them, which love, above all other motives, is likely to inspire, as our Athenian tyrants learned by experience; for the love of Aristogeiton and the constancy of Harmodius had a strength which undid their power." This last refers to a pair of lovers who helped overthrow the tyrants at Athens.

To this, our American Jews would respond: so what else would you expect from an uncircumcised Greek? While our American Christers would remind us of those scorching letters that Saint Paul mailed to the residents of Corinth and Athens.

Although the founders of our republic intended the state to be entirely secular in its laws and institutions, in actual fact, our laws are a mishmash of Judaeo-Christian superstitions. One ought never to be surprised by the intolerant vehemence of our fundamentalist Christers. After all, they started the country, and the seventeenth-century bigot Cotton Mather is more central to their beliefs than the eighteenth-century liberal George Mason, who fathered the Bill of Rights. But it is odd to observe Jews making common cause with Christian bigots.

I have yet to read anything by a Christer with an IQ above 95 that is as virulent as the journalist Joseph Epstein's statement (in

Harper's magazine): "If I had the power to do so, I would wish homosexuality off the face of this earth. I would do so because I think that it brings infinitely more pain than pleasure to those who are forced to live with it," etc. Surely, Epstein must realize that if the word Jewry were substituted for homosexuality, a majority of American Christers would be in full agreement. No Jew ought ever to mention the removal of any minority "from the face of this earth." It is unkind. It is also unwise in a Christer-dominated society where a pogrom is never *not* a possibility.

In a recent issue of *Partisan Review*, what I take to be a Catskill hotel called the Hilton Kramer wants to know why the New York intellectuals are not offering the national culture anything "in the way of wisdom about marriage and the family, for example? Anything but attacks, and often vicious attacks, on the most elementary fealties of family life?"

The hotel is worried that for the nation at large, the New York intellectual world is represented in the pages of *The New York Review of Books* "by the likes of Gore Vidal and Garry Wills." I assume that the hotel disapproves of Wills and me because we are not Jewish. The hotel then goes on to characterize me as "proselytizing for the joys of buggery." Needless to say, I have never done such a thing, but I can see how to a superstitious and ill-run hotel anyone who has worked hard to remove consenting sexual relations from the statute books (and politics) must automatically be a salesman for abominable vices, as well as a destroyer of the family and an eater of shellfish.

Finally, dizziest of all, we have the deep thoughts of Norman Podhoretz, the editor of *Commentary*, a magazine subsidized by the American Jewish Congress. In the Sixties, Podhoretz wrote a celebrated piece in which he confessed that he didn't like niggers. Now, in the Seventies, he has discovered that he doesn't like fags, either—on geopolitical rather than rabbinical grounds.

In an article called "The Culture of Appeasement" (again in *Harper's*), Podhoretz tells us that the Vietnam caper had a bad effect on Americans because we now seem not to like war at all. Of course, "The idea of war has never been as natural or as glamorous to Americans as it used to be to the English or the Germans or the French." Podhoretz obviously knows very little American history. As recently as Theodore Roosevelt, war was celebrated as the highest of all human activities. Sadly, Podhoretz compares this year's United States to England in the Thirties when, he assures us, a powerful homosexual movement made England pacifist because the fags did not want beautiful (or even ugly?) boys killed in the trenches.

Aside from the fact that quite as many faggots like war as heterosexualists (Cardinal Spellman, Senator Joe McCarthy, General Walker), the argument makes no sense. When the English were ready to fight Hitler, they fought. As for Vietnam, if we learned anything from our defeat so far from home, it was that we have no right to intervene militarily in the affairs of another nation.

But Podhoretz is not exactly disinterested. As a publicist for Israel, he fears that a craven United States might one day refuse to go to war to protect Israel from its numerous enemies. Although I don't think that he has much to worry about, it does his cause no good to attribute our country's alleged pacifism to a homosexual conspiracy. After all, that is the sort of mad thinking that inspired Hitler to kill not only 6,000,000 Jews but also 600,000 homosexualists.

In the late Sixties and early Seventies, the enemies of the Equal Rights Amendment set out to smear the movement as lesbian. All sorts of militant right-wing groups have since got into the act: the Ku Klux Klan, the John Birch Society, the Committee for the Survival of a Free Congress, Phyllis Schlafly's Eagle Forum, The Conservative Caucus, and dozens of other like-minded groups. Their aim is to deny equal rights to women through scare tactics. If the amendment is accepted, they warn us that lesbians will be able to marry each other, rape will be common, men will use women's toilets. This nonsense has been remarkably effective.

But then, as The Conservative Caucus' Howard Phillips told *The New Republic* with engaging candor, "We're going after people on the basis of their hot buttons." In the past year, the two hot buttons have proved to be sexual: ERA and gay rights legislation. Or "Save the Family" and "Save Our Children."

Elsewhere in the badlands of the nation, one Richard Viguerie is now the chief money raiser for the powers of darkness. In 1977, Viguerie told the *Congressional Quarterly*, "I'm willing to compromise to come to power. There aren't 50 percent of the people that share my view, and I'm willing to make concessions to come to power." That has a familiar Nuremberg ring.

Viguerie is said to have at least 10,000,000 names and addresses on file. He sends out mailings and raises large sums for all sorts of far-right political candidates and organizations. But Viguerie is not just a hustler. He is also an ideologue. "I have raised millions of dollars for the conservative movement over the years and I am not happy with the results. I decided to become more concerned with how the money is spent." He is now beginning to discuss the creation of a new political party.

Among groups that Viguerie works for and with is Gun Owners of America. He also works closely with Phyllis Schlafly, who dates back to Joe McCarthy and Barry Goldwater; currently, she leads the battle against the ERA. Another of Viguerie's clients is Utah's Senator Orrin Hatch, a proud and ignorant man who is often mentioned as a possible candidate for president if the far right should start a new political party.

Viguerie has vowed that "the organized conservative community is going to put in many times more than 3,000,000 [*sic*]. . . . I want a massive assault on Congress in 1978. I don't want any token efforts. We now have the talent and resources to move in a bold, massive way. I think we can move against Congress in 1978 in a way that's never been conceived of."

"Move against Congress." That sounds like revolution. Anyway, it will be interesting to see whether or not Congress will be overwhelmed in November; to see whether or not those children will actually be saved; to see whether or not fealty will be sworn by all right-thinking persons to the endangered family.*

Playboy
JANUARY 1979

---

* Mr. Viguerie was two years off. It was not until 1980 that he got the sort of president and Senate that he wanted. Meanwhile, a backlash to him is developing. Lively times are in store for us.

Pink Triangle and Yellow Star

A few years ago on a trip to Paris, I read an intriguing review in *Le Monde* of a book called *Comme un Frère, Comme un Amant*, a study of "Male Homosexuality in the American Novel and Theatre from Herman Melville to James Baldwin," the work of one Georges-Michel Sarotte, a Sorbonne graduate and a visiting professor at the University of Massachusetts. I read the book, found it interesting; met the author, found him interesting. He told me that he was looking forward to the publication of his book in the United States by Anchor Press/Doubleday. What sort of response did I think he would have? I was touched by so much innocent good faith. There will be no reaction, I said, because no one outside of the so-called gay press will review your book. He was shocked. Wasn't the book serious? scholarly? with an extensive bibliography? I agreed that it was all those things; unfortunately, scholarly studies having to do with fags do not get reviewed in the United States (this was before the breakthrough of Yale's John Boswell, whose ferociously learned *Christianity, Social Tolerance and Homosexuality* obliged even the "homophobic" *New York Times* to review it intelligently). If Sarotte had written about the agony and wonder of being female and/or Jewish and/or divorced, he would have been extensively reviewed. Even a study of black literature might have got attention (Sarotte is beige), although blacks are currently something of a nonsubject in these last days of empire.

I don't think that Professor Sarotte believed me. I have not seen him since. I also have never seen a review of his book or of Roger Austen's *Playing the Game* (a remarkably detailed account of American writing on homosexuality) or of *The Homosexual as Hero in Contemporary Fiction* by Stephen Adams, reviewed at much length in England and ignored here, or of a dozen other books that have been sent to me by writers who seem not to understand why an activity of more than casual interest to more than one-third of the male population of the United States warrants no serious discussion. That is to say, no serious *benign* discussion. All-out attacks on faggots are perennially fashionable in our better periodicals.

I am certain that the novel *Tricks* by Renaud Camus (recently translated for St. Martin's Press by Richard Howard, with a preface by Roland Barthes) will receive a perfunctory and hostile response out there in book-chat land. Yet in France, the book was treated as if it were actually literature, admittedly a somewhat moot activity nowadays. So I shall review *Tricks*. But first I think it worth bringing out in the open certain curious facts of our social and cultural life.

The American passion for categorizing has now managed to create two nonexistent categories—gay and straight. Either you are one or you are the other. But since everyone is a mixture of inclinations, the categories keep breaking down; and when they break down, the irrational takes over. You *have* to be one or the other. Although our mental therapists and writers for the better journals usually agree that those who prefer same-sex sex are not exactly criminals (in most of our states and under most circumstances they still are) or sinful or, officially, sick in the head, they must be, somehow, evil or inadequate or dangerous. The Roman Empire fell, didn't it? because of the fags?

Our therapists, journalists, and clergy are seldom very learned. They seem not to realize that most military societies on the rise tend to encourage same-sex activities for reasons that should be obvious to anyone who has not grown up ass-backward, as most Americans have. In the centuries of Rome's great military and political success, there was no differentiation between same-sexers and other-sexers; there was also a lot of crossing back and forth of the sort that those Americans who *do* enjoy inhabiting category-gay or category-straight find hard to deal with. Of the first twelve Roman emperors, only one was exclusively heterosexual. Since these twelve men were pretty tough cookies, rigorously trained as warriors, perhaps our sexual categories and stereotypes are—can it really be?—false. It was not until the sixth century of the empire that same-sex sex was proscribed by church and state. By then, of course, the barbarians were within the gates and the glory had fled.

Today, American evangelical Christians are busy trying to impose on the population at large their superstitions about sex and the sexes and the creation of the world. Given enough turbulence in the land, these natural fascists can be counted on to assist some sort of authoritarian—but never, never totalitarian—political movement. Divines from Santa Clara to Falls Church are particularly fearful of what they describe as the gay liberation movement's attempt to gain "special rights and privileges" when all that the same-sexers want is to be included, which they are not by law and custom, within the framework of the Fourteenth Amendment. The divine in Santa Clara believes that same-sexers should be killed. The divine in Falls Church believes that they should be denied equal rights under the law. Meanwhile, the redneck divines have been joined by a group of New York Jewish publicists who belong to what they proudly call "the new class" (*né arrivistes*), and these lively hucksters have now managed to raise fag-baiting to a level undreamed of in Falls Church—or even in Moscow.

In a letter to a friend, George Orwell wrote, "It is impossible to mention Jews in print, either favorably or unfavorably, without getting into trouble." But there are times when trouble had better be got into before mere trouble turns into catastrophe. Jews, blacks and homosexualists are despised by the Christian and Communist majorities of East and West. Also, as a result of the invention of Israel, Jews can now count on the hatred of the Islamic world. Since our own Christian majority looks to be getting ready for great adventures at home and abroad, I would suggest that the three despised minorities join forces in order not to be destroyed. This seems an obvious thing to do. Unfortunately, most Jews refuse to see any similarity between their special situation and that of the same-sexers. At one level, the Jews are perfectly correct. A racial or

religious or tribal identity is a kind of fact. Although sexual preference is an even more powerful fact, it is not one that creates any
particular social or cultural or religious bond between those so-
minded. Although Jews would doubtless be Jews if there was no
anti-Semitism, same-sexers would think little or nothing at all about
their preference if society ignored it. So there *is* a difference between the two estates. But there is no difference in the degree of
hatred felt by the Christian majority for Christ-killers and Sod-
omites. In the German concentration camps, Jews wore yellow
stars while homosexualists wore pink triangles. I was present when
Christopher Isherwood tried to make this point to a young Jewish
movie producer. "After all," said Isherwood, "Hitler killed six hundred thousand homosexuals." The young man was not impressed.
"But Hitler killed six *million* Jews," he said sternly. "What are
you?" asked Isherwood. "In real estate?"

Like it or not, Jews and homosexualists are in the same fragile
boat, and one would have to be pretty obtuse not to see the common danger. But obtuseness is the name of the game among New
York's new class. Elsewhere,* I have described the shrill fag-baiting
of Joseph Epstein, Norman Podhoretz, Alfred Kazin, and the Hilton Kramer Hotel. *Harper's* magazine and *Commentary* usually
publish these pieces, though other periodicals are not above printing the odd exposé of the latest homosexual conspiracy to turn the
United States over to the Soviet Union or to structuralism or to
Christian Dior. Although the new class's thoughts are never much
in themselves, and they themselves are no more than spear carriers
in the political and cultural life of the West, their prejudices and
superstitions do register in a subliminal way, making mephitic the
air of Manhattan if not of the Republic.

A case in point is that of Mrs. Norman Podhoretz, also known
as Midge Decter (like Martha Ivers, *whisper* her name). In September of last year, Decter published a piece called "The Boys on
the Beach" in her husband's magazine, *Commentary*. It is well
worth examining in some detail because she has managed not only
to come up with every known prejudice and superstition about
same-sexers but also to make up some brand-new ones. For sheer
vim and vigor, "The Boys on the Beach" outdoes its implicit model,
The Protocols of the Elders of Zion.

Decter notes that when the "homosexual-rights movement first

* "Sex Is Politics," *Playboy*, January 1979. See pages 149–165 in this volume.

burst upon the scene," she was "more than a little astonished." Like so many new-class persons, she writes a stilted sort of genteel-gentile prose not unlike—but not very like, either—*The New Yorker* house style of the 1940s and '50s. She also writes with the authority and easy confidence of someone who knows that she is very well known indeed to those few who know her.

Decter tells us that twenty years ago, she got to know a lot of pansies at a resort called Fire Island Pines, where she and a number of other new-class persons used to make it during the summers. She estimates that 40 percent of the summer people were heterosexual; the rest were not. Yet the "denizens, homosexual and heterosexual alike, were predominantly professionals and people in soft, marginal businesses—lawyers, advertising executives, psychotherapists, actors, editors, writers, publishers, etc." Keep this in mind. Our authoress does not.

Decter goes on to tell us that she is now amazed at the recent changes in the boys on the beach. Why have they become so politically militant—and so ill groomed? "What indeed has happened to the homosexual community I used to know—they who only a few short years ago [as opposed to those manly 370-day years] were characterized by nothing so much as a sweet, vain, pouting, girlish attention to the youth and beauty of their bodies?" Decter wrestles with this problem. She tells us how, in the old days, she did her very best to come to terms with her own normal dislike for these half-men—and half-women, too: "There were also homosexual women at the Pines, but they were, or seemed to be, far fewer in number. Nor, except for a marked tendency to hang out in the company of large and ferocious dogs, were they instantly recognizable as the men were." Well, if I were a dyke and a pair of Podhoretzes came waddling toward me on the beach, copies of Leviticus and Freud in hand, I'd get in touch with the nearest Alsatian dealer pronto.

Decter was disturbed by "the slender, seamless, elegant and utterly chic" clothes of the fairies. She also found it "a constant source of wonder" that when the fairies took off their clothes, "the largest number of homosexuals had hairless bodies. Chests, backs, arms, even legs were smooth and silky. . . . We were never able to determine just why there should be so definite a connection between what is nowadays called their sexual preference [previously known to right-thinking Jews as an abomination against Jehovah] and their smooth feminine skin. Was it a matter of hormones?"

Here Decter betrays her essential modesty and lack of experience.
In the no doubt privileged environment of her Midwestern youth,
she could not have seen very many gentile males without their
clothes on. If she had, she would have discovered that gentile men
tend to be less hairy than Jews except, of course, when they are
not. Because the Jews killed our Lord, they are forever marked
with hair on their shoulders—something that no gentile man has
on *his* shoulders except for John Travolta and a handful of other
Italian-Americans from the Englewood, New Jersey, area.

It is startling that Decter has not yet learned that there is no
hormonal difference between men who like sex with other men and
those who like sex with women. She notes, "There is also such a
thing as characteristic homosexual speech . . . it is something of an
accent redolent of small towns in the Midwest whence so many
homosexuals seemed to have migrated to the big city." Here one
detects the disdain of the self-made New Yorker for the rural or
small-town American. "Midwest" is often a code word for the fly-
overs, for the millions who do not really matter. But she is right in
the sense that when a group chooses to live and work together,
they do tend to sound and look alike. No matter how crowded and
noisy a room, one can always detect the new-class person's nasal
whine.

Every now and then, Decter does wonder if, perhaps, she is gen-
eralizing and whether this will "no doubt in itself seem to many of
the uninitiated a bigoted formulation." Well, Midge, it does. But
the spirit is upon her, and she cannot stop because "one cannot
even begin to get at the truth about homosexuals without this kind
of generalization. They are a group so readily distinguishable."
Except of course, when they are not. It is one thing for a group of
queens, in "soft, marginal" jobs, to "cavort," as she puts it, in a
summer place and be "easily distinguishable" to her cold eye just
as Jewish members of the new class are equally noticeable to the
cold gentile eye. But it is quite another thing for those men and
women who prefer same-sex sex to other-sex sex yet do not choose
to be identified—and so are not. To begin to get at the truth about
homosexuals, one must realize that the majority of those millions
of Americans who prefer same-sex sex to other-sex sex are obliged,
sometimes willingly and happily but often not, to marry and have
children and to conform to the guidelines set down by the heterosexual dictatorship.

Decter would know nothing of this because in her "soft, marginal" world, she is not meant to know. She does remark upon those fairies at the Pines who did have wives and children: "They were for the most part charming and amusing fathers, rather like favorite uncles. And their wives . . . drank." This dramatic ellipsis is most Decterian.

She ticks off Susan Sontag for omitting to mention in the course of an essay on camp "that camp is of the essence of homosexual style, invented by homosexuals, and serving the purpose of domination by ridicule." The word "domination" is a characteristic new-class touch. The powerless are always obsessed by power. Decter seems unaware that all despised minorities are quick to make rather good jokes about themselves before the hostile majority does. Certainly Jewish humor, from the Book of Job (a laff-riot) to pre-*auteur* Woody Allen, is based on this.

Decter next does the ritual attack on Edward Albee and Tennessee Williams for presenting "what could only have been homosexual relationships as the deeper truth about love in our time." This is about as true as the late Maria Callas's conviction that you could always tell a Jew because he had a hump at the back of his neck—something Callas herself had in dromedarian spades.

Decter makes much of what she assumes to be the fags' mockery of the heterosexual men at the Pines: "Homosexuality paints them [heterosexuals] with the color of sheer entrapment," while the fags' "smooth and elegant exteriors, unmussed by traffic with the detritus of modern family existence, constituted a kind of sniggering reproach to their striving and harried straight brothers." Although I have never visited the Pines, I am pretty sure that I know the "soft, marginal" types, both hetero and homo, that hung out there in the 1960s. One of the most noticeable characteristics of the self-ghettoized same-sexer is his perfect indifference to the world of the other-sexers. Although Decter's blood was always at the boil when contemplating these unnatural and immature half-men, they were, I would suspect, serenely unaware of her and her new-class cronies, solemnly worshiping at the shrine of The Family.

To hear Decter tell it, fags had nothing to complain of then, and they have nothing to complain of now: "Just to name the professions and industries in which they had, and still have, a significant presence is to define the boundaries of a certain kind of privilege: theatre, music, letters, dance, design, architecture, the visual arts, fashion at every level—from head, as it were, to foot, and from inception to retail—advertising, journalism, interior decoration,

antique dealing, publishing . . . the list could go on." Yes. But these
are all pretty "soft, marginal" occupations. And none is "dominated" by fags. Most male same-sexers are laborers, farmers,
mechanics, small businessmen, schoolteachers, firemen, policemen,
soldiers, sailors. Most female same-sexers are wives and mothers.
In other words, they are like the rest of the population. But then
it is hard for the new-class person to realize that Manhattan is not
the world. Or as a somewhat alarmed Philip Rahv said to me after
he had taken a drive across the United States, "My God! There are
so many of them!" In theory, Rahv had always known that there
were a couple of hundred million gentiles out there, but to see
them, in the flesh, unnerved him. I told him that I was unnerved,
too, particularly when they start showering in the Blood of the
Lamb.

Decter does concede that homosexualists have probably not
"established much of a presence in basic industry or government
service or in such classic [new-classy?] professions as doctoring
and lawyering but then for anyone acquainted with them as a
group the thought suggests itself that few of them have ever made
much effort in these directions." Plainly, the silly billies are too
busy dressing up and dancing the hully-gully to argue a case in
court. Decter will be relieved to know that the percentage of same-
sexers in the "classic" activities is almost as high, proportionately,
as that of Jews. But a homosexualist in a key position at, let us say,
the Department of Labor will be married and living under a good
deal of strain because he could be fired if it is known that he likes
to have sex with other men.

Decter knows that there have always been homosexual teachers,
and she thinks that they should keep quiet about it. But if they keep
quiet, they can be blackmailed or fired. Also, a point that would
really distress her, a teacher known to be a same-sexer would be a
splendid role model for those same-sexers that he—or she—is teaching. Decter would think this an unmitigated evil because men and
women were created to breed; but, of course, it would be a perfect
good because we have more babies than we know what to do with
while we lack, notoriously, useful citizens at ease with themselves.
That is what the row over the schools is all about.

Like most members of the new class, Decter accepts without
question Freud's line (*Introductory Lectures on Psychoanalysis*)
that "we actually describe a sexual activity as perverse if it has
given up the aim of reproduction and pursues the attainment of

pleasure as an aim independent of it." For Freud, perversion was any sexual activity involving "the abandonment of the reproductive function." Freud also deplored masturbation as a dangerous "primal affliction." So did Moses. But then it was Freud's curious task to try to create a rational, quasi-scientific basis for Mosaic law. The result has been not unlike the accomplishments of Freud's great contemporary, the ineffable and inexorable Mary Baker Eddy, whose First Church of Christ Scientist he was able to match with *his* First Temple of Moses Scientist.

Decter says that once faggots have "ensconced" themselves in certain professions or arts, "they themselves have engaged in a good deal of discriminatory practices against others. There are businesses and professions [which ones? She is congenitally short of data] in which it is less than easy for a straight, unless he makes the requisite gesture of propitiation to the homosexual in power, to get ahead." This, of course, was Hitler's original line about the Jews: they had taken over German medicine, teaching, law, journalism. Ruthlessly, they kept out gentiles; lecherously, they demanded sexual favors. "I simply want to reduce their numbers in these fields," Hitler told Prince Philip of Hesse. "I want them proportionate to their overall number in the population." This was the early solution; the final solution followed with equal logic.

In the 1950s, it was an article of faith in new-class circles that television had been taken over by the fags. Now I happen to have known most of the leading producers of that time and, of a dozen, the two who were interested in same-sex activities were both married to women who . . . did not drink. Neither man dared mix sex with business. Every now and then an actor would say that he had not got work because he had refused to put out for a faggot producer, but I doubt very much if there was ever any truth to what was to become a bright jack-o'-lantern in the McCarthy *Walpurgisnacht*.

When I was several thousand words into Decter's tirade, I suddenly realized that she does not know what homosexuality is. At some level she may have stumbled, by accident, on a truth that she would never have been able to comprehend in a rational way. Although to have sexual relations with a member of one's own sex is a common and natural activity (currently disapproved of by certain elements in this culture), there is no such thing as a homosexualist any more than there is such a thing as a heterosexualist. That is one of the reasons there has been so much difficulty with nomenclature. Despite John Boswell's attempts to give legitimacy to the word "gay," it is still a ridiculous word to use as a common identification for Frederick the Great, Franklin Pangborn and Eleanor Roosevelt. What makes some people prefer same-sex sex derives from whatever impulse or conditioning makes some people prefer other-sex sex. This is so plain that it seems impossible that our Mosaic-Pauline-Freudian society has not yet figured it out. But to ignore the absence of evidence is the basis of true faith.

Decter seems to think that yesteryear's chic and silly boys on the beach and today's socially militant fags are simply, to use her verb, "adopting" what she calls, in her tastefully appointed English, a lifestyle. On the other hand, "whatever disciplines it might entail, heterosexuality is not something adopted but something accepted. Its woes—and they have of course nowhere been more exaggerated than in those areas of the culture consciously or unconsciously influenced by the propaganda of homosexuals—are experienced as the woes of life."

"Propaganda"—another key word. "Power." "Propitiation." "Domination." What *does* the new class dream of?

Decter now moves in the big artillery. Not only are fags silly and a nuisance but they are, in their unrelenting hatred of heterosexualists, given to depicting them in their plays and films and books as a bunch of klutzes, thereby causing truly good men and women to falter—even question—that warm, mature heterosexuality that is so necessary to keeping this country great while allowing new-class persons to make it materially.

Decter is in full cry. Fags are really imitation women. Decter persists in thinking that same-sexers are effeminate, swishy, girlish. It is true that a small percentage of homosexuals are indeed effeminate, just as there are effeminate heterosexualists. I don't know why this is so. No one knows why. Except Decter. She believes that this sort "of female imitation pointed neither to sympathy with nor flattery of the female principle." Yet queens of the sort she is writing about tend to get on very well with women. But Decter can only cope with two stereotypes: the boys on the beach, mincing about, and the drab political radicals of gay liberation. The millions of ordinary masculine types are unknown to her because they are not identifiable by voice or walk and, most important, because they have nothing in common with one another except the desire to have same-sex relations. Or, put the other way around, since Lyndon Johnson and Bertrand Russell were both heterosexualists, what character traits did *they* have in common? I should think none at all. So it is with the invisible millions—now becoming less invisible—of same-sexers.

But Decter knows her Freud, and reality may not intrude: "The desire to escape from the sexual reminder of birth and death, with its threat of paternity—that is, the displacement of oneself by others—was the main underlying desire that sent those Fire Island homosexuals into the arms of other men. Had it been the opposite desire—that is, the positive attraction to the manly—at least half the boutiques, etc.," would have closed. Decter should take a stroll down San Francisco's Castro Street, where members of the present generation of fags look like off-duty policemen or construction workers. They have embraced the manly. But Freud has spoken. Fags are fags because they adored their mothers and hated their poor, hard-working daddies. It is amazing the credence still given this unproven, unprovable thesis.

Curiously enough, as I was writing these lines, expressing yet again the unacceptable obvious, I ran across Ralph Blumenthal's article in *The New York Times* (August 25), which used "unpublished letters and growing research into the hidden life of Sigmund Freud" to examine "Freud's reversal of his theory attributing neurosis in adults to sexual seduction in childhood." Despite the evidence given by his patients, Freud decided that their memories of molestation were "phantasies." He then appropriated from the high culture (a real act of hubris) Oedipus the King, and made him a complex. Freud was much criticized for this theory at the time —particularly by Sandor Ferenczi. Now, as we learn more about Freud (not to mention about the sexual habits of Victorian Vienna as reported in police records), his theory is again under attack. Drs. Milton Klein and David Tribich have written a paper titled "On Freud's Blindness." They have studied his case histories and observed how he ignored evidence, how "he looked to the child and only to the child, in uncovering the causes of psychopathology." Dr. Karl Menninger wrote Dr. Klein about these findings: "Why oh why couldn't Freud believe his own ears?" Dr. Menninger then noted, "Seventy-five per cent of the girls we accept at the Villages have been molested in childhood by an adult. And that's today in Kansas! I don't think Vienna in 1900 was any less sophisticated."

In the same week as Blumenthal's report on the discrediting of

the Oedipus complex, researchers at the Kinsey Institute reported
(*The Observer*, August 30) that after studying 979 homosexualists
("the largest sample of homosexuals—black and white, male and
female—ever questioned in an academic study") and 477 heterosexualists, they came to the conclusion that family life has nothing
to do with sexual preference. Apparently, "homosexuality is deep-
rooted in childhood, may be biological in origin, and simply shows
in more and more important ways as a child grows older. It is not
a condition which therapy can reverse." Also, "homosexual feelings begin as much as three years before any sort of homosexual
act, undermining theories that homosexuality is learned through
experience." There goes the teacher-as-seducer-and-perverter myth.
Finally, "Psychoanalysts' theories about smothering mum and absent dad do not stand investigation. Patients may tend to believe
that they are true because therapists subtly coach them in the ap-
propriate memories of their family life."

Some years ago, gay activists came to *Harper's*, where Decter
was an editor, to demonstrate against an article by Joseph Epstein,
who had announced, "If I had the power to do so, I would wish
homosexuality off the face of the earth." Well, that's what Hitler
had the power to do in Germany, and did—or tried to do. The
confrontation at *Harper's* now provides Decter with her theme.
She tells us that one of the demonstrators asked, "Are you aware
of how many suicides you may be responsible for in the homosexual community?" I suspect that she is leaving out the context
of this somewhat left-field *cri de coeur*. After all, homosexualists
have more to fear from murder than suicide. I am sure that the actual conversation had to do with the sort of mischievous effect that
Epstein's Hitlerian piece might have had on those fag-baiters who
read it.

But Decter slyly zeroes in on the word "suicide." She then de-
velops a most unusual thesis. Homosexualists hate themselves to
such an extent that they wish to become extinct either through in-
viting murder or committing suicide. She notes that in a survey of
San Francisco's homosexual men, half of them "claimed to have had
sex with at least five hundred people." This "bespeaks the obliter-
ation of all experience, if not, indeed, of oneself." Plainly Decter has
a Mosaic paradigm forever in mind and any variation on it is
abominable. Most men—homo or hetero—given the opportunity
to have sex with 500 different people would do so, gladly; but most

men are not going to be given the opportunity by a society that wants them safely married so that they will be docile workers and loyal consumers. It does not suit our rulers to have the proles tom-catting around the way that our rulers do. I can assure Decter that the thirty-fifth president went to bed with more than 500 women and that the well-known . . . but I must not give away the secrets of the old class or the newly-middle-class new class will go into shock.

Meanwhile, according to Decter, "many homosexuals are now-adays engaged in efforts at self-obliteration . . . there is the appal-ling rate of suicide among them." But the rate is not appreciably higher than that for the rest of the population. In any case, most who do commit—or contemplate—suicide do so because they can-not cope in a world where they are, to say the least, second-class citizens. But Decter is now entering uncharted country. She also has a point to make: "What is undeniable is the increasing longing among the homosexuals to do away with themselves—if not in the actual physical sense then at least spiritually—a longing whose chief emblem, among others, is the leather bars."

So Epstein will not be obliged to press that button in order to get rid of the fags. They will do it themselves. Decter ought to be pleased by this, but it is not in her nature to be pleased by anything that the same-sexers do. If they get married and have children and swear fealty to the family gods of the new class, their wives will . . . drink. If they live openly with one another, they have fled from woman and real life. If they pursue careers in the arts, heteros will have to be on guard against vicious covert assaults on heterosexual values. If they congregate in the fashion business the way that Jews do in psychiatry, they will employ only those heterosexuals who will put out for them.

Decter is appalled by the fag "takeover" of San Francisco. She tells us about the "ever deepening resentment of the San Francisco straight community at the homosexuals' defiant displays and power ['power'!] over this city," but five paragraphs later she contradicts herself: "Having to a very great extent overcome revulsion of com-mon opinion, are they left with some kind of unappeased hunger that only their own feelings of hatefulness can now satisfy?"

There it is. *They are hateful.* They know it. That is why they want to eliminate themselves. "One thing is certain." Decter finds a lot of certainty around. "To become homosexual is a weighty act." She still has not got the point that one does not choose to have

same-sex impulses; one simply has them, as everyone has, to a
greater or lesser degree, other-sex impulses. To deny giving physical expression to those desires may be pleasing to Moses and Saint
Paul and Freud, but these three rabbis are aberrant figures whose
nomadic values are not those of the thousands of other tribes that
live or have lived on the planet. Women's and gay liberation are
simply small efforts to free men and women from this trio.

Decter writes, "Taking oneself out of the tides of ordinary mortal
existence is not something one does from any longing to think oneself ordinary (but only following a different 'life-style')." I don't
quite grasp this sentence. Let us move on to the next: "Gay Lib
has been an effort to set the weight of that act at naught, to define
homosexuality as nothing more than a casual option among op-
tions." Gay lib has done just the opposite. After all, people are what
they are sexually not through "adoption" but because that is the
way they are structured. Some people do shift about in the course
of a life. Also, most of those with same-sex drives do indeed "adopt"
the heterosexual life-style because they don't want to go to prison
or to the madhouse or become unemployable. Obviously, there *is*
an option but it is a hard one that ought not to be forced on any
human being. After all, homosexuality is only important when
made so by irrational opponents. In this, as in so much else, the
Jewish situation is precisely the same.

Decter now gives us not a final solution so much as a final conclusion: "In accepting the movement's terms [hardly anyone has,
by the way], heterosexuals have only raised to a nearly intolerable
height the costs of the homosexuals' flight from normality." The
flight, apparently, is deliberate, a matter of perverse choice, a misunderstanding of daddy, a passion for mummy, a fear of responsibility. Decter threads her clichés like Teclas on a string: "Faced
with the accelerating round of drugs, S-M and suicide, can either
the movement or its heterosexual sympathizers imagine they have
done anyone a kindness?"

Although the kindness of strangers is much sought after, gay
liberation has not got much support from anyone. Natural allies
like the Jews are often virulent in their attacks. Blacks in their
ghettos, Chicanos in their barrios, and rednecks in their pulpits also
have been influenced by the same tribal taboos. That Jews and
blacks and Chicanos and rednecks all contribute to the ranks of the
same-sexers only increases the madness. But the world of the Dec-
ters is a world of perfect illogic.

Herewith the burden of "The Boys on the Beach": since homo-sexualists choose to be the way they are out of idle hatefulness, it has been a mistake to allow them to come out of the closet to the extent that they have, but now that they are out (which most are not), they will have no choice but to face up to their essential hate-fulness and abnormality and so be driven to kill themselves with promiscuity, drugs, S-M and suicide. Not even the authors of *The Protocols of the Elders of Zion* ever suggested that the Jews, who were so hateful to them, were also hateful to themselves. So Decter has managed to go one step further than the *Protocols'* authors; she is indeed a virtuoso of hate, and thus do pogroms begin.

Tricks is the story of an author—Renaud Camus himself—who has twenty-five sexual encounters in the course of six months. Each of these encounters involves a pick-up. Extrapolating from Camus's sexual vigor at the age of 35, I would suspect that he has already passed the 500 mark and so is completely obliterated as a human being. If he is, he still writes very well indeed. He seems to be hav-ing a good time, and he shows no sign of wanting to kill himself, but then that may be a front he's keeping up. I am sure that Decter will be able to tell just how close he is to OD'ing.

From his photograph, Camus appears to have a lot of hair on his chest. I don't know about the shoulders, as they are covered, mod-estly, with a shirt. Perhaps he is Jewish. Roland Barthes wrote an introduction to *Tricks*. For a time, Barthes was much admired in American academe. But then, a few years ago, Barthes began to write about his same-sexual activities; he is now mentioned a bit less than he was in the days before he came out, as they say.

Barthes notes that Camus's book is a "text that belongs to litera-ture." It is not pornographic. It is also not a Homosexual Novel in that there are no deep, anguished chats about homosexuality. In fact, the subject is never mentioned; it just is. Barthes remarks, "Homosexuality shocks less [well, he is—or was—French], but continues to be interesting; it is still at that stage of excitation where it provokes what might be called feats of discourse [see "The Boys on the Beach," no mean feat!]. Speaking of homosexuality permits those who aren't to show how open, liberal, and modern they are; and those who are to bear witness, to assume responsibility, to mili-tate. Everyone gets busy, in different ways, whipping it up." You can say that again! And Barthes does. But with a nice variation. He makes the point that you are never allowed *not* to be categorized.

But then, "say 'I am' and you will be socially saved." Hence the passion for the either/or.

Camus does not set out to give a panoramic view of homosexuality. He comments, in *his* preface, on the variety of homosexual expressions. Although there is no stigma attached to homosexuality in the French intellectual world where, presumably, there is no equivalent of the new class, the feeling among the lower classes is still intense, a memento of the now exhausted (in France) Roman Catholic Church's old dirty work ("I don't understand the French Catholics," said John Paul II). As a result, many "refuse to grant their tastes because they live in such circumstances, in such circles, that their desires are not only for themselves inadmissible but inconceivable, unspeakable."

It is hard to describe a book that is itself a description, and that is what *Tricks* is—a flat, matter-of-fact description of how the narrator meets the tricks, what each says to the other, where they go, how the rooms are furnished, and what the men do. One of the tricks is nuts; a number are very hairy—the narrator has a Decterian passion for the furry; there is a lot of anal and banal sex as well as oral and floral sex. *Frottage* flows. Most of the encounters take place in France, but there is one in Washington, D.C., with a black man. There is a good deal of comedy, in the Raymond Roussel manner.

Tricks will give ammunition to those new-class persons and redneck divines who find promiscuity every bit as abominable as same-sex relations. But that is the way men are when they are given freedom to go about their business unmolested. One current Arab ruler boasts of having ten sexual encounters a day, usually with different women. A diplomat who knows him says that he exaggerates, but not much. Of course, he is a Moslem.

The family, as we know it, is an economic, not a biological, unit. I realize that this is startling news in this culture and at a time when the economics of both East and West require that the nuclear family be, simply, God. But our ancestors did not live as we do. They lived in packs for hundreds of millennia before "history" began, a mere 5,000 years ago. Whatever social arrangements human society may come up with in the future, it will have to be acknowledged that those children who are needed should be rather more thoughtfully brought up than they are today and that those adults who do not care to be fathers or mothers should be let off the hook. This is beginning, slowly, to dawn. Hence, the rising hysteria in the land. Hence, the concerted effort to deny the human ordinariness of same-sexualists. A recent attempt to portray such a person sympathetically on television was abandoned when the Christers rose up in arms.

Although I would never suggest that Truman Capote's bright wit and sweet charm as a television performer would not have easily achieved for him his present stardom had he been a *hetero-sexualist*, I do know that if he had not existed in his present form, another would have been run up on the old sewing machine because that sort of *persona* must be, for a whole nation, the stereotype of what a fag is. Should some macho film star like Clint Eastwood, say, decide to confess on television that he is really into same-sex sex, the cathode tube would blow a fuse. That could never be allowed. That is all wrong. That is how the Roman Empire fell.

There is not much *angst* in *Tricks*. No one commits suicide—but there is one sad story. A militant leftist friend of Camus's was a teacher in the south of France. He taught 14-year-old members of that oldest of all the classes, the exploited laborer. One of his pupils saw him in a fag bar and spread the word. The students began to torment what had been a favorite teacher. "These are little proles," he tells Camus, "and Mediterranean besides—which means they're obsessed by every possible macho myth, and by homosexuality as well. It's all they can think about." One of the boys, an Arab, followed him down the street, screaming "Faggot!" "It was as if he had finally found someone onto whom he could project his resentment, someone he could hold in contempt with complete peace of mind."

This might explain the ferocity of the new class on the subject. They know that should the bad times return, the Jews will be singled out yet again. Meanwhile, like so many Max Naumanns (Naumann was a German Jew who embraced Nazism), the new class passionately supports our ruling class—from the Chase Manhattan Bank to the Pentagon to the Op-Ed page of *The Wall Street Journal*—while holding in fierce contempt faggots, blacks (see Norman Podhoretz's "My Negro Problem and Ours," *Commentary*, February 1963), and the poor (see Midge Decter's "Looting and Liberal Racism," *Commentary*, September 1977). Since these neo-Naumannites are going to be in the same gas chambers as the blacks and the faggots, I would suggest a cease-fire and a common front against the common enemy, whose kindly voice is that of Ronald Reagan and whose less than kindly mind is elsewhere in the boardrooms of the Republic.

The Nation
NOVEMBER 14, 1981

How to Find God
and Make Money

Both *Publishers Weekly* and *Christian Bookseller* agree that
1978 will be a "bumper year" for evangelical literature. Particularly popular is the first-person confession of a washed-up or
caught-up-with celebrity who has found God. Rinsed in the Blood
of the Lamb, the redeemed celebrity is presented with what looks
to be a real book, bearing a personalized dust jacket—that is, he
will be credited with having written a memoir composed by someone else. Sinwise, mis-labeling is less than deadly; it is also big
business. Celebrity-sinner books are sold by the millions through
hundreds of bookstores and dozens of book clubs that cater to
fundamentalist Christians. Last year over $600 million worth of
"Christian books" were sold in the United States.

If the redeemed and revived celebrity can so much as tote a tune
(Pat Boone, Anita Bryant), there are countless stops not only along
but above and below the Bible Belt where large audiences will pay
to observe a reborn celebrity. For those who cannot sing songs, a
patter of penitence will do. *Ci-devant* revolutionary, rapist, and
couturier Eldridge Cleaver's repentance number is a heart-warming
crowd-pleaser wherever chiggers burrow and Jesus saves.

Watergate criminals are also in demand. When the inspiring Charles Colson (author of *Born Again*) and the inspired Jeb S. Magruder (author of *An American Life*) confess to all sorts of small sins and crimes not unlike those that Shakespeare's Cardinal Wolsey sang of in *his* final aria, the audience is able to enjoy if not pity and awe a certain amount of catharsis.

Christian Bookseller reports on some new good books: "Master's Press announced a first print run of 300,000 copies of its spring release, *Looking Good*, the biography of Freddie Prinze by Mary Pruetzel, the late comedian's mother. . . . Mrs. Pruetzel's purpose in writing Freddie's biography is to spare other young hopefuls the tragic fate which befell her son." Celebrity, sex, drugs, suicide—*as told by a Mother!* Not only will Master's Press be in the chips this year, but any young and hopeful Puerto Rican Magyar who wants to be a comic will know what to look out for en route to the next presidential Inaugural Eve Gala.

Also scheduled for 1978 is *Christ and the Media* by Malcolm Muggeridge. According to *Christian Bookseller* this "English radio and television personality who became a Christian late in life, is pessimistic about the present and future influence of television on human morality. He observes that television station owners, producers, writers and performers—like the films—operate under no established code of moral values. They are free to create their own morality as they go along." Plainly, this is a bad thing. Plainly, an established code would be a good thing and Harold M. Voth, M.D., might be just the man to come up with one.

Dr. Voth's latest book is *The Castrated Family*, a "critical assessment of the women's movement, gay liberation, unisex, open marriage and role blurring . . . phenomena [that] are destroying the American family." Ann Landers thinks that "Dr. Voth has said a mouthful," while from far-off Monte Carlo H.S.H. Princess Grace hopes that the book "will be read as widely as possible."

Thank God I Have Cancer! by Clifford Oden has best seller written all over it. Arlington House tells us that "When Rev. Oden learned he had cancer eight years ago he turned to God in prayer. He asked God to show him how to cope. Now he is living proof that cancer can be controlled by natural means—without surgery, without radiation or chemotherapy." Meanwhile, Alba Books gives us *Sexuality Summary* by W. F. Allen. "A clear treatment of four problem areas: homosexuality, abortion, contraception and premarital sex." Since a great many of the new books deal with these four problem areas, it is obvious that Evangelical Christians want those areas cleaned up, *and quick*.

According to the *National Catholic Register* Harold J. Brown's *The Reconstruction of the Republic* shows us how this can be done. "Prof. Brown makes a telling criticism of government without Christianity, and does not spare even the Constitution, which omits the name of God. In the process he exposes the fallacies of welfarism and the Equal Rights Amendment. A meaty volume that requires study and action." The word "action" reminds us of those of our Roman Catholics who dislike the American Constitution and its beautiful appendage the Bill of Rights. Yet if the Inventors had been so unkind and superstitious as to work *their* God into the fabric of the Constitution, the United States would have been a stern and illiberal Protestant republic from which Roman Catholics might very well have been excluded. Fortunately, the Inventors tended to deism, and so were able to eliminate deity from our secular republic.

One of the busiest of the religio-publishers is Christian Herald Books, located at 40 Overlook Drive, Chappaqua, NY 10514. Christian Herald publishes books about missionaries in the Amazon jungle ("larger than life true adventures") as well as "triumphant encounters with the Divine" and of course retold Old Testament stories about the likes of Hagar ("a powerful novel of love, conflict and faith"). Christian Herald also owns at least four book clubs if, as I suspect, "Christian Book Club for Today's Woman," "Family Bookshelf," "Farm Journal Family Bookshelf," and "Grit Family Bookshelf" are all tentacles to the Christian Herald octopus. A deduction gleaned from a close analysis of the club advertisements: *each operates out of 40 Overlook Drive*. Further analysis reveals that the president of one of the clubs is Fenwick Loomer; his editor is Evelyn Bence. Mr. Loomer is also president of a second club but in this enterprise Ms. Bence's job is filled by Gary Sledge (remember that name). A third club is managed by Douglas Andrews; a fourth by Frank Cummings. Assuming that each of these names represents a different person, we have some idea of the shadowy conclave up there on Overlook Drive.

To date, Christian Herald has not hit the really big time. That is, none of its books has sold more than one million copies. But they are definitely fighting the good fight, and doing the Lord's work. If they have yet to sell more than two million copies of a book like *I've Got to Talk to Somebody, God*, by the dread Marjorie

Holmes (whose *Two for Galilee* I once reviewed), they have at least been able to put into fiery orbit a celebrity-sinner book called *This Too Shall Pass* written by Mrs. Bert (LaBelle) Lance, "with Gary Sledge" (editor of Family Bookshelf).

Properly speaking, LaBelle is neither a celebrity nor a sinner even though she was much photographed and written about during the early years of the Carter administration or, to be precise, months. Since devotees of the celebrity-sinners are interested not in her but in Bert, LaBelle's dark glory is entirely of the reflected kind. She has committed no lurid crimes; as for her sins, I am sure that they add up to nothing more than a twinge or two of pride at being married to a guy as swell as Bert Lance. Certainly, the magazine *Christian Life* ("The Wonderful Way of Living") thinks the world of both Bert and LaBelle; so much so, that the cover story of the April issue is devoted to "The Lance Ordeal: Let God Have the Burden." The author of this sympathetic account is Wesley J. Pippert, who reveals to us "The secret of the Lance's [*sic*] strength during public scrutiny."

The Pippert account of the agony of the Lances makes almost as good reading as the adjacent article, "Exercising Your Authority Over Satan." Apparently, Satan can be defeated not only by Faith but by the repetition of sacred texts guaranteed to undo the wicked incantations of those who walk up and down and all about this great republic, peddling abortion, contraception, and the Equal Rights Amendment. Ultimately, the writer tells us, "the battle will be won or lost according to which side uses its mouths right." Among the bad-mouthers are the residents of the Moslem world where "the powers of darkness have expressed themselves . . . through those Islamic chants. And let me say in all love, without being controversial, for in some ways Islam is a good religion, it just has one problem: its god is the devil."

Apropos Islam, it should be noted that earlier this year Bert tried to obtain control of Financial General Bankshares, Inc., a $2.2 billion holding company that owns banks in four states. Bert's associates in this caper (currently halted by order of the Federal District Court of the District of Columbia) are—aside from La-Belle—such devil-worshipers as Sheikh Kamal Adham, Faisal Saud Al-Fulaij, Sheikh Sultan Bin Azid Al-Nahyan, Sheikh Mohammed Bin Zaid Al-Nahyan, Abdullah Darwaish, and the Pakistani financial wizard Agha Hassen Abedi, who recently paid off Bert's $3.4

million bank loan, simply because he liked the cut of Bert's Twice-Born jib.

Christian Life identifies Wesley J. Pippert as "a professional news correspondent with UPI"; he is also "an approved supply pastor with the United Methodist Church" whose special concern "as a Christian reporter is how the mass media can better handle the moral aspects of public issues." Although Rev. Pippert is in no doubt about the moral correctness of Bert Lance, he tends to hurry through the events that caused Bert to resign as budget director last fall. A year ago last January Bert "reported [to the Senate Finance Committee] assets of $7.9 million and debts of $5.3 million. He also agreed to sell 190,000 shares of stock in the National Bank of Georgia, Atlanta, in which he held controlling interest." Four months later, "there were news reports that a surge in the prime rate and the pay-cut Lance had taken were hindering his ability to keep up the interest payments on his debts."

As a Christian reporter and supply pastor, Rev. Pippert finds nothing wrong in any of this. In fact, if the increase in the prime rate was in any way attributable to Bert's policies then that would be a definite plus for Bert Lance, Fiscal Conservative. Another plus is that pay cut. Yet the money that Bert saved the American taxpayer would not have made much of a dent in interest payments he was obliged to make on $5.3 million worth of loans.

"Lance had been accused of permitting $450,000 in overdrafts by himself and his family at the family-owned bank in Calhoun," etc. There were new hearings. Although Bert handled himself well, The Mass Media would not let up. Finally, "His eyes welling, President Carter went on nationwide television to announce his friend's resignation. . . . Then [the?] Lances flew home to Georgia. . . . Despite his sense of peace, Lance had serious questions about what had happened. 'It's important we not lose the freedom of the presumption of innocence,' he told this reporter." Bert turned a cold eye on The Mass Media. " 'God has a laser beam that's a whole lot stronger than that other laser beam,' he said in a reference to the beam of the television camera."

When Rev. Pippert asked LaBelle to confirm whether or not the Lances' lavish $2 million fifty-room-plus Atlanta home was for sale, she said that it was not. After all, " 'We were not on the verge of bankruptcy, but if we were, who cares?' This was typical of lovely, long-haired Mrs. Lance. A talk with her does not dwell on the

material world for long. Inevitably conversation with her turns to
the spiritual, for that's where her heart is."

Bert's heart is very much in the same place. "Lance led the White
House Bible study," Rev. Pippert tells us, "but prefers not to talk
about it."

> "That's something that's very personal to everyone over there.
> I sort of took a pledge with that group that we really wouldn't
> talk about it. We got together on a very personal basis."
> Lance did say that Carter, who had a conflict at that hour, ex-
> pressed a desire to come.
> Lance also did considerable lay speaking to religious groups.

Now Rev. Wesley J. Pippert gives way to Mr. Gary Sledge of
40 Overlook Drive. LaBelle has a tale to unfold and unfold it she
does ("with Gary Sledge") in the pages of *This Too Shall Pass*.
Between the two of them they manage to illuminate the Bert Lance
Continuing Scandal not at all. Nevertheless, many good things are
said—indeed, good news is everywhere spread, for the book is dedicated to the Lances' old family friend "the Glory of God through
his Son Jesus Christ."

The prologue is datelined "Calhoun, Ga." First sentence: "This
too shall pass." When (and if) "this" passes, "hopefully we grow
wiser, more patient, more loving." LaBelle tells us that not only has
she been going through a pretty awful time lately but "Let me just
list the human afflictions that have touched my life: alcoholism,
drugs, broken homes, suicide, death, violence, serious illness, car
accidents, jailings, homosexuality, murder, adultery, runaway children." Sly Mr. Sledge knows that television series are usually shot
in series of thirteen. Each of LaBelle's thirteen human afflictions
would make for at least one powerful episode in a high-rated series.

But after this scorching teaser, LaBelle neglects to Tell All. No
doubt on the ground that we are all so used to suicide, murder, and
runaway children in our daily lives (i.e., television). Instead, La-
Belle zeroes in on something truly hated and feared out there on
the circuit, The Mass Media. As a Christian, LaBelle *tries* to forgive
the press. If she fails, . . . well, it is the effort that counts and if
Jesus does not want LaBelle for a sunbeam at the end of life's
journey, it will not have been for want of her (and Mr. Sledge's)
trying.

"Our family is not so different from any other. But I'd like you to walk with me down the Lance road of life, if only to illustrate how wonderful is the Lord on whom we rely." Actually, the Lances are quite a bit different from most people. For one thing, they have managed to acquire a whole lot of money real fast. For another, Bert was for many years a chief adviser and lender of money to what may prove to be our most mysterious president. Nevertheless, the fact that Carter and Lance in tandem were for a time allowed to preside over the republic's affairs does indeed illustrate the loony sense of humor as well as true mystery of our Lord and His ways.

LaBelle begins at a high moment: the morning of the day that Bert is going to talk to the president about resigning as director of the Office of Management and Budget. For months the scandal has been breaking all around them. LaBelle is aroused from a . . . what else, Mr. Sledge? "fitful sleep" by "laughter and many loud voices and the sound of shuffling feet." Whose laughter? whose feet? The Mass Media are outside in the street. "We were under seige [*sic*], as we had been throughout September."

Bert brings her breakfast in bed. Things look bad. Bert leaves for the White House. LaBelle dares not look at the *Washington Post* because "recently there had been a story on the front page . . . about my brother Banks' death two years before. The writer implied that our family's financial situation was rocky, that Bert was somehow responsible, and that this was the reason my brother had taken his own life. All that was untrue."

According to LaBelle, Beverly Banks David committed suicide "when his high expectations for himself were not realized, he felt unreasonable guilt or failure." This is dignified reticence. We are given no revelations of the sort promised in the prologue. Yet there is evidence that, wittingly or unwittingly as Mr. Sledge might say, LaBelle's brother had been very much involved in Bert's shenanigans at the National Bank of Georgia. In fact, according to the SEC, thirteen months *after* the death of Beverly Banks David, his bank account was $73,401 overdrawn, presumably by the Holy Ghost.

Later that afternoon, Bert comes home, having "played tennis with President Carter. . . . He looked exhausted. . . . I could see the suppressed anger in his face, the tiredness and the letting go. . . . Then at supper in the garden, we asked God to give us wisdom and strength and to show us his [LaBelle knows God too well to capitalize the pronoun] will. . . . God was not far off. He was near. We talked to him intimately and often." Actually, it was Jimmy Carter who was far off by now, sweating ice over the so-called Lance Affair.

Like the stern Nixon women of an earlier epoch, LaBelle was against resignation. But Bert had had it. He was going to resign even though "I had a dream about what could be accomplished in this job." The first Kuwaiti Mutual Fund? The first International Bank of Georgia and Abu Dhabi? Dreams, dreams. . . .

The next day LaBelle hightailed it over to the White House to put the arm on Jimmy. "The President was very cordial, very gracious. . . . He always is a friend to everyone in our family on a person-to-person basis, despite the formalities of his office. I think the President believes strongly that Christ's love and concern can only be shown in this way." But Jimmy was concerned about that old devil The Mass Media. "He spoke honestly about his public relations problem caused by Bert's name being in the news so long." Although LaBelle *knew* that she was filled to the brim with Christ when she told Jimmy that Bert should remain in office, Jimmy was every bit as filled with Christ when he came to the conclusion that Bert should get his ass out of town.

Like Saint Jerome battling with the pagan shade of Cicero, La-Belle and Mr. Sledge wrestle with this exquisite theological problem. "I knew that the President had presented his views in the light of faith. He, just as Bert and I, had prayed about this situation and each of us reached different conclusions—but each of us had come to realize the profound love in Christ we shared." Thus LaBelle papers over the inexplicable plurality of Truth.

Since Jimmy and LaBelle can't both be right, she surrenders if not to the Holy Ghost to the Gallup Poll: "I have often learned [that] God's purpose and my intentions are not always the same. Yet everything comes in his own time!" A striking image, worthy of Ecclesiastes. Back at the house ("I was suddenly tired"), LaBelle dealt compassionately with The Mass Media at the door. Then, "I went back to the TV but only the afternoon game shows were on, so I turned off the set and read a daily devotional book."

The rest of *This Too Shall Pass* is a somewhat mechanical ghost-story of LaBelle's family and early life, marriage and motherhood, riches and heartbreak, and (above all) a steadfast Faith. Inevitably, she falls from a horse; inevitably, she is told that she "must remount with dignity." Daddy owned the Calhoun bank while Bert's father had been president of Young Harris, a small Methodist College in northeast Georgia. As a child, Bert had experienced "an exciting mix of intellectual conversation and theological discussion." Then he moved to Calhoun where he went to school with LaBelle, who "had a dream. I wanted to be an actress on Broadway or in the movies. See Hollywood and the Pacific Ocean." But, luckily, she chose to "think and work for Christ. The Christian road is a hard one, but it is the most rewarding road." And so it proved to be for Bert and LaBelle.

LaBelle did not go with Bert to an outdoor political barbecue, attended by "a young state senator named Carter. . . . Bert was attracted initially by Jimmy's forthright approach and community conscience." Apparently, they were as alike as two black-eyed peas in a pod. Each had so much in common with the other: "Concern for progress in Georgia . . . raised in a small town . . . strong commitment to public service . . . boyhood dreams of going to sea . . . both were involved in agribusiness, Jimmy as a farmer and warehouser of peanuts, Bert as the financial underwriter . . . born-again Christians." Civil rights? LaBelle passes on that one. Martin Luther King is not a name to conjure with amongst those who read this sort of inspirational Christian literature.

In due course, Jimmy becomes governor; he appoints Bert head of the Bureau of Transportation. Bert donates his salary to charity. When "Jimmy had hopes of higher office . . . [Bert] presented Jimmy with a set of small medals of all the states, saying he now had dominion over one—someday he hoped he would have dominion over all." As soon as Jimmy's term of office ended, he proceeded to seek dominion over all the states while Bert stayed home and tried to dominate Georgia. "We announced Bert's candidacy [for governor] at a party held out at Lancelot, at which Bert spoke from the bed of an old wagon. . . ." Bert lost. Jimmy won.

Bert was offered the big job at Management and Budget. Should he take it? He agonizes with LaBelle: " 'It would mean a dramatic cut in salary,' Bert said. 'But it's a matter of duty. A citizen owes something to his country. I can't turn my back on a nation that's given us so much. In a free society we all must pay the "rent." ' " The dream . . . always the dream!

The Lances join the Carters in Washington. LaBelle was soon "encircled by new friends and prayer partners. Shortly after we got settled in Georgetown, I invited Cabinet wives to join me in a prayer group which met at our house." LaBelle also "taught a Bible class for senior citizens at the Dumbarton Avenue Methodist Church. . . ."

Then, on May 23, *Time* magazine struck. Something about irregular bank loans. LaBelle was impervious at first: "I knew Bert would never do anything illegal." But The Mass Media had tasted blood. They did not let up until they had sent Bert and LaBelle back to Calhoun, their finances tangled but their faith in God more resolute than ever. The Lances were also bucked up by the president, who promptly sent them abroad as "co-chairmen of the Friendship Force—America's people-to-people outreach to other nations. Rosalynn Carter is the very active honorary chairman."

That's all LaBelle has to say about this organization. *Christian Life* is a bit more explicit. Apparently, this "non-profit, non-government organization designed to promote world peace through friendships" was invented by Rev. Wayne Smith of Decatur, Georgia. "The exchanges last about ten days. . . . Once there, the ambassadors stay in guest homes, live, work and share with their hosts" for eight days. Each "ambassador" shells out $250 for an "embassy" of ten days, but can that possibly cover the costs of the trip? If it doesn't, who pays? But then, whatever the Lances get mixed up in tends to be mysterious—like the Lord Himself.

Has it come to this? Franz Joseph would mutter, as he gazed down at the mob of shouting dress extras below his window at Schönbrunn palace in Burbank, California. Cut to the hunting lodge at old-world Mayerling. Sulky Crown Prince Rudolf wonders, what does it all mean? as he draws a bead on LaBelle . . . I mean Maria Vetsera. Slow dissolve to the funeral cortege, to the grieving Franz Joseph, to Hitler riding through the streets of Vienna.

Rhetorical questions never get answered either in Golden Age movies or in modern-day United States. At most, grand juries, congressional committees, district courts sometimes manage to extract a few pale perjuries from the odd scapegoat. Presumably, this will happen in the case of Bert Lance when he goes before a grand jury in Atlanta to answer charges of criminal misapplication of bank funds. Three federal agencies are also on his tail for assorted crimes while his secret attempt to take over Financial General Bankshares, Inc. has been temporarily stopped by a federal judge. Will Bert be found guilty? And if so, of what is he actually guilty?

With some pride, the Inventor-owners of the United States announced that their republic would be "a government of laws and not of men." The world applauded. It never occurred to any Enlightenment figure in the eighteenth century that law was not preferable to man. The republic was then given to lawyers to govern. Predictably, lawyers make laws, giving work to other lawyers. As a result of two centuries of law-making every aspect of an American's life has either been prescribed for or proscribed by laws that even as they are promulgated split amoeba-like to create more laws. The end to this Malthusian nightmare of law metastasized is nowhere in sight.

Plaintively, Bert acknowledged this state of affairs in his last appearance before the Senate. He maintained that he had not really broken any law, while desperately signaling to the senators that if you were to obey every dumb law on the statute books you could do no business at all. The senator-lawyers would doubtless have been more understanding if their client-constituents had not been watching them on television.

One rationale for the necessity of new laws is the need to protect that vague entity known to lawyers as the public, to corporations as the consumer. Yet each virtuous law promptly creates counterlaws designed to serve those special interests that do not have at heart the public's interest. As a result virtually any polluter of rivers, corrupter of politicians, hustler of snake-oil who can afford expensive legal counsel is able to sail with the greatest of ease through the legislative chambers and courtrooms of the republic. This is the way that we are now, and that is the way we have always been. Nevertheless, from time to time, the system of ownership requires a sacrificial victim to show that the system truly works and that no one is above the law—except those who are.

What sustains a system that is plainly unjust if not illegal? The Lance affair suggests an answer. One third of the American population claim to be twice-born Christians. Although redemption is big on the evangelical Christian circuit, punishment of sinners is even bigger. To the fundamentalist Christian mind, evil is everywhere and every day is a lovely day, as John Latouche's lyric goes, for an *auto-da-fé*. According to hard-core white fundamentalists, Jews are forever guilty of the murder of our Lord. As children of Ham, blacks are eternally inferior to whites. The Pauline injunction that slaves obey their masters still applies in the sense that those without money must serve those with money, for money is the most tangible sign of God's specific love. Sexual activity outside marriage must be punished by law in the here-and-now as well as by God in eternity. The unremitting rage of the fundamentalist Christian against so many varieties of sin is the source of innumerable laws that have bred, in turn, other laws of the sort that now enmesh Bert Lance, the Georgia Laocoön.

Bert is now being sacrificed by his own kind, and he still can't believe it. When Bert and LaBelle inveigh against The Mass Media, they are sending out distress signals in Twice-Born Code. The Mass Media means Jews. Surely the Christers will rally to the defense of an innocent man traduced by those elders of Zion who have gained control of the nation's television and press in order to destroy the moral fiber of God's own country. But code phrases can no longer save Bert's bacon. Like Nixon, he got caught. And like Nixon he must be made to suffer by those for whom the infliction of pain is not only a Christian duty but an abiding pleasure.

It says a good deal for Jimmy Carter's essential decency or timidity or both that he has not yet put together a populist (and popular) Christian crusade to "save" those whose very birth and deeds are offensive to the God of the Twice-Born. But should he ever be so minded, there are more than enough laws already on the books to help him in his holy task.

Fortunately, Jimmy's friends Bert and LaBelle have the consolation of Holy Scripture in their dark hours. As the grand jury convenes in Atlanta, Bert is certain to turn to Luke 11:52: "Woe to you lawyers! For you have taken away the key of knowledge; you did not enter yourselves, and you hindered those who were entering."

Meanwhile, *Quo vadis, Jimmy?**

The New York Review of Books
JUNE 29, 1978

---

* Back to Plains. The un-twice-born Ronald (where *is* the rest of him?) Reagan put together the Christian crusade that, rightfully, should have been Carter's juggernaut.

Rich Kids

Privileged Ones is the fifth and last of Robert Coles's *Children of Crisis* series. In four earlier volumes Dr. Coles interviewed a wide range of American children—Eskimos, Appalachians, migrant workers. Now he deals with the children of what he calls "The Well-Off and the Rich in America."

Dr. Coles is a professional child psychiatrist ("There are, after all, only a few hundred such men and women in the country"); he is currently at Harvard. According to the publisher, he has written twenty-four books. Except for *Children of Crisis*, I cannot say that I really know his work. From time to time I see articles by him; whenever I do, I feel a warm glow. I like thee, Dr. Coles, I know not why. Perhaps it is because I am interested in many of his large subjects (economic injustice, children, Middle America). Certainly, I admire his uninhibited liberalism; his obvious compassion for those he deals with. The fact that I seldom actually finish reading anything that he writes probably has to do with my own perhaps irrational conviction that Dr. Coles's heart is so entirely in all the right places (mouth, boots, upon the sleeve) that nothing he has to say will ever surprise me despite the fact that he has traveled far and reasonably wide because "One hopes; one hopes against hope that somehow it will make a little difference; only a little, but still some, if people mostly unknown to almost all of us get better known to more of us." This generous sentiment is from the preface to the penultimate volume *Eskimos, Chicanos, Indians.** Yet no matter how far afield Dr. Coles goes, he is seldom able to tell us anything that we did not already know.

I suspect that this gift for inducing *déjà vu* may very well be the most subtle form of teaching. Where Plato makes us think by asking questions, Dr. Coles makes us *feel* by giving answers—in the form of monologues attributed to various children, an enjoyable if somewhat questionable technique (even Dr. Coles is disturbed by a form of "narrative that excludes myself as much as possible, and brings [the reader] directly to the children. . . . I may well have made a mistake, given the limitations of words, not to mention my own shortcomings").

Children of Crisis is a work of high seriousness, and a great deal of labor (if not work) has gone into the compilation of so many interviews with so many children over so many years. The persona of Dr. Coles is truly attractive . . . and it is the persona that one is most conscious of while reading him. Thanks no doubt to "the limitations of words" he is present, like God, in every aspect of his creation and, unlike God, he must be a most agreeable companion for a child, causing a minimum of that sort of dislocation Lévi-Strauss notes in *Tristes tropiques*: the moment that the anthropologist appears on the scene a pristine culture ceases, by definition, to be what it was and becomes something else again in order to accommodate the researcher-invader and his preconceptions.

Dr. Coles is attractively modest; he does not claim to know all the questions—as opposed to answers. In a sense, *Children of Crisis* could be called *The Education of Robert Coles*. Although he has a strong if oddly undefined sense of the way the world ought to be, he knows perfectly well that he is apt to impose his own world view on the children he talks to. In fact, the most beguiling aspect of his work is the pains that he takes not to do what, of course, he cannot help doing: expressing through the children his outrage at a monstrously unjust society. As a result, we get to know a lot about the mind (or feelings) of Dr. Coles. This is no bad thing.

* Atlantic/Little, Brown, 587 pp., $15.00

On the other hand, the children he interviewed during the last twenty years are somewhat shadowy.

In *Privileged Ones* Dr. Coles talks to the children of the rich. As he describes his method of work, he worries whether or not the phrase "children of crisis" really applies to them. The original "crisis" of the earlier studies was the integration of America's public schools and its effect on not-rich children. In theory, the rich don't have to worry about integrated public schools if they don't want to; their children can always go elsewhere. Finally (and rightly, I think), Dr. Coles thinks that the "crisis" does include the squire's children (Dr. Coles's approach is not unlike Horatio Alger's, whose cast of characters always included a "purse-proud" squire's son who treats badly poor pluck-and-luck Luke, who eventually works hard and makes money and has the satisfaction of one day condescending to his old enemy who has lost all his money). It was a black parent who told Dr. Coles that the rich are the people he should be talking to because "they own us" (this was in New Orleans). A sensible observation; and suggestion.

Dr. Coles set about the work at hand in his usual way. "I do *not* interview children with tests, tape-recorders, questions. I call upon them as a visitor and eventually, one hopes, a friend." How he comes to meet them is somewhat mysterious. He tells us, "In 1960 I started visiting regularly five quite well-to-do New Orleans families. . . . These were not the 'first' families of New Orleans, but they were far from the last in rank." He tells us that he had been so much with the victims of our economic system that he felt "ill at ease" with the New Orleans bourgeoisie, although they were "my own kind." So Saint Francis must have felt whenever he stopped off in Assisi to visit the folks, only to find them still busy netting and eating those very same little birds he liked to chat with. Yet Dr. Coles is able to give the rich almost the same compassionate attention that he gave the less "advantaged" (his verb) families.

> I never came to their parents as a stranger, suddenly at the door with a brazenly insistent set of inquiries. I met these upper-income families as an outgrowth of work that often they had good reason to know about: as growers and plantation owners; as important citizens.

This does not explain very much. For instance, was Dr. Coles ever called in professionally? Several of the children he talked to had already had dealings with that somber eminence known as "the school psychologist." Were they difficult children? And did the parents turn to Dr. Coles? If so, did they know what *he* was doing?

The most extraordinary omission in this work is the parents. Although we hear a good deal about them at secondhand through the children, Dr. Coles seldom records his own impression of the parents. As a result, his Privileged Ones often sound like voices in one of Beckett's enervating plays—literally unrelated to any recognizable world. He does warn us that his method requires, "at times, not only changes of name and place of residence, but the substantial alteration of other significant information. The point has been to struggle for representative accounts. I have not hesitated, at times, to condense remarks drastically or to draw upon the experiences of several children in the interest of a composite picture." I am afraid that the result not only makes the children sound all alike (Dr. Coles has no ear for the way people speak), but since we are given so little precise data about any of the families, there is a flat sameness of tone as well as of subject. Dr. Coles's education (like that of Henry Adams) starts with certain things already absolutely known and contrary data is either excluded or made to fit certain preconceptions.

What are Dr. Coles's absolutes? At the start, he makes clear "my political sympathies, my social and economic views. . . . I worked for years in the South and SNCC and CORE, the civil rights movement." He reminds us that the first volume of the series was the result of the crisis brought on by the integration of Mississippi schools and that the second volume dealt with the perpetual crisis (exploitation) of migrant workers: "I dedicated a book I wrote on Erik H. Erikson's psychoanalytic work to Cesar Chavez." Also, "I have written an assortment of muckraking articles in connection with the social, racial, and economic problems of the South," etc. Finally, "My heroes—of this century, at least—are James Agee and George Orwell, Walker Percy and Flannery O'Connor, Simone Weil and Georges Bernanos, William Carlos Williams, and Dorothy Day—none of them great admirers of this nation's upper-income, propertied families."

Although I have not read every work by the writers named, I have read something of each and I think that one can safely say that Bernanos never had a word to say about America's propertied families. Flannery O'Connor was interested not in class but in grace. Walker Percy is a southern aristocrat who has not shown, to date, any leveling social tendencies. No doubt Orwell deplored our "well-off and rich families" as he did their British equivalents, but he did not write about them. Neither Simone Weil nor William Carlos Williams, M.D., seems quite relevant. Dorothy Day obviously contributed to Dr. Coles's education as did, I fear, James Agee, whose early ersatz-Biblical style has not had a good influence on Dr. Coles's over-fluent prose. Like so many good-hearted, soft-headed admirers of the Saint James (Agee) version of poverty in America, *Let Us Now Praise Famous Men*, Dr. Coles is enthralled by the windy, woolly style of the saint, unaware that the only numinous presence in that book is Walker Evans, whose austere photographs are so at odds with Agee's tumescent (the pornographers have stolen "turgid"; we'll never get it back) text.

In any case, somehow or other, Dr. Coles got to talk to a number of nicely "advantaged" children in, variously, Alaska, New Mexico, New Orleans, a San Antonio barrio, an Atlanta black ghetto, "north of Boston," "west of Boston," and "well north of Boston" (the last three phrases reverberate for the Massachusetts-bred author in much the same way that Combray and Balbec did for Proust). The geographic range is wide, and interesting. Once Dr. Coles got to know the children (aged, roughly, six to eleven or twelve at first encounter), he would encourage them to draw pictures for him. The pictures are included in the book and I am sure that they reveal a good deal about the artists.

Since Dr. Coles gives the impression of being a thoroughly nice man, the children were probably as candid as he thinks they were. Rather sweetly, he admits that he liked *them* even though, with his credentials (Cesar Chavez, Georges Bernanos, Walker Percy), he feared that he might be put off by their advantaged-ness. I am sure that they liked him, too. But then it is not possible to dislike an author who dedicates a book: "To America's children, rich and well-off as well as poor, in the hope that some day, one day soon, all boys and girls everywhere in the world will have a decent chance to survive, grow, and affirm themselves as human beings." Plainly, Bishop Coles will not rest easy as long as a single child on this earth is obliged to negate himself as a vegetable or mineral.

The American vice is explanation. This is because there is so little conversation (known as "meaningful dialogue" to the explainers) in the greatest country in the history of the greatest world in the Milky Way. Dr. Coles is a born explainer and prone to loose rhetoric; given his "credentials," this is as it should be. But it is somewhat disturbing to find that most of the children are also great explainers. Admittedly, Dr. Coles is homogenizing their characters and prose in the interests of "representativeness" and "compositiveness"; as a result, not only do they sound like him, they also come through as a batch of born-explainers, faithfully reflecting the explanatory style of parents, teachers, television commercials.

But despite the grimly didactic tendencies of our future rulers, the kids themselves are often interesting; particularly when Dr. Coles gets down to facts. In an excellent early chapter called "Comfortable, Comfortable Places," Dr. Coles gives us a sharp look at the way the rich live nowadays. He describes the air-conditioned ranch houses in the Southwest, the Georgian and Colonial manors west and north and well north of Boston, the Gothic mansions in New Orleans' Garden District. He has a gift for the expensive detail. He notes the almost universal desire of the rich to live in the country (hangover from the days of the British Ascendancy?). They acquire ranches, farms, estates; go richly native. Pools, tennis courts, stables are taken for granted. For many parents a life "without golf . . . would be unbearable, even hard to imagine." Although Dr. Coles describes the obsession that the rich have with sports, he does not analyze the significance of the games that they play, and oblige their children to play. He seems to think that sports are indulged in either for the sake of health or to show off wealth (the private golf course, the ski run).

In the case of the new rich (his usual subject), expensive sports may indeed be a sign of status. But for the old rich, games are a throwback to a warrior heritage, real or imagined. A competence with weapons and horses was a necessity for the noble. Later, which such things were of no use to desk-bound magnates, horses, weapons, games continued to exert an atavistic appeal. Also, as late as my own youth, it was taken for granted that since making a living was not going to be much of a problem or even (in some cases) a necessity, the usual hard round of money-making with all its excitements and insecurities was not to be one's lot. Therefore, time must be filled—hence, games. Certainly physical activity is better than drinking, gambling, lechery . . . the traditional hazards of great families, not to mention fortunes.

As a child, at each birthday or Christmas, I came to dread the inevitable tennis racquet, Winchester rifle, skis: these objects were presented to me in much the same way that the pampered dog in the television commercial is tempted with every sort of distasteful dog food until, finally, he goes up the wall when given The Right Brand. In any case, The Right Brand proved to be books . . . not proper substance for the growing boy of forty years ago; or even today, if Dr. Coles's findings are correct. I don't believe a single child that he talked to mentions a book to him (did he mention any books to them?). But television is noted. And sports. And school. And parents. And servants. Servants!

Dr. Coles notes that in the South the servants are black; in the North they are sometimes black, but more usually (in the houses of the true nobles) white. Dr. Coles records what the children have to say about servants. But he does not probe very deeply. He does not seem to understand to what extent, prepuberty, "privileged children" are brought up not by parents but by servants. Governesses, nannies, mademoiselles (our spelling) are still very much a part of the scene even in the age of the baby-sitter, and they can be more important to the child than his parents. Although Dr. Coles records a good deal of what the children have to say about the people who work in the house or around the place, he is not (except in one case) sensitive to the deep and complex relationships that exist between, say, nurse and child. But then Dr. Coles is after different game: the attitude of the rich child toward economic inferiors.

Dr. Coles is good at showing the subtle and not-so-subtle ways in which class lines are drawn by parents and toed by children. One must never be rude or unkind to those less fortunate. Above all, one must never embarrass (recurring word) the lower orders by asking them to dinner or by going to visit their house (or "home," as Dr. Coles would say—a word seldom used by the nobles). Incidentally, all schoolteachers and most doctors are counted as plebes. This news will come as a particular jolt to our medicos, who are not only well-to-do but when espied on a dim day on a green fairway might pass for upper class.

The last time that I saw W. H. Auden, he announced, apropos nothing at all, "*I* am upper middle class. My father was a doctor. In England that is upper middle class." Like the Baron de Charlus enumerating his titles for the benefit of Madame Verdurin, Auden discoursed for ten minutes on the social importance of his family. As an old corsair in the class wars, I waited for him to pause; then raised the Jolly Roger. I told him that in my youth we were tended by Washington's "leading society physician" (the Homeric epithet always put before his name in the city's social columns). He would

come to our house in not-so-nearby Virginia. Dressed in morning
coat and striped trousers, he would dispense aspirin (and morphine
to the family junkie); then, if the company at table was not too
grand, he would be *invited for lunch.* Auden received this bit of
cutlass-work with the bland announcement, "*I* am upper middle
class." And repeated himself, word for word.

Dr. Coles notes a significant difference between rich and poor
children. The poor tend to live in a long unchanging present while
the rich have a future to look forward to. For the rich there is
always "next year" when they will go to Switzerland to ski or to
the West Indies to scuba-dive. Early on, rich children are trained
to think of themselves as having a certain "entitlement" (Dr. Coles's
not so bad synonym for "privilege"—from the Latin for "private
law") to a way of life that despite numerous perils and often
onerous obligations is bound to be satisfactory and worthwhile.
Unlike the present-trapped poor, each child of privilege is acutely
conscious of his own specialness. Dr. Coles defines this self-
consciousness most elegantly: "With none of the . . . children I
have worked with" (well, disregard those two inelegant "withs")
"have I heard such a continuous and strong emphasis put on the
'self.' In fact, other children rarely if ever think about themselves
in the way children of well-to-do and rich parents do—with insistence, regularity, and, not least, out of a learned sense of obliga-
tion. These privileged ones are children who live in homes with
many mirrors. They have mirrors in their rooms, larger mirrors in
adjoining bathrooms. . . ." *Mirrored Ones* or *Reflected Ones* might
have been an even better title than *Privileged Ones.* At his best,
Dr. Coles is himself something of a mirror, with fun-house tendencies.

Certain themes emerge from these monologues. The collapse of
the financial order in the early Thirties made a lasting impression
on the parents of these children. The Depression convinced them
of the essential fragility of what is now known as the consumer society. Menaced, on the one hand, by labor unions and, on the other,
by the federal government, even the richest American family feels
insecure. It is fascinating that this unease . . . no, paranoia (somehow or other *they* will ruin us) still persists after so many years of
prosperity for the rich. But then, the privileged had a number of
frights in the Thirties. One of my first memories was the march on
Washington of war veterans in 1932. Demanding bonuses for
having served in World War I, they were nicknamed Boners. I

thought them Halloween skeletons. Then I saw them at the Capitol. They looked like comic-strip hobos. But there was nothing comic about the rocks that they heaved at my grandfather's car. In due course, General MacArthur and his corps of photographers sent the Boners home; nevertheless, we *knew* that one day they would come back and kill us all. Like Cavafy's urbanites, we waited with a certain excitement for the barbarians to return and sack the city.

Dr. Coles's children also fear the Boners. Only now they are called communists or liberals, blacks or Chicanos; and the federal government is in league with them. Worse, the Boners are no longer encamped outside the city; they have occupied the city. All streets are dangerous now. Apartment houses are fortresses; and even the suburbs and exurbs are endangered by "them," and (recurrent theme) there is nowhere to go. Although some of Dr. Coles's children talk of France and England as relative paradises (curious, the fascination with Europe), most are fatalistic. As an Alaskan girl puts it, "I hear Daddy tell Mom that he feels like taking all his money out of the bank and getting a compass and spinning it, and wherever it ends up pointing to, we would go there. But if it pointed straight north, we couldn't go to live near the North Pole." Meanwhile the son of a Boston banker reports that, "It's hard to trust the help these days." He worries about the house being robbed: "Someone tips off the crooks." As for Boston, his mother "doesn't like to walk even a block in the city when it gets dark. . . ."

Dr. Coles's principal interest is how the rich regard the poor. This is a good subject. But one wishes that he was a bit less direct and on target in his approach. After all, there are a lot of ways to come at the subject. For instance, many of the children are pubescent or even adolescent; yet sex is hardly mentioned. Now the question of sexual role is every bit as political, in the true sense, as conditioned attitudes toward money, class, and race. Dr. Coles nowhere deals with the *idea* of the family ("fealty" to which is so excitedly sworn by certain childless lowbrow moralists). For instance, what do the young girls he talked to think of motherhood? Most of the girl children (*genus* privileged) that I know are adamant about *not* having children. They believe that the planet is overcrowded, that resources are limited, that the environment is endangered. Their vehemence is often startling—if, perhaps, short-lived. Dr. Coles notes none of this. But then *his* "crisis" was racial integration.

Except for one anecdote about a New Orleans girl who liked to contemplate a nearby cemetery, wondering "who 'those people' were," death is hardly present in these tales. Although Dr. Coles handles with delicacy the New Orleans girl's "morbidity," he seems not to have been interested in what the other children had to say on a subject of enormous concern to children. The moment that a child comprehends not only the absoluteness but the inevitability of his own death, he is obliged, for better or worse, to come to terms with how best to live in the world. For a rich child to whom all things seem possible, the knowledge of death often brings on a vastation not unlike the one that helped to propel to enlightenment the uniquely over-advantaged Prince Siddhartha.

But if death is absent in Dr. Coles's testaments, God is all over the place. Since Dr. Coles has so generalized the families that he writes about, it is hard to tell just what their actual beliefs are. I would guess that none is Jewish or Roman Catholic. I would assume that the southern or southwestern families are Protestant with fundamentalist tendencies of the twice-born variety. West, north, and well north of Boston, the rich tend to belong to the highly refined Episcopal Church where talk of God is considered bad taste. Yet I was startled by how many of Dr. Coles's families say grace before meals; go to church; refer to God. I never heard grace said at table in any house that I visited as a child. Yet God and religion mean so much to so many of Dr. Coles's families that I can't help thinking he himself is enthralled by that tripartite deity whose sense of fun has made sublunary life so strenuous and odd.

In describing a disaster dream, "My father asked God to spare us," says a girl with a pair of alcoholic parents. A New Mexico boy wonders if Indians "pray to the same God his parents ask him to beseech before going to sleep. His parents are Presbyterians, attend church with their children every Sunday, and encourage in them prayer at the table and upon retiring." The son of a black entrepreneur notes his father's appeals to God to forgive him if he has wronged anyone in the course of making money. A southern girl notes that "Christ didn't want people to look down on the poor...." The *good* poor, that is. One child is critical of his father's treatment of migrant labor; he is regarded with some unease by his family as "a believing Christian." I suspect that Dr. Coles may himself be a believing Christian (like Bernanos, O'Connor, Weil, et al.). If he is, it is possible that he has exaggerated the importance of religion in the lives of the families that he deals with. But I propose this only tentatively. After all, a recent poll assured us that one-third of the American population (mostly unrich) claims to be twice-born.

According to Dr. Coles's research, the children of the rich (poor, too, but in a different way) pass through an altruistic phase at about the age of ten or eleven. They become aware not only of injustice but of hypocrisy. They question seriously the ancient parental injunction: do as I say, not as I do. Thanks to television, an unexpected agent of revolution, a white child can watch a black child being menaced by a mob (thus compassion begins), while television serials like "The Adventures of Robin Hood" can have a positively subversive effect. After all, to rob the rich in order to give to the poor is not entirely unlike what he has been taught in Sunday School. Eventually, there is a showdown between parent and child. "Robin Hood" is replaced by "Gilligan's Island" and all's right with the world—for the time being, anyway. Predictably, parents get a good deal of help from schoolteachers who also have a stake in maintaining things as they are. Dr. Coles's children are uncommonly shrewd when it comes to analyzing their teachers. They know that the teachers are terrified of saying anything that might distress the parents. The children also know when a teacher does get out of line, there is hell to pay: the subject of one of Dr. Coles's best tales.

The stories that comprise *Privileged Ones* seem to me to belong more to moral literature than to science. I assume that psychology still pretends to be a science. Dr. Coles has used conversations with actual children in order to write a series of short stories. Since the author is the least disinterested of men, these stories are essentially polemical and so, to my mind, entirely honorable if not exactly "scientific." Dr. Coles's mind tends to the political and the moral rather than to the abstract or the empirical. He believes that the economic system by which this country maintains its celebrated standard of living (for a few) is eminently unfair. Millions of men, women, and children are financially exploited in order to support one percent of the population in opulence and the rest in sufficient discomfort to keep them working at jobs that they dislike in order to buy things that they do not need in order to create jobs to make money to be able to buy, etc. This is not a just society. It may not last much longer. But for the present, the children of the rich are as carefully conditioned to the world as it is as are those of the poor.

In story after story, Dr. Coles shows a child at the moment he becomes aware of the problems of those who work his father's mine, or harvest his father's crops. Then he is enlightened. He is told that the world is a cruel place where big fish eat little fish and Daddy is a big fish. Family and teachers unite; convince the child that there is not much he can do now—or, perhaps, ever. The world is as it is. Perhaps, later, something might be done. Just wait. Meanwhile. . . . But the waiting is not long. Metamorphosis is at hand. Parents and teachers know that the principal agent of social conformity is puberty. As Old Faithful DNA triggers, on schedule, certain hormones, the bright outward-looking compassionate ten-year-old becomes like everyone else. Or sixteen equals cynicism equals a car.

From the cradle, our economic rulers-to-be are imbued with a strong sense of what they are entitled to, which is, technically speaking, 25 percent of the wealth of the United States. To make sure that they will be able to hold on to this entitlement, most of the boys and one of the girls want to be—what else?—lawyers. Dr. Coles keens: "it is unfair that a few be so very privileged and that the overwhelming majority be either hard-pressed or barely able to make do." He also worries that his own social-meliorizing views might have colored these stories because "one has to distinguish between social criticism and psychological observation." I can't think why. At least not in the case of Robert Coles. Whatever pretensions he may have as a scientific observer, he is essentially a moralist and, in these interesting stories, he has shown how the ruling class of an unjust society perpetuates itself through the indoctrination of its young.

Unfortunately, Dr. Coles does nothing much with his material. He is hortatory; good-hearted; vague. Were he less timid, he might have proposed a kind of socialism as partial solution to the "crisis." But like those collusive schoolteachers he writes about and resembles, he keeps within the familiar framework of a political system which is itself not only in crisis but the crisis. Although Dr. Coles's notes on contemporary children are in themselves of no particular urgency, they might one day serve as useful appendices to some yet to be written synthesizing work in which our peculiar society is looked at plain from an economic or political or (why not?) religious point of view.

The New York Review of Books
FEBRUARY 9, 1978

Theodore Roosevelt: An American Sissy

In Washington, D.C., there is—or was—a place where Rock Creek crosses the main road and makes a ford which horses and, later, car could cross if the creek was not in flood. Half a hundred years ago, I lived with my grandparents on a wooded hill not far from the ford. On summer days, my grandmother and I would walk down to the creek, careful to avoid the poison ivy that grew so luxuriously amid the crowded laurel. We would then walk beside the creek, looking out for crayfish and salamanders. When we came to the ford, I would ask her to tell me, yet again, what happened when the old President Roosevelt—not the current President Roosevelt—had come riding out of the woods on a huge horse just as two ladies on slow nags had begun a slow crossing of the ford.

"Well, suddenly, Mr. Roosevelt screamed at them, 'Out of my way!'" My grandmother imitated the president's harsh falsetto. "Stand to one side, women. *I am the President.*" What happened next? I'd ask, delighted. "Oh, they were both soaked to the skin by his horse's splashing all over them. But then, the very next year," she would say with some satisfaction, "*nice* Mr. Taft was the president." Plainly, there was a link in her mind between the Event at the Ford and the change in the presidency. Perhaps there was. In those stately pre-personal days you did not call ladies women.

The attic of the Rock Creek house was filled with thousands of books on undusted shelves while newspapers, clippings, copies of the *Congressional Record* were strewn about the floor. My grandmother was not a zealous housekeeper. There was never a time when rolled-up Persian rugs did not lie at the edge of the drawing room, like crocodiles dozing. In 1907, the last year but one of Theodore Roosevelt's administration, my grandfather came to the Senate. I don't think that they had much to do with each other. I found only one reference to TR—as he was always known—on the attic floor. In 1908, when Senator Gore nominated William Jennings Bryan for president, he made an alliterative aside, "I much prefer the strenuosity of Roosevelt to the sinuosity of Taft."

Years later I asked him why he had supported Bryan, a man who had never, in my grandfather's own words, "developed." "He was too famous too young. He just stopped in his thirties." So why had he nominated Bryan for president? Well, at the time there were reasons: he was vague. Then, suddenly, the pale face grew mischievous and the thin, straight Roman mouth broke into a crooked grin. "After I nominated him at Denver, we rode back to the hotel in the same carriage and he turned to me and said, 'You know, I base my political success on just three things.'" The old man paused for dramatic effect. What were they? I asked. "I've completely forgotten," he said. "But I do remember wondering why he thought he was a success."

In 1936, Theodore Roosevelt's sinuous cousin Franklin brought an end to my grandfather's career in the Senate. But the old man stayed on in Rock Creek Park and lived to a Nestorian age, convinced that FDR, as it was always known, was our republic's Caesar while his wife, Eleanor, Theodore's niece, was a revolutionary. The old man despised the whole family except Theodore's daughter Alice Longworth.

Alice gave pleasure to three generations of our family. She was as witty—and as reactionary—as Senator Gore; she was also deeply resentful of her distant cousin Franklin's success while the canonization of her own first cousin Eleanor filled her with horror. "Isn't Eleanor no-ble," she would say, breaking the word into two syllables, each hummed reverently. "So very, *very* good!" Then she would imitate Eleanor's buck teeth which were not so very unlike her own quite prominent choppers. But Alice did have occasional, rare fits of fairness. She realized that what she felt for her cousins was "Simply envy. *We* were the President Roosevelt family. But then along came the Feather Duster," as she habitually referred to Franklin, "and we were forgotten." But she was exaggerating, as a number of new books attest, not to mention that once beautiful Dakota cliff defaced by the somber Gutzon Borglum with the faces of dead pols.

It is hard for Americans today to realize what a power the Roosevelts exerted not only in our politics but in the public's imagination. There had been nothing like them since the entirely different Adamses and there has been nothing like them since—the sad story of the Kennedys bears about as much resemblance to the Roosevelts as the admittedly entertaining and cautionary television series *Dallas* does to Shakespeare's chronicle plays.

From the moment in 1898 when TR raced up Kettle Hill (incorrectly known as San Juan) to April 12, 1945, when Franklin Roosevelt died, the Roosevelts were at the republic's center stage. Also, for nearly half that fifty-year period, a Roosevelt had been president. Then, as poignant coda, Eleanor Roosevelt, now quite alone, acted for seventeen years as conscience to a world very different from that of her uncle TR or even of FDR, her cousin-husband.

In the age of the condominium and fast foods, the family has declined not only as a fact but as a concept. Although there are, presumably, just as many Roosevelts alive today as there were a century ago, they are now like everyone else, scattered about, no longer tribal or even all of the same class. Americans can now change class almost as fast—downward, at least—as they shift from city to city or job to job. A century ago, a member of the patriciate was not allowed to drop out of his class no matter how little money he had. He might be allowed to retire from the world, like TR's alcoholic brother Elliott, in order to cultivate his vices, but even Elliott remained very much a part of the family until death—not his own kind—declassed him.

As a descendant of Theodore Roosevelt said to David McCullough, author of *Mornings on Horseback*, "No writer seems to have understood the degree to which [TR] was part of a clan." A clan that was on the rise, socially and financially, in nineteenth-century New York City. In three generations the Roosevelts had gone from hardware to plate glass to land development and banking (Chemical). By and large, the Roosevelts of that era were a solemn, hardworking, uninspired lot who, according to the *New York World*, had a tendency "to cling to the fixed and the venerable." Then, suddenly, out of this clan of solid burghers erupted the restless Theodore and his interesting siblings. How did this happen? *Cherchez la mère* is the usual key to the unexpected—for good or ill—in a family's history.

During Winston Churchill's last government, a minister found him in the Cabinet room, staring at a newspaper headline: one of his daughters had been arrested, yet again, for drunkenness. The minister said something consoling. Churchill grunted. The minister was then inspired to ask: "How is it possible that a Churchill could end up like this?" To which the old man replied: "Do you realize just *what* there was between the first Duke of Marlborough and *me*?" Plainly, a genetic disaster area had been altered, in Winston's case, by an American mother, Jennie Jerome, and in Theodore Roosevelt's case by a southern mother, named Mittie Bulloch, a beautiful, somewhat eccentric woman whom everyone delighted in even though she was not, to say the least, old New York. Rather, she was proudly southern and told her sons exciting stories of what their swashbuckling southern kin had done on land and sea. In later life, everyone agreed that Theodore was more Bulloch than Roosevelt just as his cousin Franklin was more Delano—or at least *Sara* Delano—than Roosevelt.

Mr. McCullough's book belongs to a new and welcome genre: the biographical sketch. Edmund Wilson in *Patriotic Gore* and Richard Hofstadter in *The American Political Tradition* were somewhat specialized practitioners of this art but, by and large, from Plutarch to Strachey, it has been more of a European than an American genre. Lately, American biography has fallen more and more into the hands not of writers but of academics. That some academics write very well indeed is, of course, perfectly true and, of course, perfectly rare. When it comes to any one of the glorious founders of our imperial republic, the ten-volume hagiography is now the rule. Under the direction of a tenured Capo, squads of graduate students spend years assembling every known fact, legend, statistic. The Capo then factors everything into the text, like sand into a cement mixer. The result is, literally, monumental, and unreadable. Even such minor figures as Ernest Hemingway and Sinclair Lewis have been accorded huge volumes in which every letter, telegram, drunken quarrel is memorialized at random.

"Would *you* read this sort of book?" I asked Mark Schorer, holding up his thick life of Sinclair Lewis. He blinked, slightly startled by my bad manners. "Well," he said mildly, politely, "I must say I never really *liked* Lewis's work all that much."

Now, as bright footnotes to the academic texts, we are offered such books as Otto Friedrich's *Clover* and Jean Strouse's *Alice James*. These sketches seem to me to belong to literature in a way that Schorer's *Sinclair Lewis* or Dumas Malone's *Jefferson and His Time* do not—the first simply a journeyman compilation, the second a banal hagiography (with, admittedly, extremely valuable footnotes). In a sense, the reader of Malone et al. is obliged to make his own text out of the unshaped raw material while the reader of Strouse or Friedrich is given a finished work of literature that supplies the reader with an idiosyncratic view of the subject. To this genre *Mornings on Horseback* belongs: a sketch of Theodore Roosevelt's parents, brothers and sisters, wife, and self until the age of twenty-eight. Mr. McCullough has done a good swift job of sketching this family group.

Unfortunately, he follows in the wake not of the usual dull, ten-volume academic biography of the twenty-sixth president but of the first volume of Edmund Morris's *The Rise of Theodore Roosevelt*. This is bad luck for Mr. McCullough. Morris's work is not only splendid but covers the same period as Mr. McCullough, ending some years later with the death of McKinley. Where Mr. McCullough scores is in the portrait of the family, particularly during Theodore's youth. Fortunately, there can never be too much of a good thing. Since Morris's work has a different, longer rhythm, he does not examine at all closely those lesser lives which shaped —and explain, somewhat—the principal character.

Theodore Roosevelt, Senior, was a man of good works; unlike his wife Mittie. "She played no part in his good works, and those speculations on life in the hereafter or the status of one's soul, speculations that appear in Theodore's correspondence . . . are not to be found in what she wrote. She was not an agnostic exactly," writes McCullough, but at a time when the church was central to organized society she seems more than slightly indifferent or, as her own mother wrote, "If she was only a Christian, I think I could feel more satisfied."

Mittie's lack of religion was to have a lasting effect on her granddaughter Eleanor, the future Mrs. Franklin Delano Roosevelt. In 1870 Mittie placed her eldest child, Anna—known as Bamie—in

Les Ruches, a girls' school at Fountainebleau. The school's creator
was Mlle. Marie Souvestre, "a woman of singular poise and great
culture, but also an outspoken agnostic . . . as brief as Bamie's time
there would be, Mlle. Souvestre's influence would carry far." Indeed it did. In the next generation Bamie's niece Eleanor was also
sent to school with Mlle. Souvestre, now removed to Allenwood in
England. One of Mlle. Souvestre's teachers was Dorothy Bussy, a
sister of Lytton Strachey and the pseudonymous as well as epony-
mous author of *Olivia* by Olivia, a story of *amitiés particulières* in a
girls' school.

Bamie was not to marry until she was forty, while Eleanor's dislike of heterosexuality was lifelong ("*They* think of nothing else,"
she once said to me, grimly—and somewhat vaguely, for she never
really said exactly who "they" were); it would seem that Mlle.
Souvestre and her school deserve a proper study—before M. Roger
Peyrefitte gets to it. Certainly, Eleanor had learned Mlle. Souvestre's lesson well: this world is the one that we must deal with
and, if possible, improve. Eleanor had no patience with the other-
worldly. Neither had her uncle TR. In a letter to Bamie, the future
president says that he is marrying for a second time—the first wife
had died. As a highly moral man, he is disgusted with himself. So
much so that "were I sure there were a heaven my one prayer
would be I might never go there, lest I should meet those I loved
on earth who are dead."

A recurrent theme in this family chronicle is ill health. Bamie
had a disfiguring curvature of the spine. Elliott had what sounds
like epileptic fits. Then, at thirty-four, he was dead of alcoholism,
in West 102nd Street, looked after by a mistress. Theodore, Junior's
general physical fragility was made intolerable by asthma. Mr.
McCullough has done a good deal of research into asthma, that
most debilitating and frightening of nervous afflictions. "Asthma
is repeatedly described as a 'suppressed cry for the mother'—a cry
of rage as well as a cry for help." Asthmatics live in constant terror
of the next attack, which will always seem to be—if indeed it is
not—terminal.

Parenthetically, I ran into the Wise Hack not long ago—in the
lobby of the Beverly Hills Hotel. Where else? He is now very old,
very rich: he owns a lot of Encino. Although he will no longer
watch a movie made after 1945, he still keeps an eye on "the
product." He knows all the deals. "One funny thing," he said,
wheezing from emphysema—not asthma. "You know, all these hot-

shot young directors they got now? Well, every last one of them is a fat sissy who likes guns. And every last one of them has those thick glasses and the asthma." But before I could get him to give me the essential data, as Mrs. Wharton used to say, he had been swept into the Polo Lounge by the former managing editor of *Liberty*.

I must say that I thought of the Wise Hack's gnomic words as I read Mr. McCullough's account of TR's asthma attacks, which usually took place on a Sunday "which in the Victorian era was still the Lord's day . . . the one day of the week when the head of the household was home from work. . . ." Sunday also involved getting dressed up and going to church, something TR did not like. On the other hand, he enjoyed everyone's attention once the attacks had ended. Eventually, father and son came under the spell of a Dr. Salter, who had written that "organs are made for action, not existence; they are made to *work*, not to be; and when they *work* well, they can *be* well." You must change your life, said Rilke's Apollo. And that is what the young TR did: he went to a gymnasium, became an outdoorsman, built up his fragile body. At Harvard he was five foot eight inches tall and weighed one hundred twenty-five pounds. In later life, he was no taller but he came to weigh more than two hundred pounds; he was definitely a butter-ball type, though a vigorous one. He also wore thick glasses; liked guns.

Unlike the sissies who now make violent movies celebrating those who kill others, Theodore was a sissy who did not know that he was one until he was able to do something about it. For one thing, none of the Roosevelt children was sent to school. They were tutored at home. The boys seemed not to have had a great deal to do with other boys outside their own tribe. When Theodore went to Harvard, he was on his own for the first time in his life. But even at Harvard, Mittie would not allow him to room with other boys. He had an apartment in a private house; and a manservant. At first, he was probably surprised to find that he was unpopular with the other students; but then he was not used to dealing with those he did not know. He was very much a prig. "I had a headache," he writes in his diary, aged eleven, "and Conie and Ellie made a tremendous noise playing at my expense and rather laughed when I remonstrated."

At Harvard, he was very conscious of who was and who was not a gentleman. "I stand 19th in the class. . . . Only one gentleman stands ahead of me." He did not smoke; he got drunk on only one occasion—when he joined the Porcellian Club; he remained "pure" sexually. He was a lively, energetic youth who spoke rapidly, biting off his words as if afraid there would not be enough breath for him to say what he wanted to say. Properly bespectacled and gunned since the age of thirteen, he shot and killed every bird and animal that he could; he was also a fair taxidermist. Toward the end of his Harvard career, he was accepted as what he was, a not unattractive New York noble who was also very rich; his income was $8,000 a year, about $80,000 in today's money. In his last two years at Harvard "clothes and club dues . . . added up to $2,400, a sum the average American family could have lived on for six years."

In later years, Theodore was remembered by a classmate as "a joke . . . active and enthusiastic and that was all," while a girl of his generation said "he was not the sort to appeal at first." Harvard's President Eliot, who prided himself on knowing no one, remembered Theodore as "feeble" and rather shallow. According to Mr. McCullough, he made "no lasting male friendships" at Harvard, but then, like so many men of power, he had few attachments outside his own family. During the early part of his life he had only one friend—Henry Cabot (known as La-de-dah) Lodge, a Boston aristo-sissy much like himself.

The death of his father was a shattering experience; and the family grew even closer to one another than before. Then Theodore fell in love and added a new member to the clan. When TR met Alice Lee, she was seventeen and he was nineteen. "See that girl," he said to Mrs. Robert Bacon at a party. "I am going to marry her. She won't have me, but I am going to have *her*." Have her he did. "Alice," said Mrs. Bacon years later, "did not want to marry him, but she did." They were married October 27, 1880, on Theodore's twenty-second birthday. They lived happily ever after—for four years. Alice died of Bright's disease, shortly after giving birth to their daughter; a few hours earlier, in the same house, Mittie had died of typhoid fever. The double blow entirely changed Theodore's life. He went west to become a rancher, leaving little Alice with his sister Bamie. That same year Elliott also became a father when his wife, Anna Hall, give birth to Eleanor.

In 1876, as General Grant's second administration fell apart in a storm of scandal and the winds of reform gathered force, New

York State's great lord of corruption, Senator Roscoe Conkling, observed with characteristic sour wit: "When Dr. Johnson defined patriotism as the last refuge of a scoundrel, he ignored the enormous possibilities of the word reform." Since good Republicans like Theodore Roosevelt, Senior, could not endure what was happening to their party and country, they joined together to cleanse party, country.

As a member of the New York delegation to the Republican convention at Cincinnati, Theodore, Senior, helped deny both Conkling and James G. Blaine, another lord of corruption, the nomination for president. After a good deal of confusion the dim but blameless Rutherford B. Hayes was nominated. Although Hayes was not exactly *elected* president, he became the president as a result of the Republican Party's continued mastery of corruption at every level of the republic.

The new president then offered Theodore, Senior, the Collectorship of the Port of New York, a powerhouse of patronage and loot that had been for some years within Conkling's gift. And so it remained: thanks to Conkling's efforts in the Senate, Theodore, Senior, was denied the Collectorship. A week after this rejection, he wrote his son at Harvard to say that, all in all, he was relieved that he was not to be obliged to "purify our Customhouse." Nevertheless, he was glad that he had fought the good fight against the "machine politicians" who "think of nothing higher than their own interests. I fear for your future. We cannot stand so corrupt a government for any great length of time." This was the last letter from father to son. Two months later Theodore, Senior, was dead of cancer, at the age of forty-six.

Although TR worshiped his father, he does not seem to have been particularly interested in the politics of reform. During the Collectorship battle, he had wanted to be a naturalist; later he thought of writing, and began to compose what proved to be, or so one is told, a magisterial study of the early years of the American navy, *The Naval War of 1812*. He also attended Columbia Law School until 1881, when he got himself elected to the New York State Assembly. He was twenty-three years old; as lively and bumptious as ever.

Much had been made of what a startling and original and noble thing it was for a rich young aristo to enter the sordid politics of New York State. Actually, quite a number of young men of the ruling class were going into politics, often inspired by fathers who had felt, like Theodore, Senior, that the republic could not survive so much corruption. In fact, no less a grandee than the young William Waldorf Astor had been elected to the Assembly (1877) while, right in the family, TR's Uncle Rob had served in Congress, as a Democrat. There is no evidence that Theodore went into politics with any other notion than to have an exciting time and to rise to the top. He had no theory of government. He was, simply, loyal to his class—or what he called, approvingly, "our kind." He found the Tammany politicians repellent on physical and social as well as political grounds.

To TR's credit, he made no effort at all to be one of the boys; quite the contrary. He played the city dude, to the hilt. In Albany, he arrived at his first Republican caucus, according to an eye-witness, "as if he had been ejected by a catapult. He had on an enormous great ulster . . . and he pulled off his coat; he was dressed in full dress, he had been to dinner somewhere. . . ." Even then, his high-pitched voice and upper-class accent proved to be a joy for imitators, just as his niece Eleanor's voice—so very like his— was a staple of mimics for fifty years. To the press, he was known, variously, as a "Jane-Dandy," "his Lordship," "Oscar Wilde," "the exquisite Mr. Roosevelt." He sailed above these epithets. He was in a hurry to . . . do what?

Mr. McCullough quotes Henry James's description of a similar character in *The Bostonians* (published five years after Theodore's entry into politics): "He was full of purpose to live . . . and with a high success; to become great, in order not to be obscure, and powerful not to be useless." In politics, it is character rather than ideas that makes for success; and the right sort of character combined with high energy can be fairly irresistible. Although TR was the most literary of our post–Civil War presidents, he had a mind that was more alert to fact than to theory. Like his father, he was against corruption and machine politicians, and that was pretty much that—until he met Samuel Gompers, a rising young trade unionist. Gompers took the dude around the tenements of New York City; showed him how immigrants were forced to live, doing such sweated labor as making cigars for wealthy firms. TR had planned to oppose a bill that the Cigarmaker's Union had sponsored, outlawing the manufacture of cigars "at home." After all, TR was a laissez-faire man; he had already opposed a minimum wage of $2.00 a day for municipal workers. But the tour of the tenements so shocked the dude that he supported the Cigar Bill.

TR also began to understand just how the United States was governed. Predictably, he found the unsavory Jay Gould at the center of a web that involved not only financiers but judges and newspaper proprietors and, to his horror, people that he knew socially. He describes how a kindly friend of the family, someone whom he referred to as a "member of a prominent law firm," explained the facts of life to him. Since *everyone*, more or less openly, did business with the likes of Jay Gould, TR was advised to give up "the reform play" and settle down as a representative member of the city's ruling—as opposed to governing—class. This was the sort of advice that was guaranteed to set him furiously in motion. He had found, at last, the Horatio-at-the-bridge role that he had been looking for. He took on the powers that be; and he coined a famous phrase, "the wealthy criminal class." Needless to say, he got nowhere in this particular battle, but by the time he was twenty-six he had made a national name for himself, the object of the exercise. He had also proven yet again that he could take it, was no sissy, had what Mark Sullivan was to call "a trait of ruthless righteousness."

In 1884, TR was a delegate to the Republican convention where, once again, James G. Blaine was a candidate. Like his father before him, TR joined the reformers; and together they fought to eliminate Blaine; but this time the gorgeous old trickster finally got the nomination, only to lose the election to Grover Cleveland. But by the time Cleveland was elected, the young widower and ex-assemblyman was playing cowboy in the Dakota Badlands. Just before TR disappeared into the wilderness, he made what was to be the most important decision of his career. In 1884 the reform Republicans deserted Blaine much as the antiwar Democrats were to abandon Hubert Humphrey in 1968. But TR had already made up his mind that he was going to have a major political career and so, cold-bloodedly, he endorsed Blaine: "I have been called a reformer but I am a Republican." For this show of solidarity with the Grand Old Party, he lost the decent opinion of the reformers and gained the presidency. He might have achieved both, but that would have required moral courage, something he had not been told about.

Give a sissy a gun and he will kill everything in sight. TR's slaughter of the animals in the Badlands outdoes in spades the butcheries of that sissy of a later era, Ernest Hemingway. Elks, grizzly bears, blacktail bucks are killed joyously while a bear cub is shot, TR reports proudly, "clean through . . . from end to end" (the Teddy bear was yet to be invented). "By Godfrey, but this is fun!" TR was still very much the prig, at least in speech: "He immortalized himself along the Little Missouri by calling to one of his cowboys, 'Hasten forward quickly here!' " Years later he wrote: "There were all kinds of things of which I was afraid at first, ranging from grizzly bears to 'mean' horses and gunfighters; but by acting as if I was not afraid I gradually ceased to be afraid."

There is something strangely infantile in this obsession with dice-loaded physical courage when the only courage that matters in political or even "real" life is moral. Although TR was often reckless and always domineering in politics, he never showed much real courage, and despite some trust-busting, he never took on the great ring of corruption that ruled and rules in this republic. But then, he was born a part of it. At best, he was just a dude with the reform play. Fortunately, foreign affairs would bring him glory. As Lincoln was the Bismarck of the American states, Theodore Roosevelt was the Kaiser Wilhelm II, a more fortunate and intelligent figure than the Kaiser but every bit as bellicose and conceited. Edith Wharton described with what pride TR showed her a photograph of himself and the Kaiser with the Kaiser's inscription: "President Roosevelt shows the Emperor of Germany how to command an attack."

I once asked Alice Longworth just why her father was such a war-lover. She denied that he was. I quoted her father's dictum: "No triumph of peace is quite as great as the supreme triumph of war." A sentiment to be echoed by yet another sissy in the next generation: "*Meglio un giorno da leone che cento anni da pecora.*" "Oh, well," she said, "that's the way they all sounded in those days." But they did not all sound that way. Certainly Theodore, Senior, would have been appalled, and I doubt if Eleanor really approved of Uncle Teddy's war-mongering.

As president TR spoke loudly and carried a fair-sized stick. When Colombia wouldn't give him the land that he needed for a canal, he helped invent Panama out of a piece of Colombia; and got his canal. He also installed the United States as the policeman of the Western Hemisphere. In order to establish an American hegemony in the Pacific, TR presided over the tail-end of the slaughter of more than half a million Filipinos who had been under the illusion that after the Spanish-American War they would be free to set up an independent republic under the leadership of Emilio Arguinaldo. But TR had other plans for the Philippines. Nice Mr. Taft was made the governor-general and one thousand American teachers of English were sent to the islands to teach the natives the sovereign's language.

Meanwhile, in the aftermath of the Boxer Rebellion, TR's "open-door policy" to China had its ups and downs. In 1905 the Chinese boycotted American goods because of American immigration policies, but the United States was still able to establish the sort of beachhead on the mainland of Asia that was bound to lead to what TR would have regarded as a bully fine war with Japan. Those of us who were involved in that war did not like it all that much.

In 1905, the world-famous Henry James came, in triumph, to Washington. He was a friend of Secretary of State John Hay and of Henry Adams. "Theodore Rex," as James called the president, felt obliged to invite the Master to the White House even though TR had denounced James as "effete" and a "miserable little snob" —it takes one to know one—while James thought of TR as "a dangerous and ominous Jingo." But the dinner was a success. James described the president as a "wonderful little machine . . . quite exciting to see. But it's really like something behind a great plate-glass window on Broadway." TR continued to loathe "the tone of satirical cynicism" of Henry James and Henry Adams while the Master finally dismissed the president as "the mere monstrous embodiment of unprecedented and resounding noise."

Alice Longworth used to boast that she and her father's viceroy Taft were the last Westerners to be received by the Dowager Empress of China. "We went to Peking. To the Forbidden City. And there we were taken to see this strange little old lady standing at the end of a room. Well, there was no bowing or scraping for us. So we marched down the room just behind the chamberlain, a eunuch, like one of those in that book of yours, *Justinian*, who slithered on his belly toward her. After he had announced us, she gave him a kick and he rolled over like a dog and slithered out." What had they talked about? She couldn't recall. I had my impression that she rather liked the way the empress treated her officials.

In the years before World War II, Alice was to be part of a marital rectangle. The heart having its reasons, Alice saw fit to conduct a long affair with the corrupt Senator William Borah, the so-called lion of Idaho, who had once roared, "I'd rather be right than president," causing my grandfather to murmur, "Of course, he was neither." In 1940, when the poor and supposedly virtuous Borah died, several hundred thousand dollars were found in his safety deposit box. Where had the money come from? asked the press. "He was my friend," said Senator Gore, for public consumption, "I do not speculate." But when I asked him who had paid off Borah, the answer was blunt. "The Nazis. To keep us out of the war." Meanwhile, Alice's husband, the Speaker of the House Nicholas Longworth, was happily involved with Mrs. Tracy (another Alice) Dows.

Rather late in life, Alice Longworth gave birth to her only child. In *The Making of Nicholas Longworth*, by Longworth's sister Clara de Chambrun, there is a touching photograph of Longworth holding in his arms a child whose features are unmistakably those of a lion's cub. "I should have been a grandmother, not a mother," Alice used to say of her daughter. But then, she had as little maternal instinct toward her only child as TR had had paternal instinct for her. When Nicholas Longworth died in 1931, Alice Dows told me how well Alice Longworth had behaved. "She asked me to go with her in the private train that took Nick back to Ohio. Oh, it was very moving. Particularly the way Alice treated me, as if *I* was the widow, which I suppose I was." She paused; then the handsome, square-jawed face broke into a smile and she used the Edwardian phrase: "Too killing."

When Alice Dows died she left me a number of her books. Among them was *The Making of Nicholas Longworth*, which I have just read. It is a loving, quite uninteresting account of what must have been a charming, not very interesting man. On the page where Alice Dows makes her appearance "one evening at Mrs. Tracy Dows's home. . . ," she had placed a four-leaf clover—now quite faded: nice emblem for a lucky lot.

In the electronic era, letter-writing has declined while diaries are kept only by those ill-educated, crazed, lone killers who feel obliged to report, in clinical detail, just how crazed and solitary they are as they prepare to assassinate political leaders. Except for Christopher Isherwood, I can think of no contemporary literary figure who has kept, for most of a lifetime, a journal. *The Diaries of Anaïs Nin* were, of course, her fiction. Fortunately, the pre-electronic Roosevelts and their friends wrote countless letters and journals and books, and Mr. McCullough has done a good job of selection; one is particularly grateful for excerpts from the writings of Elliott Roosevelt, a rather more natural and engaging writer than his industrious but not always felicitous older brother. Mr. McCullough's own style is easy to the point of incoherence. "The horse he rode so hard day after day that he all but ruined it," sounds more like idle dictation than written English. But, all in all, he has succeeded in showing us how a certain world, now lost, shaped the young Theodore Roosevelt. I think it worth noting that Simon and Schuster has managed to produce the worst set of bound galleys that I have ever read. There are so many misspellings that one has no sense of TR's own hit-or-miss approach to spelling, while two pages are entirely blank.

Now that war is once more thinkable among the thoughtless, Theodore Roosevelt should enjoy a revival. Certainly, the New Right will find his jingoism appealing, though his trust-busting will give less pleasure to the Honorable Society of the Invisible Hand. The figure that emerges from the texts of both Mr. McCullough and Mr. Morris is both fascinating and repellent. Theodore Roosevelt was a classic American sissy who overcame—or appeared to overcome—his physical fragility through "manly" activities of which the most exciting and ennobling was war.

As a politician-writer, Theodore Roosevelt most closely resembles Winston Churchill and Benito Mussolini. Each was as much a journalist as a politician. Each was a sissy turned showoff. The not unwitty Churchill—the most engaging of the lot—once confessed that if no one had been watching him he could quite easily have run away during a skirmish in the Boer War. Each was a romantic, in love with the nineteenth-century notion of earthly glory, best personified by Napoleon Bonaparte, whose eagerness to do in *his* biological superiors led to such a slaughter of alpha-males that the average French soldier of 1914 was markedly shorter than the soldier of 1800—pretty good going for a fat little fellow, five foot four inches tall—with, to be fair, no history of asthma.

As our dismal century draws to a close, it is fairly safe to say that no matter what tricks and torments are in store for us, we shall not see *their* like again. Faceless computer analysts and mindless cue-card readers will preside over our bright noisy terminus.

The New York Review of Books
AUGUST 13, 1981

The State of the
Union Revisited (1980)

F ive years and two presidents ago, I presented in the pages of
Esquire my own State of the Union Address, based on a chat
I'd been giving in various parts of the republic. Acting as a sort of
shadow president, I used to go around giving a true—well, Heisen-
berg's uncertainty principle being what it is, a *truer* report on the
state of the union than the one we are given each year by that loyal
retainer of the Chase Manhattan Bank, the American president,
who is called, depending on the year, Johnson, Nixon, Ford, Carter. Although the presidents now come and go with admirable
speed, the bank goes on forever, constantly getting us into deeper
and deeper trouble of the sort that can be set right—or wrong—
only by its man in the Oval Office. One of the bank's recent capers
has got the Oval One and us into a real mess. The de-Peacock-
Throned King of Kings wanted to pay us a call. If we did not give
refuge to the Light of the Aryans (Banksman David Rockefeller
and Banksman Henry Kissinger were the tactical officers involved),
the heir of Cyrus the Great would take all his money out of the
bank, out of Treasury bonds, out of circulation in North America.
Faced with a choice between loss of money and loss of honor and

good sense, Banksman Carter chose not to lose money. As a result, there will probably be a new president come November. But whether it is this Banksman or that, Chase Manhattan will continue to be served and the republic will continue to be, in Banksman Nixon's elegant phrase, shafted.

In 1973, Banksman D. Rockefeller set up something called the Trilateral Commission in order to bring together politicians on the make (a tautology if there ever was one) and academics like Kissinger, the sort of gung-ho employee who is always eager to start a war or to improve the bank's balance sheet. Not long after the Trilateral Commission came into being, I started to chat about it on television. Although I never saw anything particularly sinister in the commission itself (has any commission ever *done* anything?), I did think it a perfect symbol of the way the United States is ruled. When Trilateral Commission member Carter was elected president after having pretended to be An Outsider, he chose his vice-president and his secretaries of state, defense, and treasury, as well as the national security adviser, from Chase Manhattan's commission. I thought this pretty bold—even bald.

To my amazement, my warnings were promptly heeded by, of all outfits, the American Right, a group of zanies who ought deeply to love the bank and all its works. Instead, they affect to fear and loathe the Trilateral Commission on the ground that it is, somehow or other, an integral part of that international monolithic atheistic godless communist conspiracy that is bent on forcing honest American yeomen to get up at dawn and walk to work for the state as abortionists and fluoride dispensers. Needless to say, although the American right wing is a good deal stupider than the other fragile political wings that keep the republic permanently earthbound, their confusion in this matter is baffling. The bank is very much their America.

Although there has never been a left wing in the United States, certain gentle conservatives like to think of themselves as liberals, as defenders of the environment, as enemies of our dumber wars. I would think that they'd have seen in the bank's Trilateral Commission the perfect symbol of why we fight our dumber wars, why we destroy the environment. But not a single gentle liberal voice has ever been raised against the bank. I suppose this is because too many of them work for the Bank. . . . I shall now use the word Bank (capitalized, naturally) as a kind of shorthand not just for the Chase Manhattan but also for the actual ownership of the United

States. To quote from my earlier State of the Union message: "Four point four percent own most of the United States. . . . This gilded class owns 27 percent of the country's real estate. Sixty percent of all corporate stock, and so on." The Bank is the Cosa Nostra of the 4.4 percent. The United States government is the Cosa Nostra of the Bank.

For more than a century, our educational system has seen to it that 95.6 percent of the population grow up to be docile workers and consumers, paranoid taxpayers, and eager warriors in the Bank's never-ending struggle with atheistic communism. The fact that the American government gives back to the citizen-consumer very little of the enormous revenues it extorts from him is due to the high cost of what the Bank—which does have a sense of fun—calls freedom. Although most industrial Western (not to mention Eastern European) countries have national health services, the American taxpayer is not allowed this amenity because it would be socialism, which is right next door to godless communism and free love, followed by suicide in the long white Swedish night. A major part of our country's revenue must always go to the Pentagon, which then passes the money on to those client states, industries, and members of Congress with which the Bank does business. War is profitable for the Bank. Health is not.

Five years ago, incidentally, I said: "The defense budget is currently about a quarter of the national budget—$85 billion. . . . [It] is now projected for the end of the decade to cost us $114 billion. This is thievery. This is lunacy." The requested defense budget for the first year of our brand-new decade is $153.7 billion, which is still thievery, still lunacy—and highly inflationary to boot. But since the defense budget is at the heart of the Bank's system of control over the United States, it can never be seriously reduced. Or, to put it another way, cut the defense budget and the Bank will start to die.

Since my last State of the Union Address, the election law of 1971 has come into its ghastly own. The first effect of the law was to give us the four-year presidential campaign. The second treat we got from it was the presidency of Banksman Jimmy Carter. It is now plain that anyone who can get elected president under the new ground rules ought not to be allowed to take office.

For once, even the dullest of the Bank's depositors is aware that something is wrong. Certainly, there have never been quite so many demonstrably dim Banksmen running for president as there are in

1980. Part of this is historical: not since the country's bright dawn have first-rate people gone into politics. Other countries take seriously their governance. Whatever one might think of the politics of Giscard d'Estaing and Helmut Schmidt, each is a highly intelligent man who is proud to hold a place in government—unlike his American equivalent, who stays out of politics because the Bank fears the superior man. As a result, the contempt in which Carter is held by European and Japanese leaders is not so much the fault of what I am sure is a really swell Christian guy as it is due to the fact that he is intellectually inferior to the other leaders. They know history, economics, geography. He doesn't—and neither do his rivals. The Bank perfers to keep the brightest Americans hidden away in the branch offices. The dull and the docile are sent to Congress and the White House.

I don't know any thoughtful person who was not made even more thoughtful by the recent Canadian election. The new prime minister was not popular. He made mistakes. In the course of a half-hour vote of no confidence, the government fell. There was a nine-and-a-half-week campaign that cost about $60 million. At its end, the old prime minister was back. In a matter of weeks there had been a political revolution. If the United States had had a parliamentary system last April, we would have been relieved of Jimmy Carter as chief of government after his mess in the Iranian desert. But he is still with us, and the carnival of our presidential election goes on and on, costing tens of millions of dollars, while the candidates smile, shake hands, and try to avoid ethnic jokes and the demonstration of any semblance of intelligence. Although the economy is in a shambles and the empire is cracking up, the political system imposed upon us by the Bank does not allow any candidate to address himself seriously to any issue. I know that each candidate maintains, in some cases accurately, that he has superb position papers on all the great issues; but no one pays any attention— further proof that the system doesn't work. After all, since the Bank owns the media, the Bank is able to decide who and what is newsworthy and just how much deeptalk its depositors can absorb. Plainly, the third American republic is drawing to a close, and we must now design for ourselves a fourth republic, a democratic society not dedicated to war and the Bank's profits. Third republic? Fourth republic? What am I talking about? Let me explain.

The first American republic began with the revolution in 1776 and ended with the adoption of the Constitution in 1788. The first republic was a loose confederation of thirteen autonomous states. The second republic was also a fairly loose affair until 1861, when the American Bismarck, Abraham Lincoln, took the mystical position that no state could ever leave the Union. When the southern states disagreed, a bloody war was fought in order to create "a more perfect [sic] union." At war's end, our third and most imperial republic came into existence. This republic was rich, belligerent, hungry for empire. This republic's master was the Bank. This republic became, in 1945, the world's master. Militarily and economically, the third American republic dominated the earth. All should then have been serene: the mandate of Heaven was plainly ours. Unfortunately, the Bank made a fatal decision. To keep profits high, it decided to keep the country on a permanent wartime footing. Loyal Banksman Harry S Truman deliberately set out to frighten the American people. He told us that the Soviet Union was on the march while homegrown Reds were under every bed—all this at a time when the United States had atomic weapons and the Russians did not, when the Soviet Union was still in pieces from World War II and we were incredibly prosperous.

Those who questioned the Bank's official line were called commies or soft on communism. Needless to say, in due course, the Soviet Union did become the powerful enemy that the Bank requires in order to keep its control of the third republic. The business of our third republic is war, or defense, as it's been euphemistically called since 1949. As a result, of the thirty-five years since the end of World War II, the United States has managed to be at war (hot and cold) for thirty; and if the Bank has its way, we shall soon be at war again, this time on a really large scale. But then, as Banksman Grover Cleveland so presciently observed almost a century ago, "the United States is not a country to which peace is necessary."

There comes a time, however, when the waging of war is too dangerous even for Banksmen. There also comes a time when the crude politics of getting the people to vote against their own interests by frightening them with the Red Menace simply doesn't work. We are now in such a time. Clearly, a new sort of social arrangement is necessary.

The fact that half of those qualified to vote don't vote in presidential elections is proof that the third republic is neither credible nor truly legitimate. The fact that the Bank's inspired invention, the so-called two-party system (which is really one single Banks-party), is now collapsing is further proof that the fourth republic will require political parties that actually represent the various groups and classes in the country and do not simply serve the Bank. By breaking out of the two-party system this year, Banksman John Anderson has demonstrated in the most striking way that, like the Wizard of Oz, the two-party system never existed.

The time has come to hold another constitutional convention. Those conservatives known as liberals have always found this notion terrifying, because they are convinced that the powers of darkness will see to it that the Bill of Rights is abolished. This is always a possibility, but sometimes it's best to know the worst all at once rather than to allow those rights to be slowly taken away from us by, let us say, the present majority of the Supreme Court, led by Banksman Burger.

In the development of a new Constitution, serious attention should be paid to the Swiss political arrangement. Its cantonal system is something that might work for us. The United States could be divided into autonomous regions: northern California, Oregon, and Washington would make a fine Social Democratic society, while the combined states of Texas, Arizona, and Okla-homa could bring back slavery and the minstrel show. There ought to be something for everybody to choose from in the United States, rather than the current homogenized overcentralized state that the Bank has saddled us with. The Swiss constitution has another attrac-tive feature: the citizens have the right to hold a referendum and rescind, if they choose, a law. No need for a Howard Jarvis to yodel in the wilderness: the Jarvis Effect would be institutionalized.

Ideally, the fourth republic should abandon the presidential sys-tem for a parliamentary one. The leader of a majority in Congress would form the government. Out of respect for the rocks at Mount Rushmore, we would retain the office of president, but the president would be a figurehead and not what he is today—a dictator who is elected by half the people from a very short list given them by the Banksparty.

Five years ago I got a good reaction with this: "I propose that no candidate for any office be allowed to buy space on television or in any newspaper or other medium. This will stop cold the present system where presidents and congressmen are bought by corpora-tions and gangsters. . . . Instead, television (and the rest of the media) would be required by law to provide prime time (and space) for the various candidates.

"I would also propose a four-week election period as opposed to the current four-year one. Four weeks is more than enough time to present the issues. To show us the candidates in interviews, debates, *un*controlled encounters in which we can actually see who the candidate really is, answering tough questions, his record up there for all to examine."

One aspect of our present patchwork Constitution that should be not only retained but strengthened is that part of the First Amendment that says "Congress shall make no law respecting an establishment of religion, or prohibiting the free exercise thereof" —which, according to Justice Hugo Black, "means at least this: Neither a state nor the Federal Government can . . . pass laws which aid one religion, aid all religions, or prefer one religion over another. Neither can [they] force nor influence a person to go to or remain away from church against his will or force him to profess a belief or disbelief in any religion." This is clear-cut. This is noble. This has always been ignored—even in the two pre-Bank republics. Religion, particularly the Judaeo-Christian variety, is hugely favored by the federal government. For one thing, the revenues of every religion are effectively tax-exempt. Billions of dollars are taken in by the churches, temples, Scientological basements, and Moonie attics, and no tax need be paid. As a result, various fundamentalist groups spend millions of dollars propagandizing over the airwaves, conducting savage crusades against groups that they don't like, mixing in politics. Now, a church has as much right as an individual to try to persuade others that its way is the right way, but not even the Bank is allowed to advertise without first doing its duty as a citizen and paying (admittedly too few) taxes.

The time has come to tax the income of the churches. After all, they are essentially money-making corporations that ought to pay tax at the same rate secular corporations do.* When some of the Founders proposed that church property be tax-exempt, they meant the little white church house at the corner of Elm and Main—not the $25-billion portfolio of the Roman Catholic Church, nor the even weirder money-producing shenanigans of L. Ron Hubbard, a science fiction writer who is now the head of a wealthy "religion" called Scientology, or of that peculiar Korean gentleman who may

* Or did, pre-Reagan.

or may not be an agent of Korean intelligence but who is certainly the boss of a "religion" that takes in many millions of tax-free dollars a year.

Until the height of the cold war in the 1950s, the American government kept God in his place—in heaven, presumably. But the Bank-created anti-communist hysteria of the era gave the Christers a wonderful opportunity to do such things as get Congress to put "In God We Trust" on the money—a sly gesture, come to think of it: God and the dollar joined, as it were, in holy matrimony, a typical Bank ploy. Needless to say, the Founders would have been horrified. Here are two comments *not* to be found in any American public-school book. Thomas Jefferson: "The day will come when the mystical generation of Jesus, by the Supreme Being as his father, in the womb of a virgin, will be classed with the fable of the generation of Minerva in the brain of Jupiter." John Adams (in a letter to Jefferson): "Twenty times, in the course of my late reading, have I been on the point of breaking out. 'This would be the best of all possible worlds, if there was no religion in it.'" But since the Bank approves of most religions ("Slaves, obey thy masters" is an injunction it finds irresistible), superstition continues to flourish. On the other hand, if we were to tax the various denominations, a good many religions would simply wither away, on the ground that they had ceased to be profitable to their managers.

Five years ago, I was eager to make changes that would benefit society without costing any money. I see now, in a curious way, that most of those changes were tied up with religion. Although our Constitution forbids the government to favor any religion, the government favors *all* religions by allowing them to escape paying taxes. Although the federal government has not gone so far as to oblige everyone to believe that Jesus was divine, a number of Moses–Jesus–Saint Paul laws are on the books, causing all sorts of havoc and making a joke of our pretense of being a free or even a civilized society. In 1975, I said: "Roughly eighty percent of police work in the United States has to do with the regulation of our private morals. By that I mean controlling what we drink, eat, smoke, put into our veins—not to mention trying to regulate with whom and how we have sex, with whom and how we gamble. As a result, our police are among the most corrupt in the Western world." This used to cause some distress with certain audiences. But I'd trudge on: "Therefore, let us remove from the statute books all laws that have to do with *private* morals—what are called victimless crimes.

If a man or woman wants to be a prostitute, that is his or her affair. It is no business of the state what we do with our bodies sexually. Obviously laws will remain on the books for the prevention of rape and the abuse of children, while the virtue of our animal friends will continue to be protected by the SPCA." Relieved laughter. He can't really mean that sin should go unpunished, no matter what those old WASP atheists who started the country had in mind.

"All drugs should be legalized and sold at cost to anyone with a doctor's prescription." Gasps! Cries! Save our children! I pointed out that our children would be saved from the playground pusher because there would be no profit for the pusher—a brand-new thought. "Legalization will also remove the Mafia and other big-time drug dispensers from the scene, just as the repeal of Prohibition eliminated the bootleggers of whiskey forty years ago." I didn't add that the absolute political corruption of the United States can be traced to that "noble experiment" when the Christers managed to outlaw whiskey—an unconstitutional act if there ever was one. As a result, practically everyone broke the law, and gradually lawlessness became a habit, while organized crime became a huge business of Banklike proportions (and connections).

"Obviously drug addiction is a bad thing. But in the interest of good law and good order, the police must be removed from the temptation that the current system offers them and the Bureau of Narcotics should be abolished." That would be the trick of the week! If the bureau were ever to eliminate all drugs, the bureau would be itself eliminated. Therefore . . . The logic is clear. But few can follow it, because the brainwashing has been too thorough.

"I worry a good deal about the police because traditionally they are the supporters of fascist movements, and America is as prone to fascism as any other country. Individually, no one can blame the policeman. He is the way he is because Americans have never understood the Bill of Rights. Since sex, drugs, alcohol, gambling, are proscribed by various religions, the states have made laws against them." I was too tactful in those days to add that the enslavement of the blacks (accursed descendants of Ham) and the persecution of the Jews (Christ-killers forever) and homosexualists (a duet of male angels *claim* to have been threatened with rape by a number of men in downtown Sodom), as well as the deep dislike and mistrust of woman as unclean, all derive from that book that Jimmy Carter likes to read regularly in Spanish and that Presidents Adams and Jefferson did not really like to read at all.

During the 1960 presidential campaign, Richard Nixon referred
to John Kennedy's Catholicism six times in practically a single
breath; he then said, piously, that he did not think religion ought to
play any part in any political election—unless, maybe, *the candidate had no religion* (and Nixon shuddered ever so slightly). As
the First Criminal knew only too well, religion is the most important force not only in American politics but in world politics, too.
Currently, the ninth-century Imam at Qom is threatening an Islamic
holy war against Satan America. Currently, the fifth-century-B.C.
prime minister of Israel is claiming two parcels of desirable real
estate because an ancient text says that Jews once lived there. Currently, the eleventh-century Polish pope is conducting a series of
tours in order to increase his personal authority and to shore up a
church whose past excesses caused so much protest that a rival
Protestant church came into being—and it, in turn, hates . . .

Religion is an endless and complicated matter, and no one in his
right mind can help agreeing with John Adams. Unfortunately,
most of the world is not in its right mind; and the Bank can take
some credit for this. For years, relations were kept tense between
poor American whites and poor blacks (would you let your sister
marry one?), on the ground that if the two groups ever got together in a single labor union, say, they could challenge the Bank's
authority. Religion is also the basis of those laws governing personal
conduct that keep the prisons overcrowded with people who get
drunk, take dope, gamble, have sex in a way that is not approved
by the holy book of a Bronze Age nomad tribe as reinterpreted by
a group of world-weary Greeks in the first centuries of the last
millennium.

The thrust of our laws at the beginning of the country—and
even now—is to make what these religions regard as sin secular
crimes to be punished with fines and prison terms. The result? Last
year the United States shelled out some $4 billion to keep 307,000
sinners locked up. Living conditions in our prisons are a famous
scandal. Although the National Advisory Commission on Criminal
Justice Standards and Goals declared in 1973 that "prisons should
be repudiated as useless for any purpose other than locking away
people who are too dangerous to be allowed at large in a free
society," there are plans to build more and more prisons to brutalize
more and more people who are, for the most part, harmless. In
much of Scandinavia, even vicious criminals are allowed a degree
of freedom to work so that they can lead useful lives, turning over

a part of the money that they earn to their victims. At present, at least five American states are experimenting with a compensatory system. All agree that the new way of handling so-called property offenders is a lot cheaper than locking them up at a cost that, in New York State, runs to $26,000 a year—more than enough to send a lively lad to Harvard, where he will soon learn how to commit his crimes against property in safe and legal ways.

But since the Bank is not happy with the idea of fewer prisons, much less with the idea of fewer crimes on the books, the Bank has now come up with something called the Omnibus Crime Bill. This has been presented in the Senate by Banksman Kennedy as S. 1722 and in the House of Representatives by Banksman the Reverend Robert F. Drinan as H.R. 6233. Incidentally, Banksman Drinan will presently give up his seat in the House at the order of the Polish pope, who says that he does not want his minions in politics, which is nonsense. A neo-fascist priest sits as a deputy in the Italian Parliament, just across the Tiber from the Vatican. Father Drinan, alas, is liberal. He does not favor the Right to Life movement. On the other hand, he is a loyal Banksman—hardly a conflict of interest, since the Vatican has an account with the Bank, administered until recently by Michele Sindona, a master criminal.

The point of these two bills is as simple as the details are endlessly complex: the Bank wants more power to put in prison those people who challenge its authority. At the moment it looks as if this repressive legislation will become law, because, as Republican Senator James A. McClure has pointed out, the Omnibus Crime Bill is now "a law unto itself, a massive re-creation whose full implications are known only by its prosecutorial draftsmen (in the Justice Department)." Some features:

If, during a war, you should advise someone to evade military service, to picket an induction center, to burn a draft card, *you* can go to jail for five years while paying a fine of $250,000 (no doubt lent you by the bank at 20 percent).

If, as a civilian, you speak or write against a war in such a way that military authorities think you are inciting insubordination, you can get up to ten years in prison or pay a fine of $250,000, or both. If, as a civilian, you write or speak against a war or against conditions on a military installation, and if the Bank is conducting one of its wars at the time (according to the bill—by omission—a war is not something that Congress declares anymore), you can get ten years in prison and pay the usual quarter-million-dollar fine. If the

Bank is not skirmishing some place, you can go to jail for only five years while forking out a quarter mill.

If you break a federal law and tell your friendly law enforcer that you did not break that federal law, and if he has corroboration from another friendly cop that you did, you have made a False Oral Statement to a Law Enforcement Officer, for which you can get two years in the slammer after paying the customary quarter mill.

Anyone who refuses to testify before a grand jury, court, or congressional committee, even though he has claimed his constitutional (Fifth Amendment) right against self-incrimination, can be imprisoned if he refuses to exchange his constitutional right to remain silent for a grant of *partial* immunity from prosecution.

The Bank's deep and abiding love of prison requires that alternatives to prison not be encouraged. According to a 1978 Congressional Research Service report, this bill (then S. 1437), enacted and enforced, would add anywhere from 62.8 to 92.8 percent to our already overcrowded federal prisons. The Bank's dream, plainly, is to put all its dissident depositors either in prison or, if they're young enough, into the army, where they lose most of their civil rights.

Needless to say, the press gets it in the chops. If you're a newspaperman and you refuse to identify your sources for a story, you are Hindering Law Enforcement, for which you can get the usual five and pay the usual quarter. If you receive documentary proof that the government is breaking the law or that its officials are corrupt, you may be guilty of Defrauding the Government, and you can get the old five and pay a quarter. On the other hand, if you are a public servant who blows the whistle on government corruption or criminality, you can get only two and pay a quarter: the Bank has a certain compassion for apostate tellers.

Finally, a judge will have the right to put any person accused of any crime in prison before he has been tried, and that same judge can then deny the accused bail for any reason that appeals to him. This provision means the end of the basis of our legal system: you are innocent until you are proved guilty. According to the *Los Angeles Times*: "What is contemplated in S. 1722 is a fundamental reordering of the relationship between the people and the government, with the dominant emphasis placed on the power of the government. . . . Under the proposed radical revisions of federal criminal law now before Congress, we would be less free and ultimately less secure." But (at this writing) this huge, complex assault on our liberties continues to sail through the Congress, guided by Banksman Kennedy and Popesman Drinan, and it looks fairly certain to pass.*

When I first gave my State of the Union talk in 1975, I said, "In an age of chronic and worsening shortages, I would propose that all natural resources—oil, coal, minerals—be turned over to the people, to the government." I still think nationalization a good idea. Also, our government should deal directly with the oil-producing states, eliminating, as middleman, the oil companies. A dollar that Mobil Oil does not earn will be a dollar that an American gets to keep. I also proposed that "since none of us trusts our government to do anything right—much less honest—national resources should be a separate branch of the government, co-equal with the other three but interconnected so that Congress can keep a sharp eye on its funding and the courts on its fairness. The president, any president, on principle, should be kept out of anything that has to do with the economy."

Plainly, there is panic in the boardroom of the Bank. A number of things have started to go wrong all at once. Since energy will soon be in short supply to all the world, the third republic will be particularly hard hit, because the Bank is not capable of creating alternatives to the conventional unrenewable (and so highly profitable) sources of energy, any more than the Bank was able to anticipate the current crisis of small car versus gas-guzzler, something that consumer-depositors had figured out some time ago when they demonstrated a preference for small economic models by buying foreign cars.

The empire is cracking up because the Banksmen have never had a very clear world view. On the one hand, they are superb pragmatists. They will do business with Mao, Stalin, Franco, the Devil, if profits can be made that way. On the other hand, simultaneously, they must continue to milk this great cow of a republic; and the only way they know to get their hands on our tax dollars is to frighten us with the menace of godless communism, not easily done when you're seen to be doing business quite happily with these godless predators. The final madness occurred when Banksman Nixon went to Peking and Moscow in search of new accounts (which he got on terms unfavorable to us) while continuing to rail against

---

* The bill was defeated in the fall of 1980 by the lame-duck Congress. Like Dracula, it is sure to rise again. Next time it will pass.

those two ruthless, inexorable enemies of all that we hold dear.
This sort of schizophrenia has switched off the public and made
our government a source of wonder and despair to its allies.

When Banksman Nixon was audited and found wanting, the
Bank itself came under scrutiny of a sort that it is not used to.
Lowly consumer-depositors now speak of a national "crisis of confidence." The ordinarily docile media have even revealed a few tips
of the iceberg—no, glacier—that covers with corruption our body
politic.

Now the masters of the third republic are striking back. They are
loosening the CIA's leash, which had been momentarily shortened
(or so they told us). They have also come up with a new charter
for the FBI that is now before the Senate (S. 1612). In testimony
before the Judiciary Committee, law professor emeritus T. I. Emerson of Yale was highly critical of the new powers given the FBI.
"The natural tendency of any system of law enforcement," he
testified, "is to formulate its doctrines, train its personnel, and utilize
its machinery to support social stability and thwart social change."
Among the features of the new charter that Emerson found dangerous was the right to initiate an investigation where there is a
suspicion, in the agency's eyes, that a person "will engage" in illegal
activity. This means that anyone is a potential target of the FBI
because anyone might somehow, someday, do something illegal.
The FBI also wants access to the financial records of political
associations—an invasion of political as well as personal freedom.
Finally, the new charter will pretty much remove the agency from
any outside scrutiny. In so doing, it will create something that our
pre-Bank republics refused to countenance: a centralized national
police force. Well, as that wily old fox Benjamin Franklin once
hinted, sooner or later every republic becomes a tyranny.

For 169 years, from the halls of Montezuma to the shores of
Tripoli, the United States was a military success, able to overlook
the odd scalped general or the White House that the British so
embarrassingly burned to the ground in 1814. With considerable
dash, we tore a chunk of land away from Mexico (which the Mex-
icans are now, sensibly, filling up again); next, we killed a million or so Filipinos (no one has ever determined just how many)
in order to establish ourselves as a regnant Pacific power at the beginning of this century; but then, after we got through two world
wars in fine shape, something started to go wrong. In fact, since
1945 nothing has gone right for us. The war in Korea was a draw.

The war in Vietnam was a defeat. Our constant meddling in the affairs of other countries has made us not only widely hated but, rather more serious, despised. Not unlike the Soviet Union, our opposite number, we don't seem able to maintain our helicopters properly or to gauge in advance the world's reactions to our deeds or to have sufficient intelligence to know when to make a run for it and when to stand still. What's wrong?

Those born since World War II have been taught to believe that the CIA has always been an integral part of American life. They don't know that the agency is only thirty-three years old, that it is essentially illegal not only in its activities (overthrowing a Chilean president here, an Iranian prime minister there) but also in its charter. The Constitution requires that "a regular Statement and Account of the Receipts and Expenditures of all Public Money shall be published from time to time." The CIA does no such thing: it spends billions of dollars a year exactly as it pleases. Although forbidden by law to operate inside the United States, the CIA has spied on American citizens at home, in merry competition with numerous other intelligence agencies whose single interest is the control of the American people in the name of freedom. Most Americans have heard of the FBI and the Treasury men and the Secret Service (though few Americans have a clear idea of what they actually do or of how much money they spend). On the other hand, hardly anyone knows about the National Security Agency, a miniature CIA run by the Defense Department. It has been estimated that in 1975, the NSA employed 20,000 civilians, used between 50,000 and 100,000 military personnel, and had a budget of $1 billion. Needless to say, the NSA is quite as illegal as the CIA— more so, in fact. The CIA was chartered, messily but officially, by Congress; but the NSA was created secretly by presidential directive in 1952, and Congress has never legalized the agency.

All good Americans want the budget balanced, and the liquidation of the CIA and the NSA would probably save anywhere from $10 billion to $20 billion a year. For those who are terrified that we won't have enough information about our relentless and godless enemy, the State Department is a most expensive piece of machinery whose principal purpose is—or was—the gathering of information about all the countries of the world. For underground, James Bond stuff, we should rely on the organization that was so useful to us when we were successful: army intelligence. Meanwhile, as a free society—the phrase no longer has much humor in it—we ought not to support tens of thousands of spies, secret agents, and dirty-tricksters, on the practical ground that a rich, lawless, and secret agency like the CIA could, with no trouble at all, take over the United States—assuming that it has not already done so.

The Bank hopes to maintain its power through the perpetuation of that garrison state it devised for us after World War II. This can be done only by involving the country in a series of small wars that will keep tax money flowing from the citizens to the Treasury to the Pentagon to the secret agencies and, eventually, to the Bank. Meanwhile, to stifle criticism, the Bank has ordered an all-out attack on the civil liberties of the people. There is little doubt that, from Banksman Kennedy to Banksman Thurmond, the entire political spectrum in the United States (which is always a single shade of green, just like the money) will work to take away as many of our traditional freedoms as it can. Happily, the Bank's marvelous incompetence, which gave us Nixon and Carter and is now offering (at this writing) Reagan or Bush "versus" Carter or Kennedy, is of a kind that is bound to fail. For one thing, everyone knows that small wars have a way of escalating; and though Banksmen Nixon and Bush view with what looks like equanimity World War III, the rest of the world—including, with luck, an aroused American citizenry—may call a halt to these mindless adventures for private profit. Finally, Anderson's candidacy *could* pull the plug on the two-party-system-that-is-really-one-party apparatus that has kept the Bank in power since the 1870s.*

Meanwhile, a new constitutional convention is in order. The rights guaranteed by the Founders in the old Constitution should be reinforced; the presidential form of government should be exchanged for a more democratic parliamentary system; the secret agencies should be abolished; the revenues of the country should go to create jobs, educational and health systems, alternative forms of energy, and so on. All those things, in fact, that the Bank says we can never afford. But I am sure that what countries less rich than ours can do, we can do.

Where will the money come from? Abolish the secret agencies, and gain at least $20 billion a year. Cut the defense budget by a third, and gain perhaps $50 billion. Tax the thousand and one religions, and get untold billions more. Before you know it, the chief

---

* "I believe in the two-party system," said Mr. Anderson in the course of his campaign, nicely pulling the plug on himself.

financial support of a government become gross and tyrannous will no longer be the individual taxpayer, that perennial patsy, but the Bank, whose entry into receivership will be the aim of the fourth, the good, the democratic republic that we must start to create sometime between now and 1984.

Esquire
AUGUST 1980

The Real
Two-Party System

I n the United States there are two political parties of equal size.
One is the party that votes in presidential elections. The other is
the party that does not vote in presidential elections. This year the
party that votes is divided into four parts: the Democratic, Republican, Libertarian and Citizens—and a number of fragments, including the independent candidacy of Republican John Anderson.
Forty-eight percent of the party that votes are blue-collar or
service workers; the rest tend to be white, middle-class and over
twenty-one years old. Seventy-five percent of the party that does
not vote are blue-collar or service workers in combination with
most of the eighteen-to-twenty-year-olds—whatever their estate.

Presidential elections are a bit like the Grammy Awards, where
an industry of real interest to very few people honors itself ful-
somely [correct use of this adverb] on prime-time television. Since
the party that does not vote will never switch on, as it were, the
awards ceremony, the party that does vote has to work twice as
hard to attract attention to get a rating.

As a result, media-men, -women and -persons analyze at length
and in bright shallow the three principal candidates of the one

party. To read, hear and watch the media-types, one would think that the election really mattered. Grave subjects are raised: Will Ronald Reagan get us into a war with the forests once he has uni-laterally zapped the trees in order to stop the pollution of Mount St. Helens? Will Jimmy Carter be able to balance the budget as he keeps, simultaneously, the interest rates high for the bankers and low for the homeowners? Will John Anderson ever again debate anyone on prime-time television, other than Regis Philbin, who is not national? These are the great issues in the year of our Lord 1980.

And it is the year of our Lord, in spades. Once- and twice-born Christians haven't been on such a rampage since World War I when they managed to add an amendment to the Constitution making it a crime for Americans to drink alcohol. Ironically, the Christers seemed to have turned away from their own twice-born Carter and twice-born Anderson. They prefer once-born Reagan (presumably, the rest of him is with the Lord), because Reagan is against Satan as represented by rights for women and homosexual-ists—two groups that get a bad press in the Old Testament, and don't do much better in the New. In fact, every candidate of the party that votes is being forced this year to take a stand on abor-tion, and if the stand should be taken on law and not on the Good Book, the result can be very ugly indeed for the poor politician be-cause abortion is against God's law: "Thou shalt not kill." Since this commandment is absolute, any candidate who favors abortion must be defeated as a Satanist. On the other hand, any candidate who does not favor capital punishment must be defeated as per-missive. In the land of the twice-born, the life of the fetus is sacred; the life of the adult is not.

Were the United States in less trouble, this election would be treated the way it deserves to be treated—like the Grammy Awards: those who are amused by such trivia will tune in; the rest will not. But the next president—even though he will simply be a continuation of the previous president ("clones" was the apt word used to describe Reagan and Carter by clone Kennedy) will have to face: 1) A nation whose per-capita income has dropped to ninth in the world; 2) A working population whose real discretion-ary income (money you get to spend out of what you earn) has declined 18 percent since 1973; 3) An industrial plant with the lowest productivity growth rate in the Western world—yes, we've sunk below England; 4) Double-digit inflation and high unemploy-

ment that, according to the latest Nobel prize person for economics, will go on into the foreseeable future; 5) A federal budget
of some $600 billion, of which 75 percent can never be cut back
(service on the national debt, Social Security, congressionally man-
dated programs, entitlements); 6) A mindlessly wasteful military
establishment whose clients in Congress and in the press can always
be counted on to yell, "the Russians are coming," when it is appropriations time on the Hill. And so the military budget grows while
our military capacity, by some weird law of inverse ratio, decreases.
The national debt increases.

The party that votes (to which I no longer belong) is now offering for our voting pleasure a seventy-year-old clone (if you're born
in 1911, you are now in your seventieth not sixty-ninth year)
whose life has been spent doing what a director tells him to do:
Hit the mark, Ronnie! He has now played so many parts that his
confusions and distortions of fact are even more surrealist than
those of Carter, and need not be repeated here. There is no reason
to assume that Reagan's administration would be any different
from that of Carter any more than Reagan's administration as governor of California was much different from that of Brown, Senior
—or Junior. The party that votes knows what it is doing when it
comes to giving awards on the big night. Also, the magnates who
control the party that votes are now acting upon Machiavelli's advice to the Prince: to gain perfect control over the state, keep the
people poor and on a wartime footing. Between the extortion
racket of the IRS and the bottomless pit of the Pentagon, this is
happening.

What to do? A vote for Carter, Reagan or Anderson is a vote
against the actual interests of the country. But for those who like
to vote against their interests, I would pass over the intelligent but
unadventurous Anderson as well as the old actor who knows nothing of economics ("Parity?"), foreign affairs ("Well, I've met the
King of Siam"), geography ("Pakistan?"), history ("Fascism was
really the basis of the New Deal") and return to office the inco-
herent incumbent on the ground that he cannot get it together sufficiently to start a war or a Lincoln-Douglas debate. But this is to
be negative. To be affirmative—for a compulsive voter, that is: vote
for the Citizens or Libertarian parties; each actually means something, like it or not.

Finally, if I may speak *ex cathedra*, as a leading—which is to say
following (we're all the same)—member of the party that does not

vote, I would suggest that those of you who are accustomed to vote join us in the most highly charged political act of all: not voting. When two-thirds—instead of the present half—refuse to acknowledge the presidential candidates, the election will lack all legitimacy. Then we shall be in a position to invoke Article Five of the Constitution and call a new constitutional convention where, together, we can devise new political arrangements suitable for a people who have never, in 193 years, been truly represented.

The Los Angeles Times
OCTOBER 26, 1980

The Second
American Revolution

Future generations, if there are any, will date the second American Revolution, if there is one, from the passage of California's Proposition 13 in 1978, which obliged the managers of that gilded state to reduce by more than half the tax on real estate. Historically, this revolt was not unlike the Boston Tea Party, which set in train those events that led to the separation of England's thirteen American colonies from the crown and to the creation, in 1787, of the First Constitution. And in 1793 (after the addition of the Bill of Rights) of the Second Constitution. And in 1865 of the Third Constitution, the result of those radical alterations made by the Thirteenth, Fourteenth, and Fifteenth amendments. Thus far we have had three Constitutions for three quite different republics. Now a Fourth Constitution—and republic—is ready to be born.

The people of the United States (hereinafter known forever and eternally as We) are deeply displeased with their government as it now malfunctions. Romantics who don't read much think that all will be well if we would only return, somehow, to the original Constitution, to the ideals of the founders, to a strict construction of what the Framers (nice word) of the First Constitution saw fit

to commit to parchment during the hot summer of 1787 at Philadelphia. Realists think that an odd amendment or two and better
men in government (particularly in the Oval Office, where too
many round and square pegs have, in recent years, rattled about)
would put things right.

It is taken for granted by both romantics and realists that the
United States is the greatest country on earth as well as in the history of the world, with a government that is the envy of the lesser
breeds just as the life-style of its citizens is regarded with a grinding of teeth by the huddled masses of old Europe—while Africa,
mainland Asia, South America are not even in the running. Actually, none of the hundred or so new countries that have been organized since World War II has imitated our form of government
—though, to a nation, the local dictator likes to style himself the
president. As for being the greatest nation on earth, the United
States's hegemony of the known world lasted exactly five years:
1945 to 1950. As for being envied by the less fortunate (in a *Los
Angeles Times* poll of October 1, 1980, 71 percent of the gilded
state's citizens thought that the United States had "the highest
living standard in the world today"), the United States has
fallen to ninth place in per-capita income while living standards are
higher for the average citizen in many more than eight countries.

Although this sort of information is kept from the 71 percent,
they are very much aware of inflation, high taxes, and unemployment. Because they know that something is wrong, Proposition 13,
once a mere gleam in the eye of Howard K. Jarvis, is now the law in
California and something like it has just been enacted in Massachusetts and Arkansas. Our ancestors did not like paying taxes on
their tea; we do not like paying taxes on our houses, traditionally
the only form of capital that the average middle-class American is
allowed to accumulate.

Today, thanks to the efforts of the National Taxpayers Union,
thirty state legislatures have voted in favor of holding a new constitutional convention whose principal object would be to stop the
federal government's systematic wrecking of the economic base of
the country by requiring, somewhat naïvely, a balanced federal
budget and, less naïvely, a limitation on the federal government's
power to print money in order to cover over-appropriations that
require over-borrowing, a process (when combined with a fifteen-
year decline in industrial productivity) that has led to double-digit
inflation in a world made more than usually dangerous by the

ongoing chaos in the Middle East from which the West's oil flows—or does not flow.

Even the newspapers that belong to the governing establishment of the republic are beginning to fret about that national malaise which used to trouble the thirty-ninth Oval One. Two years ago, *The New York Times* printed three articles, more in sorrow than in anger, on how, why, where, when did it all go wrong? "The United States is becoming increasingly difficult to govern," the *Times* keened, "because of a fragmented, inefficient system of authority and procedures that has developed over the last decade and now appears to be gaining strength and impact, according to political leaders, scholars and public interest groups across the country."

Were this not an observation by an establishment newspaper, one would think it a call for a Mussolini: "difficult to govern . . . inefficient system of authority. . . ." Surely, We the People govern, don't we? This sort of dumb sentiment is passed over by the *Times*, which notes that "the national political parties have continued to decline until they are little more than frameworks for nominating candidates and organizing Congress and some state legislatures." But this is all that our political parties have ever done (honorable exceptions are the first years of the Republican party and the only years of the Populists). The Framers did not want political parties—or factions, to use their word. So what has evolved over the years are two pieces of electoral machinery devoted to the acquiring of office—and money. Since neither party represents anything but the interests of those who own and administer the country, there is not apt to be much "choice" in any election.

Normally, *The New York Times* is perfectly happy with any arrangement of which the *Times* is an integral part. But a series of crazy military adventures combined with breathtaking mismanagement of the economy (not to mention highly noticeable all-out corruption among the politicos) has thrown into bright relief the failure of the American political system. So the thirty-ninth Oval One blames the people while the people blame the lousy politicians and wish that Frank Capra would once more pick up the megaphone and find us another Gary Cooper (*not* the second lead) and restore The Dream.

Serious establishment types worry about the Fragmentation of Power. "Our political system has become dominated by special interests," said one to the *Times*, stars falling from his eyes like crocodile tears. After all, our political system is—and was—the invention of those special interests. The government has been from the beginning the *cosa nostra* of the few and the people at large have always been excluded from the exercise of power. None of our rulers wants to change this state of affairs. Yet the heirs of the Framers are getting jittery; and sense that something is going wrong somewhere. But since nothing can ever be their fault, it must be the fault of a permissive idle electorate grown fat (literally) before our eyes, which are television. So give the drones less wages; more taxes; and put them on diets.

But the politician must proceed warily; if he does not, that 71 percent which has been conned into thinking that they enjoy the highest standard of living in the world might get suspicious. So for a while the operative word was "malaise" in political circles; and no effort was made to change anything. Certainly no one has recognized that the principal source of all our problems is the Third Constitution, which allows the big property owners to govern pretty much as they please, without accountability to the people or to anyone else, since for at least a century the Supreme Court was perhaps the most active—even reckless—part of the federal machinery, as we shall demonstrate.

There is more than the usual amount of irony in the fact that our peculiar Constitution is now under siege from those who would like to make it either more oppressive (the Right-to-Lifers who want the Constitution to forbid abortion) or from those sly folks who want to make more and more money out of their real estate shelters. But no matter what the motive for change, change is now very much in the air; and that is a good thing.

This autumn, the counsel to the president, Mr. Lloyd N. Cutler, proposed some basic changes in the Constitution.* Although Mr. Cutler's approach was tentative and highly timid (he found no fault at all with the Supreme Court—because he is a partner in a Washington law firm?), he does think that it is impossible for a president to govern under the present Constitution because the separation of powers has made for a stalemate between executive and legislative branches. Since "we are not about to revise our own Constitution so as to incorporate a true parliamentary system," he proceeded to make a number of suggestions that would indeed give us a quasi-parliamentary form of government—president, vice

* *Foreign Affairs*, Fall 1980.

president, and representative from each congressional district would all be elected at the same time for a four-year term (Rep. Jonathan Bingham has such a bill before the House); half the Cabinet to be selected from the Congress where they would continue to sit—and answer questions as in England; the president would have the power, once in his term, to dissolve the Congress and hold new elections—and the Congress would have the power, by a two-thirds vote, to call for a new presidential election; et cetera. Mr. Cutler throws out a number of other notions that would involve, at most, amendments to the Constitution; he believes that a new constitutional convention is a "non-starter" and so whatever change that is made must originate in the government as it now is even though, historically, no government has ever voluntarily dissolved itself.

Mr. Cutler also suffers from the malaise syndrome, contracted no doubt while serving in the Carter White House: "The public—and the press—still expect the President to govern. But the President cannot achieve his overall program, and the public cannot fairly blame the President because he does not have the power to legislate and execute his program." This is perfect establishment nonsense. The president and the Congress together or the president by himself or the Supreme Court on its own very special power trip can do virtually anything that they want to do as a result of a series of usurpations of powers that have been taking place ever since the Second Constitution of 1793.

When a president claims that he is blocked by Congress or Court, this usually means that he does not want to take a stand that might lose him an election. He will then complain that he is stymied by Congress or Court. In 1977, Carter could have had an energy policy *if* he had wanted one. What the president cannot get directly from Congress (very little if he knows how to manage those princes of corruption), he can often obtain through executive order, secure in the knowledge that the House of Representatives is not apt to exercise its prerogative of refusing to fund the executive branch: after all, it was nearly a decade before Congress turned off the money for the Vietnam war. In recent years, the presidents have nicely put Congress over a barrel through the impounding of money appropriated for projects displeasing to the executive. Impounded funds combined with the always vast Pentagon budget and the secret revenues of the CIA give any president a plump cushion on which to rest his Pharaonic crook and flail.

Obviously, a president who does not respect the decent opinion

of mankind (namely, *The New York Times*) can find himself
blocked by the Court and impeached by Congress. But the Nixon
misadventure simply demonstrated to what extremes a president
may go before his money is turned off—before the gates of Lewis-
berg Federal Penitentiary, like those to Hell or Disneyland, swing
open.

Carter could have given us gas rationing, disciplined the oil
cartels, encouraged the development of alternative forms of energy.
He did none of those things because he might have hurt his chances
of reelection. So he blamed Congress for preventing him from
doing what he did not want to do. This is a game that all presidents
play—and Congress, too. Whenever the Supreme Court strikes
down a popular law which Congress has been obliged to enact
against its better judgment, the Supreme Court gets the blame for
doing what the Congress wanted to do but dared not. Today
separation of powers is a useful device whereby any sin of omission
or commission can be shifted from one branch of government to
another. It is naïve of Mr. Cutler to think that the president he
worked for could not have carried out almost any program *if he
had wanted to*. After all, for eight years Johnson and Nixon prose-
cuted the longest and least popular war in American history by
executive order. Congress' sacred and exclusive right to declare
war was ignored (by Congress as well as by the presidents) while
the Supreme Court serenely fiddled as Southeast Asia burned. Incidentally, it is startling to note that neither Congress nor the Court
has questioned the *principle* of executive order, even in the famous
steel seizure case.

What *was* the original Constitution all about? I mean by this, what
was in the document of 1787 as defended in the Federalist Papers
of 1787–1788 by Madison, Hamilton, and Jay. Currently, Ferdi-
nand Lundberg's *Cracks in the Constitution* is as good a case history
of that Constitution (and its two successors) as we are apt to get
this troubled season. Lundberg is the latest—if not the last—in the
great line of muckrakers (TR's contemptuous phrase for those
who could clean with Heraclean zeal the national stables which he,
among others, had soiled) that began with Steffens and Tarbell.
Luckily for us, Lundberg is still going strong.

The father of the country was the father if not of the Constitution
of the convention that met in May 1787, in Philadelphia. Washington had been troubled by the civil disorders in Massachusetts in

particular and by the general weakness of the original Articles of Confederation in general. From Mount Vernon came the word; and it was heard—and obeyed—all around the states. Quick to respond was Washington's wartime aide Alexander Hamilton, who knew exactly what was needed in the way of a government. Hamilton arrived at Philadelphia with a scheme for a president and a senate and a supreme court to serve for life—while the state governors would be appointed by the federal government.

Although neither John Adams nor John Jay was present in the flesh at Philadelphia, Jay's handiwork, the constitution of New York State (written with Gouverneur Morris and R. J. Livingston), was on view as was that of John Adams, who wrote nearly all of the Massachusetts state constitution; these two charters along with that of Maryland were the basis of the convention's final draft, a curious document which in its separation of powers seemed to fulfill not only Montesquieu's cloudy theories of separation of powers but, more precisely, was a mirror image of the British tripartite arrangement of crown, bicameral legislature, and independent judiciary. Only the aged Franklin opted for a unicameral legislature. But the other Framers had a passion for England's House of Lords; and so gave us the Senate.

Lundberg discusses at some length just who the Framers were and where they came from and how much money they had. The state legislatures accredited seventy-four men to the convention. Fifty-five showed up that summer. About half drifted away. Finally, "no more than five men provided most of the discussion with some seven more playing fitful supporting roles." Thirty-three Framers were lawyers (already the blight had set in); forty-four were present or past members of Congress; twenty-one were rated rich to very rich—Washington and the banker Robert Morris (soon to go to jail where Washington would visit him) were the richest; "another thirteen were affluent to very affluent"; nineteen were slave owners; twenty-five had been to college (among those who had *not* matriculated were Washington, Hamilton, Robert Morris, George Mason—Hamilton was a Columbia dropout). Twenty-seven had been officers in the war; one was a twice-born Christian—the others tended to deism, an eighteenth-century euphemism for agnosticism or atheism.

All in all, Lundberg regards the Framers as "a gathering of routine politicians, eyes open for the main chance of a purely material nature. . . . What makes them different from latter-day politicians is that in an age of few distractions, many—at least twenty—were readers to varying extents in law, government, history and classics."

Lundberg does not accept the traditional American view that a consortium of intellectual giants met at Philadelphia in order to answer once and for all the vexing questions of how men are to be governed. Certainly, a reading of the Federalist Papers bears out Lundberg. Although writers about the Constitution like to mention Locke, Hume, Montesquieu and the other great savants of the Enlightenment as godfathers to the new nation, Montesquieu is quoted only four times in the Federalist Papers; while Hume is quoted just once (by Hamilton) in a passage of ringing banality. Locke is not mentioned. Fans of the Framers can argue that the spirit of Locke is ever-present; but then non-fans can argue that the prevailing spirit of the debate is that of the never-mentioned but always felt Hobbes. There is one reference each to Grotius, Plato, and Polybius. There are three references to Plutarch (who wrote about great men) and three to Blackstone (who showed the way to greatness—or at least the higher solvency—to lawyers). God is mentioned three times (in the Thank God sense) by Madison, a clergyman's son who had studied theology. Jesus, the Old and New Testaments, abortion, and women's rights are not alluded to. The general tone is that of a meeting of the trust department of Sullivan and Cromwell.

Lundberg quotes Merrill Jensen as saying, "Far more research is needed before we can know, if ever, how many men actually voted for delegates to the state conventions [which chose the Framers]. An old guess that about 160,000 voted—that is, not more than a fourth or fifth of the total adult (white) male population—is probably as good as any. About 100,000 of these men voted for supporters of the Constitution and about 60,000 for its opponents." It should be noted that the total population of the United States in 1787 was about 3,000,000, of which some 600,000 were black slaves. For census purposes, each slave would be counted as three-fifths of a person within the First Republic.

The Framers feared monarchy and democracy. In order to prevent the man who would be king from assuming dictatorial powers and the people at large from seriously affecting the business of government, the Framers devised a series of checks and balances within a tripartite government that would, they hoped (none was very optimistic: they were practical men), keep the people and their passions away from government and the would-be dictator hedged 'round with prohibitions.

In the convention debates, Hamilton took on the romantic notion of the People: "The voice of the people has been said to be the voice of God; and however generally this maxim has been quoted and believed, it is not true in fact. The people are turbulent and changing; they seldom judge or determine right. Give therefore to [the rich and wellborn] a distinct, permanent share in the government." The practical old Tory Gouverneur Morris took the same view, though he expressed himself rather more serenely than the fierce young man on the make: "The rich will strive to establish their dominion and enslave the rest. They always did. They always will. The proper security against them is to form them into a separate interest." Each was arguing for a Senate of lifetime appointees, to be chosen by the state legislatures from the best and the richest. It is curious that neither envisioned political parties as the more natural way of balancing economic interests.

Since Hamilton's dark view of the human estate was shared rather more than less by the Framers ("Give all power to the many, they will oppress the few. Give all power to the few, they will oppress the many"), the House of Representatives was intended to be the principal engine of the tripartite government. Like the British Parliament, the House was given (in Hamilton's words) "The exclusive privilege of originating money bills. . . . The same house will possess the sole right of instituting impeachments; the same house will be the umpire in all elections of the President. . . ." And Hamilton's ultimate defense of the new Constitution (*Federalist Paper* No. 60) rested on the ingenious way that the two houses of Congress and the presidency were chosen: "The House of Representatives . . . elected immediately by the people, the Senate by the State legislatures, the President by electors chosen for that purpose by the people, there would be little probability of a common interest to cement these different branches in a predilection for any particular class of electors."

This was disingenuous: the electoral franchise was already so limited in the various states that only the propertied few had a hand in electing the House of Representatives and the state legislatures. Nevertheless, this peculiar system of government was a success in that neither the mob nor the dictator could, legally at least, prevail. The turbulent "democratic" House would always be reined in by the appointed senators in combination with the indirectly elected president and his veto. The Constitution gave the oligarch, to use Madison's word, full possession of the government—the object of the exercise at Philadelphia. Property would be defended, as George Washington had insisted that it should be. Since Jefferson's teeth were set on edge by the word property, the euphemism "pursuit of happiness" had been substituted in the Declaration of Independence. Much pleased with this happy phrase, Jefferson recommended it highly to the Marquis de Lafayette when he was Rights of Man-ing it in France.

The wisest and shrewdest analysis of how the House of Representatives would evolve was not provided by the would-be aristo Hamilton but by the demure James Madison. In *Federalist Paper* No. 59, Madison tried to set at ease those who feared that popular gathering in whose horny hands had been placed the national purse. Madison allowed that as the nation increased its population, the House would increase its membership. But, said he with perfect candor and a degree of complacency, "The people can never err more than in supposing that by multiplying their representatives beyond a certain limit they strengthen the barrier against the government of the few. Experience will forever admonish them that . . . they will counteract their own views by every addition to their representatives. The countenance of the government may become more democratic, but the soul that animates it will be more oligarchic" because "the greater the number composing [a legislative assembly] the fewer will be the men who will in fact direct their proceedings." Until the present—and temporary—breakdown of the so-called lower House, this has proved to be the case.

By May 29, 1790, the Constitution had been ratified by all the states. The need for a bill of rights had been discussed at the end of the convention but nothing had been done. Rather than call a second convention, the Bill of Rights was proposed—and accepted —as ten amendments to the new Constitution. A principal mover for the Bill of Rights was George Mason of Virginia, who had said, just before he left Philadelphia, "This government will set out [commence] a moderate aristocracy: it is at present impossible to foresee whether it will, in its operation, produce a monarchy, or a corrupt, tyrannical [oppressive] aristocracy: it will most probably vibrate some years between the two, and then terminate in the one or the other." The words in brackets were supplied by fellow Virginian—and notetaker—Madison. As the ancient Franklin observed brightly, sooner or later every republic becomes a tyranny. They liked reading history, the Framers.

But the wild card in the federal apparatus proved not to be the predictable Congress and the equally predictable presidency whose twistings and turnings any reader of Plutarch might have anticipated. The wild card was the Supreme Court.

Lundberg calls attention to the following language of Article III of the Constitution.

> "The Supreme Court shall have appellate jurisdiction, both as to law and fact, *with such exceptions, and under such regulations as the Congress shall make.*"
>
> The preceding twelve words [he continues] are emphasized because they are rarely alluded to in discussions about the Court. They bring out that, under the Constitution, the Supreme Court is subject to regulation by Congress, which may make exceptions among the types of cases heard, individually or by categories. Congress, in short, is explicitly empowered by the Constitution to regulate the Court, not *vice versa.*

Certainly, the Court was never explicitly given the power to review acts of Congress. But all things evolve and it is the nature of every organism to expand and extend itself.

In 1800, the outgoing Federalist President John Adams made a last-minute appointment to office of one William Marbury. The incoming Republican President Jefferson ordered his secretary of state Madison to deny Marbury that office. Marbury based his right to office on Section 13 of Congress' Judiciary Act of 1789. Federalist Chief Justice John Marshall responded with marvelous cunning. In 1803 (*Marbury* v. *Madison*) he found unconstitutional Section 13, the work of Congress; therefore, the Court was unable to go forward and hear the case. The partisan Jefferson was happy. The equally partisan Marshall must have been secretly ecstatic: he had set a precedent. In passing, as it were, Marshall had established the right of the Supreme Court to review acts of Congress.

The notion of judicial review of the Executive or of Congress was not entirely novel. Hamilton had brought up the matter in 1787 (*Federalist Paper* No. 78). "In a monarchy [the judiciary] is an excellent barrier to the despotism of the prince; in a republic it is a no less excellent barrier to the encroachments and representations of the representative body." But the other Framers did not accept, finally, Hamilton's view of the Court as a disinterested umpire with veto power over the legislative branch. Yet Hamilton had made his case most persuasively; and he has been much echoed by subsequent upholders of judicial review.

Hamilton believed that the judiciary could never be tyrannous because it lacked real power; he does admit that "some perplexity respecting the rights of the courts to pronounce legislative acts void because contrary to the Constitution, has arisen from an imagination that the doctrine would imply a superiority of the judiciary to the legislative power. It is urged that the authority which can declare the acts of another void must necessarily be superior to the one whose acts must be declared void." Since this is true and since the Constitution that Hamilton is defending does *not* give judicial review to the Supreme Court, Hamilton does a most interesting dance about the subject. The Constitution is the "fundamental law" and derives from the people. If the legislative branch does something unconstitutional it acts against the people and so a disinterested court must protect the people from their own Congress and declare the act void.

> Nor does this conclusion by any means suppose a superiority of the judicial to the legislative power. It only supposes that the power of the people is superior to both, and that where the will of the legislature, declared in its statutes, stands in opposition to that of the people, declared in the Constitution, the judges ought to be governed by the latter rather than the former.

This is breathtaking, even for Hamilton. He has now asserted that a court of life appointees (chosen from the rich and wellborn) is more interested in the rights of the people than the House of Representatives, the only more or less democratically elected branch of the government. But Hamilton is speaking with the tongue of a prophet who knows which god he serves. The future in this, as in so much else, was what Hamilton had envisaged, constitutional or not. Characteristically, by 1802, he had dismissed the Constitution as "a frail and worthless fabric."

Marshall was most sensitive to the charge of judicial usurpation of congressional primacy; and during the rest of his long tenure on the bench, he never again found an act of Congress unconstitutional. But Marshall was not finished with republic-shaping. Although he shared the Framers' passion for the rights of property, he did not share the admittedly subdued passion of certain Framers for the rights of the citizens. In 1833, Marshall proclaimed (speaking for a majority of his Court in *Barron* v. *City of Baltimore*) that the Bill of Rights was binding only upon the federal government and not upon the states. In order to pull off this caper, Marshall was obliged to separate the amendments from the Constitution proper so that he could then turn to Article VI, Paragraph 2, where it is written that this Constitution (pre–Bill of Rights) "shall be the supreme law of the land . . . any thing in the Constitution or laws of any state to the contrary not withstanding." Apparently, the first ten amendments were not an integral part of "this Constitution."

The result of Marshall's decision was more than a century of arbitrary harassment of individuals by sheriffs, local police, municipal and state governing bodies—to none of whom the Bill of Rights was held to apply. As for the federal government, the Supreme Court was only rarely and feebly willing to enforce the rights of citizens against it. It is startling to think that the Supreme Court did not seriously begin to apply the Bill of Rights to the states until the 1930s despite the Fourteenth Amendment (1868), which had spelled out the rights of citizens. Gradually, over the last thirty years, an often grudging court has doled out to the people of the United States (including Mr. Brown) most of those rights which George Mason had wanted them to have in 1793.

Fifty-four years after *Marbury* v. *Madison*, the Supreme Court found a second act of Congress unconstitutional. In order to return property to its owner (the slave Dred Scott to his master Dr. Emerson), the Supreme Court declared unconstitutional the Missouri Compromise; and made inevitable the Civil War. It was ironic that the Court which Hamilton had so Jesuitically proposed as a defender of the people against a wicked legislature should, in its anxiety to protect property of any kind, have blundered onto a stage where it had neither competence nor even provenance. (Article IV: "The Congress shall have power to dispose of and make all needful rules and regulations respecting the territory or other property belonging to the United States. . . .") But the wild card had now been played. Judicial review was a fact. The Court was now ready—give or take a Civil War or two—to come into its unconstitutional own.

In 1864, the Court struck down the income tax, denying Congress its absolute power to raise revenue; and not until the passage of the Sixteenth Amendment (1913) did Congress get back its right, in this instance, to raise taxes—which it can never *not* have had, under the Constitution. But as Lundberg says, "The Court had gained nearly eighteen years of tax-free bliss for its patrons although it was shown to be out of harmony with the thinking of the country as well as that of the framers, previous courts, and legal scholars—and the Constitution."

From March 9, 1865 (when the management of the reigning Republican party became almost totally corrupt), to 1970, ninety acts of Congress were held void in whole or in part. Most of these decisions involved property, and favored large property owners. As of 1970, the Court had also managed to overrule itself 143 times. Plainly, the Constitution that the justices keep interpreting and reinterpreting is a more protean document than the Framers suspected. "The trouble with the Constitution of the United States," wrote the *London Chronicle* a century ago, "is that nobody has ever been able to find out what it means." Or, put another way, since everybody knows what it means, much trouble must be taken to distort the meaning in order to make new arrangements for the protection of property.

Lundberg takes the position that, by and large, the Court's behavior is the result of a tacit consensus among the country's rulers: that two percent of the population—or one percent, or sixty families, or those *active* members of the Bohemian Club—owns most of the wealth of a country that is governed by the ruler's clients in the three branches of government. On those occasions when their Congress is forced by public opinion to pass laws that they do not want enacted, like the income tax of 1864, they can count either on their president's veto or on the Court's invocation of the Constitution to get Congress off the hook. The various courts are so devised, Lundberg writes, as to "rescue the legislatures and executives from their own reluctant acts."

Except for the passing of the Sixteenth Amendment, Congress has made only two serious attempts to reclaim its constitutional primacy over the Court (as opposed to a lot of unserious attempts). The first was in 1868. The House Judiciary Committee, fearful that the Court would strike down a number of reconstruction acts, reported a bill requiring that two-thirds of a court's judges must concur in any opinion adverse to the law. This bill passed the House but died in the Senate. In the same year, the House did manage to pass a law (over presidential veto) to limit certain of the Court's appellate powers. On March 19, 1869, the Court unanimously bowed to Congress, with a sideswipe to the effect that although the Constitution did vest them with appellate powers, the clause that their powers were conferred "with such exceptions and under such Regulations as Congress shall make" must be honored.

This is one of the few times that Congress has asserted directly its constitutional primacy over a Court that for the next seventy years took upon itself more and more the powers not only to review any and all acts of Congress but to make law itself, particularly when it came to preventing the regulation of corporations or denying rights to blacks. During the last forty years, although the Court has tended to stand aside on most economic matters and to intervene on racial ones, the Court's record of self-aggrandizement has been equaled only by that of the Johnny-come-lately wild card, the president.

The first fifteen presidents adjusted themselves to their roomy constitutional cage and except for an occasional rattling of the bars (the Alien and Sedition Acts) and one break-out (the Louisiana Purchase) they were fairly docile prisoners of Article II. In 1860, the election of the sixteenth president caused the Union to collapse. By the time that Abraham Lincoln took office, the southern states had organized themselves into what they called a confederacy, in imitation of the original pre-Constitution republic. As Lincoln himself had declared in 1847, any state has the moral and, implicitly, constitutional right to govern itself. But permissive Congressman Lincoln was not stern President Lincoln. Firmly he put to one side the Constitution. On his own authority, he levied troops and made war; took unappropriated money from the Treasury; suspended habeas corpus. When the aged Chief Justice Taney hurled the Constitution at Lincoln's head, the president ducked and said that, maybe, all things considered, Congress ought now to authorize him to do what he had already done, which Congress did.

Lincoln's constitutional defense for what he had done rested upon the oath that he had sworn to "preserve, protect and defend the Constitution" as well as to see to it "that the law be faithfully executed." Lincoln proved to be a satisfactory dictator; and the Union was preserved. But the balances within the constitution of the Second Republic had been forever altered. With the adoption of the Thirteenth, Fourteenth, and Fifteenth Amendments extending the vote to blacks (and, by 1920, to women and, by 1970, to eighteen- to twenty-year-olds) while ensuring, yet again, that no state can "deprive any person of life, liberty, or property without the process of law; nor deny to any person within its jurisdiction the equal protection of the laws," the Bill of Rights was at last, officially at least, largely applicable to the people who lived in the states that were again united.

Needless to say, the Supreme Court, often witty if seldom wise, promptly interpreted the word "person" to mean not only a human being but a corporate entity as well. During the next fifty years, the Court continued to serve the propertied interests against any attack from the other branches of government while ignoring, as much as possible, the rights of actual persons. Any state that tried to curb through law the excesses of any corporation was sure to be reminded by the Court that it had no such right.

But the Third Republic had been born; the electorate had been expanded; and civil rights were on the books if not engraved in letters of fire upon the hearts of the judiciary. Although the presidents pretty much confined themselves to their constitutional duties, the memory of Lincoln was—and is—a constant stimulus to the ambitious chief magistrate who knows that once the nation is at war his powers are truly unlimited, while the possibilities of personal glory are immeasurable.

At the turn of the century Theodore Roosevelt nicely arranged a war for his president, McKinley, who did not particularly want one. In 1917 Wilson arranged a war which neither Congress nor nation wanted. Since then the presidents have found foreign wars irresistible. With the surrender of Japan in 1945, the last official war ended. But the undeclared wars—or "police actions"—now began with a vengeance and our presidents are very much on the march. Through secret organizations like the CIA, they subvert foreign governments, organize invasions of countries they do not like, kill or try to kill foreign leaders while spying, illegally, on American citizens. The presidents have fought two major wars—in Korea and Vietnam—without any declaration of war on the part of Congress.

Finally, halfway through the executives' war in Vietnam, the sluggish venal Congress became alarmed—not to mention hurt—at the way they had been disregarded by Johnson Augustus. The Senate Committee on Foreign Relations began to ask such questions as, by what inherent right does a president make war whenever he chooses? On March 8, 1966, the president (through a State Department memorandum) explained the facts of life to Congress:

"since the Constitution was adopted there have been at least 125 instances in which the President has ordered the armed forces to take action or maintain positions abroad without obtaining prior Congressional authorization, starting with the 'undeclared war' with France (1798–1800). . . ." Congress surrendered as they had earlier when the inexorable Johnson used a murky happening in the Tonkin Bay to ensure their compliance to his war. It was not until many thousands of deaths later that Congress voted to stop funds for bombing the Indochinese.

How did the president break out of his cage? The bars were loosened by Lincoln, and the jimmy that he used was the presidential oath, as prescribed by the Constitution: "I do solemnly swear that I will faithfully execute the Office of President of the United States, and will to the best of my ability, preserve, protect, and defend the Constitution of the United States." Lincoln put the emphasis on the verb "defend" because he was faced with an armed insurrection. Later presidents, however, have zeroed in on the verb "execute"—as broad a verb, in this context, as any president on the loose could wish for. From this innocuous-seeming word have come the notions of inherent executive power and executive privilege, and that astonishing fact with which we have been obliged to live for half a century, the executive order.

Congress and Court can be bypassed by an executive order except on very odd occasions such as Truman's unsuccessful seizure of the steel mills. When Wilson's request to arm merchant American ships was filibustered to death by the Senate in 1917, Wilson issued an executive order, arming the ships. Later, still on his own, Wilson sent troops to Russia to support the czar; concluded the armistice of 1918; and introduced Jim Crow to Washington's public places. In 1936 Franklin Roosevelt issued a secret executive order creating what was later to become, in World War II, the OSS, and then in peacetime (sic) the CIA. This vast enterprise has never been even moderately responsive to the Congress that obediently funds it. The CIA is now the strong secret arm of the president and no president is about to give it up.

For all practical purposes the Third Republic is now at an end. The president is a dictator who can only be replaced either in the quadrennial election by a clone or through his own incompetency, like Richard Nixon, whose neurosis it was to shoot himself publicly and repeatedly in, as they say, the foot. Had Nixon not been helicoptered out of the White House, men in white would have taken him away. The fact that we are living in an era of one-term presidents does not lessen, in any way, the formidable powers of the executive.

The true history of the executive order has yet to be written. As of December 31, 1975, the presidents had issued 11,893 executive orders. The Constitution makes no allowances for them. In fact, when an order wages war or spends money, it is unconstitutional. But precedents can always, tortuously, be found for the president to "execute his office." In 1793, Washington proclaimed that the United States was neutral in the war between England and France, in contravention of the treaty of 1778 which obliged the United States to come to France's aid. In 1905 the Senate declined to approve a treaty that Theodore Roosevelt wanted to make with Santo Domingo. Ever brisk and pugnacious, TR made an agreement on his own; and a year later the Senate ratified it. In 1940 Franklin Roosevelt gave England fifty destroyers that were not his to give. But three years earlier, the Supreme Court had validated the principle of the executive *agreement* (*U.S.* v. *Belmont*); as a result, the executive agreement and the executive order are now for the usurper president what judicial review has been for the usurper Court.

Law by presidential decree is an established fact. But, as Lundberg notes, it is odd that there has been no effective challenge by Congress to this usurpation of its powers by the executive. Lundberg quotes the late professor Edward S. Corwin of Princeton, a constitutional scholar who found troubling the whole notion of government by decree: "It would be more accordant," wrote Corwin in *Court Over Constitution*,* "with American ideas of government by law to require, before a purely executive agreement to be applied in the field of private rights, that it be supplemented by a sanctioning act of Congress. And that Congress, which can repeal any treaty as 'law of the land or authorization' can do the same to executive agreements would seem to be obvious." Obvious—but ignored by a Congress more concerned with the division of the contents of the pork barrel than with the defense of its own powers.

Between a president ruling by decrees, some secret and some not, and a Court making policy through its peculiar powers of judicial review, the Congress has ceased to be of much consequence. Although a number of efforts were made in the Congress during the

---

* Princeton University Press, 1950.

Fifties to put the president back in his cage and to deflect the Court from its policymaking binges, nothing substantive was passed by a Congress which, according to Lundberg, "is no more anxious to restrict the president than it is to restrict the Supreme Court. Congress prefers to leave them both with a free hand, reserving the right at all times to blame them if such a tactic fits the mood of the electorate." When Congress rejected Carter's energy program, it was not blocking a president who might well have got around it with an executive order. Congress was simply ducking responsibility for a gasoline tax just as the president had ducked it by maliciously including them in the process. Actually, Congress does, from time to time, discipline presidents, but it tends to avoid collisions with the principle of the executive order when wielded by the lonely Oval One. So does the Supreme Court. Although the Court did stop President Truman from seizing the steel mills in the course of the Korean (by executive order) War, the Court did not challenge the principle of the executive order per se.

Since the main task of government is the collection of money through taxes and its distribution through appropriations, the blood of the Third Republic is the money-labor of a population which pays taxes to support an executive establishment of some ten million people if one includes the armed forces. This is quite a power base, as it includes the Pentagon and the CIA—forever at war, covertly or overtly, with monolithic communism. "Justice is the end of government," wrote Madison (*Federalist Paper* No. 52). "It is the end of civil society. It ever has been and ever will be pursued until it is obtained, or until liberty be lost in the pursuit." Time to start again the hard pursuit.

It was the wisdom of Julius Caesar and his heir Octavian to keep intact the ancient institutions of the Roman republic while changing entirely the actual system of government. The new dynasty reigned as traditional consuls, not as kings. They visited regularly their peers in the Senate—in J.C.'s case once too often. This respect for familiar forms should be borne in mind when We the People attend the second constitutional convention. President, Senate, House of Representatives must be kept as familiar entities just as their actual functions must be entirely altered.

Thomas Jefferson thought that there should be a constitutional convention at least once a generation because "laws and institutions must go hand in hand with the progress of the human mind. As that becomes more developed, more enlightened, as new discoveries are made, new truths disclosed, and manners and opinions change with the change of circumstances, institutions must advance also, and keep pace with the times. We might as well require a man to wear still the coat which fitted him as a boy, as a civilized society to remain ever under the regimen of their barbarous ancestors." Jefferson would be amazed to see how the boy's jacket of his day has now become the middle-aged man's straitjacket of ours. The amended Constitution of today is roomier than it was, and takes into account the national paunch; but there is little freedom to move the arms because, in Herder's words, "The State is happiness for a group" and no state has ever, willingly, spread that happiness beyond the group which controls it. The so-called "iron law of oligarchy," noted by James Madison, has always obtained in the United States.

Ten years ago Rexford Guy Tugwell, the old New Dealer, came up with Version XXXVII of a constitution that he had been working on for some years at the Center for the Study of Democratic Institutions at Santa Barbara. Tugwell promptly makes the mistake that Julius Caesar and family did not make. Tugwell changes names, adds new entities. Yet the old unwieldy tripartite system is not really challenged and the result is pretty conventional at heart because "I believe," said Tugwell, explaining his new arrangements, "in the two-party system." One wonders why.

The Framers wanted no political parties—or factions. It was their view that all right-minded men of property would think pretty much alike on matters pertaining to property. To an extent, this was—and is—true. Trilateral Commissions exist as shorthand symbols of this meeting of minds and purses. But men are hungry for political office. Lincoln felt that if the United States was ever destroyed it would be by the hordes of people who wanted to be office-holders and to live for nothing at government expense—a vice, he added dryly, "from which I myself am not free."

By 1800 there were two political parties, each controlled by a faction of the regnant oligarchy. Today, despite close to two centuries of insurrections and foreign wars, of depressions and the usurpations by this or that branch of government of powers not accorded, there are still two political parties, each controlled by a faction of the regnant oligarchy. The fact that the country is so much larger than it was makes for an appearance of variety. But the substance of the two-party system or non-system is unchanged. Those with large amounts of property control the parties which control the state which takes through taxes the people's money and gives a certain amount of it back in order to keep docile the populace while reserving a sizable part of tax revenue for the oligarchy's use in the form of "purchases" for the defense department, which is the unnumbered, as it were, bank account of the rulers.

As Walter Dean Burnham puts it, "The state is primarily in business to promote capital accumulation and to maintain social harmony and legitimacy." But expensive and pointless wars combined with an emphasis on the consumption of goods at the expense of capital creation has called into question the legitimacy of the oligarchy's government. Even the dullest consumer has got the point that no matter how he casts his vote for president or for Congress, his interests will never be represented because the oligarchy serves only itself. It should be noted that this monomania can lead to anomalies. In order to buy domestic tranquillity, Treasury money in the form of transfer-payments to the plebes now accounts for some 79 percent of the budget—which cannot, by law, be cut back.

In the 1976 presidential election, 45.6 percent of those qualified to vote did not vote. According to Burnham, of those who did vote, 48.5 percent were blue-collar and service workers. Of those who did not vote, 75 percent were blue-collar and service workers. The pattern is plain. Nearly 70 percent of the entire electorate are blue-collar and service workers. Since only 20 percent of this class are unionized, natural interest requires that many of these workers belong together in one party. But as 49 percent of the electorate didn't vote in 1980, the "two-party system" is more than ever meaningless and there is no chance of a labor party—or of any party other than that of the status quo.

The regnant minority is genuinely terrified of a new constitutional convention. They are happier with the way things are, with half the electorate permanently turned off and the other half mildly diverted by presidential elections in which, despite a semblance of activity, there is no serious choice. For the last two centuries the debate has been going on as to whether or not the people can be trusted to govern themselves. Like most debates, this one has been so formulated that significant alternative ideas are excluded at the start. "There are nations," said Herzen, "but not states." He saw the nation-state as, essentially, an evil—and so it has proved most of the time in most places during this epoch (now ending) of nation-states which can be said to have started, in its current irritable megalomaniacal form, with Bismarck in Germany and Lincoln in the United States.

James Madison's oligarchy, by its very nature, cannot and will not share power. We are often reminded that some 25 percent of the population are comprised of (in Lundberg's words) "the super-annuated, the unskilled, the immature of all ages, the illiterate, the improvident propagators, the mentally below par or disordered" as well as "another 25 percent only somewhat better positioned and liable at any turn or whirligig of circumstances to find themselves in the lower category." As Herzen, in an unhappy mood, wrote, "Who that respects the truth would ask the opinion of the first man he meets? Suppose Columbus or Copernicus had put to the vote the existence of America or the movement of the earth?" Or as a successful movie executive, in a happy mood, once put it: "When the American public walks, its knuckles graze the ground."

The constant search for external enemies by the oligarchy is standard stuff. All dictators and ruling groups indulge in this sort of thing, reflecting Machiavelli's wisdom that the surest way to maintain one's power over the people is to keep them poor and on a wartime footing. We fought in Vietnam to contain China, which is now our Mao-less friend; today we must have a showdown with Russia, in order to. . . . One has already forgotten the basis for the present quarrel. No. Arms race. That's it. They are outstripping us in warheads, or something. On and on the propaganda grinds its dismal whine. Second to none. Better to die in Afghanistan than Laguna. We must not lose the will. . . .

There are signs that the American people are beginning to tire of all of this. They are also angry at the way that their money is taken from them and wasted on armaments—although they have been sufficiently conned into thinking that armaments are as good as loafers on welfare and bureaucrats on the Treasury teat are bad. Even so, they believe that too much is being taken away from them; and that too little ever comes back.

Since Lundberg began his career as an economist, it is useful to quote him at length on how the oligarchy operates the economy—acting in strict accordance with the letter if not the spirit of the three constitutions.

The main decision that Congress and the President make that is of steady effect on the citizenry concerns appropriations—that is, how much is to be spent up to and beyond a half-trillion dollars and what for. The proceeds are supposed to come from taxes but here, in response to citizen sensitivity, the government tends to understate the cost. Because the government has taken to spending more than it takes in, the result is inflation—a steady rise in the prices of goods and services.

The difference between what it spends and what it takes in the government makes up by deviously operating the money-printing machine, so that the quantity of money in circulation exceeds the quantity of goods and services. Prices therefore tend to rise and money and money-values held by citizens decline in purchasing value. . . .

All that the government has been doing in these respects is strictly constitutional. For the Constitution empowers it, first, to lay taxes without limit (Article I, Section 8, Paragraph 1). It is empowered in the very next paragraph to borrow money on the credit of the United States—that is, the taxpayers—also without limit. . . . As to inflation, Paragraph 5 empowers the government, through Congress and the President, not only to coin money but to "regulate the value thereof." In other words, under the Constitution a dollar is worth whatever Congress and the President determine it to be by their fiscal decisions, and for nearly three decades officials, Republican and Democratic alike, have decreed that it be worth less. . . .

When Congress and president over-appropriate, the Treasury simply prints

> . . . short-term notes and bonds and sends these over to the Federal Reserve Bank, the nation's central bank. In receipt of these securities, the Federal Reserve simply credits the Treasury with a deposit for the total amount. The Treasury draws checks against these deposits. And these checks are new money. Or the Treasury may simply offer the securities for sale in the open market, receiving therefore the checks of buyers.

Since there is no legal way to control either president or Congress under the current system, it is inevitable that there would be a movement for radical reform. The National Taxpayers Union was organized to force the federal government to maintain a balanced budget. In order to accomplish this, it will be necessary to

change the Constitution. So the National Taxpayers Union has
called for a new constitutional convention. To date, thirty state
legislatures have said yes to that call. When thirty-four state
legislatures ask for a new convention, there will be one. As Professor Gerald Gunther of Stanford Law School recently wrote:

> The convention delegates would gather after popular elections—
> elections where the platforms and debates would be outside con-
> gressional control, where interest groups would seek to raise issues
> other than the budget, and where some successful candidates
> would no doubt respond to those pressures. Those convention
> delegates could claim to be legitimate representatives of the
> people. And they could make a plausible—and I believe correct—
> argument that a convention is entitled to set its own agenda. . . .*

Those who fear that Milton Friedman's cheerful visage will be
swiftly hewn from Dakota rock underestimate the passion of the
majority not to be unemployed in a country where the gap between
rich and poor is, after France, the greatest in the Western world.
Since the welfare system is the price that the white majority pays
in order to exclude the black minority from the general society,
entirely new social arrangements will have to be made if that
system is to be significantly altered.

Predictably, the oligarchs and their academic advisers view with
alarm any radical change. The Bill of Rights will be torn to shreds,
they tell us. Abortion will be forbidden by the Constitution while
prayers will resonate in the classrooms of the Most Christian Republic. The oligarchs think that the people are both dangerous and
stupid. Their point is moot. But we do know that the oligarchs are
a good deal more dangerous to the polity that the people at large.
Predictions that civil rights would have a rocky time at a new
convention ignore the reality that the conglomeration of groups at-
tending it will each have residual ethnic, ideological, religious, and
local interests whose expression they will not want stifled. It is by
no means clear that civil liberties would be submerged at a new
convention; and there is no reason why the delegates should not
decide that a Supreme Court of some sort should continue to act

---

* "Constitutional Roulette: The Dimensions of the Risk" in *The Constitution and
the Budget*, edited by W. S. Moore and Rudolph G. Penner (American Enterprise Institute for Public Policy Research, Washington and London, 1980).

as protector of the Bill of Rights—a better protector, perhaps, than the court that recently separated a Mr. Snepp from his royalties.

The forms of the first three republics should be retained. But the presidency should be severely limited in authority, and shorn of the executive order and the executive agreement. The House of Representatives should be made not only more representative but whoever can control a majority will be the actual chief of government, governing through a cabinet chosen from the House. This might render it possible for the United States to have, for the first time in two centuries, real political parties. Since the parliamentary system works reasonably well in the other industrially developed democracies, there is no reason why it should not work for us. Certainly our present system does not work, as the late election demonstrated.

Under a pure parliamentary system the Supreme Court must be entirely subservient to the law of the land, which is made by the House of Representatives; and judicial review by the Court must join the executive order on the junk-heap of history. But any parliamentary system that emerged from a new constitutional convention would inevitably be a patchwork affair in which a special niche could, and no doubt would, be made for a judicial body to protect and enforce the old Bill of Rights. The Senate should be kept as a home for wise men, much like England's House of life-Lords. One of the Senate's duties might be to study the laws of the House of Representatives with an eye to their constitutionality, not to mention rationality. There should be, at regular intervals, national referenda on important subjects. The Swiss federal system provides some interesting ideas; certainly their cantonal system might well be an answer to some of our vexing problems—particularly, the delicate matter of bilingualism.

The First Constitution will be two hundred years old in 1987— as good a date as any to finish the work of the second constitutional convention, which will make possible our Fourth Republic, and first—ah, the note of optimism!—civilization.

The New York Review of Books
FEBRUARY 5, 1981

A Note on
Abraham Lincoln

In "Patriotic Gore," Edmund Wilson wrote, "There are moments when one is tempted to feel that the cruelest thing that has happened to Lincoln since he was shot by Booth has been to fall into the hands of Carl Sandburg." The late Mr. Sandburg was a public performer of the first rank ("Ker-oh-seen!" he crooned in one of the first TV pitches for the jet-engine—ole banjo on his knee, white hair mussed by the jet-stream), a poet of the second rank (who can ever forget that feline-footed fog?) and a biographer of awesome badness. Unfortunately, the success of his four-volume *Abraham Lincoln: The War Years* was total. In the course of several million clumsily arranged words, Sandburg managed to reduce one of the most interesting and subtle men in world history to a cornball Disneyland waxwork rather like . . . yes, Carl Sandburg himself.

The real Lincoln is elsewhere. He is to be found, for those able to read old prose, in his own writings. According to Lincoln's law partner William Herndon: "He was the most continuous and severest thinker in America. He read but little and that for an end. Politics was his Heaven and his Hades metaphysics." Lincoln read and reread Shakespeare; he studied Blackstone's legal commentaries. And that was about it. Biographies bored him; he read no novels. Yet, somehow (out of continuous and severe thinking?), he became a master of our most difficult language, and the odd music to his sentences is unlike that of anyone else—with the possible exception of Walt Whitman on a clear unweepy day.

The principal source for Lincoln's pre-presidential life is Herndon. For eighteen years they were close friends as well as colleagues; they traveled the circuit together in Illinois; they shared an office in Springfield. After Lincoln was murdered, Herndon began to collect every bit of information that he could find about his fallen friend. Unlike most obscure associates of the great, Herndon was not interested in cutting Lincoln down to valet-size; or even to cash in. In fact, Herndon generously gave to any and every biographer not only his personal recollections of Lincoln but the notes that he had compiled during his long investigation of Lincoln's somewhat murky antecedents. Since Lincoln was said to have been illegitimate, Herndon talked to those who had known his mother, Nancy Hanks, and her husband, Thomas Lincoln. Herndon was told by an eyewitness that Thomas (viewed in the old swimming hole) dramatically lacked a number of those parts that are necessary for propagation. After studying all the evidence, Herndon decided that Thomas must have started out fully equipped and so was able to father Abraham off Nancy Hanks who was, according to Lincoln himself, illegitimate: "the daughter of a Virginia grandee." Romantics have often suggested that John C. Calhoun was Nancy's father. But if Lincoln knew who his real grandfather was, he never told Herndon.

The Sandburg–Mount Rushmore Lincoln is a solemn gloomy cuss, who speaks only in iambic pentameter, a tear forever at the corner of his eye—the result, no doubt, of being followed around by the Mormon Tabernacle Choir, which keeps humming "The Battle Hymn of the Republic" behind him while the future ambassador Shirley Temple Black curls up in his lap. The official Lincoln is warm, gentle, shy, modest . . . everything a great man is supposed to be in Sandburg-land but never is in life. As Lincoln's secretary John Hay put it: "No great man is ever modest. It was his intellectual arrogance and unconscious assumption of superiority that men like Chase and Sumner could never forgive."

The actual Lincoln was cold and deliberate, reflective and brilliant. In private life, he had no intimates except Herndon—and their relationship ended when he became president. In family life, Lincoln was most forbearing of Mary Todd—a highly intelligent woman who went mad; and he spoiled his sons. That was the extent of the private Lincoln. The rest was public.

Honest Abe the rail-splitter was the creation of what must have been the earliest all-out PR campaign for a politician. Lincoln was born poor; but so were a great many successful lawyers in his part of the world. By the time he was elected president, he was a well-to-do lawyer, representing the railroad interests as well as the common man. From the beginning, Lincoln knew he was going to be, somehow, great. "His ambition," wrote Herndon, "was a little engine that knew no rest."

Herndon has his biases. He disliked Mary Todd and he tends to exaggerate her bad temper while pushing the story of Lincoln's love for Anne Rutledge, a highly dubious business. Usually, when Herndon repeats secondhand stories, he says that they are just that. When he speaks with firsthand knowledge, he is to be trusted.

It will come as a terrible shock to many of those who have been twice-born in the capacious bosom of Jesus to learn that Lincoln not only rejected Christianity but wrote a small book called "Infidelity" (meaning lack of faith in God). Lincoln "read his manuscript to Samuel Hill, his employer (who) said to Lincoln: 'Lincoln, let me see your manuscript.' Lincoln handed it to him. Hill ran it in a tin-plate stove, and so the book went up in flames. Lincoln in that production attempted to show that the Bible was false: first on the grounds of reason, and, second, because it was self-contradictory; that Jesus was not the son of God any more than any man." Later, in the presidency, pressure was brought on Lincoln to start putting God into his speeches. At the beginning, he did so in the vague sense of the Almighty or heaven. Later, there is a good deal of God in the speeches but no mention of Jesus. At heart, Lincoln was a fatalist, a materialist of the school of Democritus and Lucretius.

Devotees of the Mount Rushmore school of history like to think that the truly great man is a virgin until his wedding night; and a devoted monogamist thereafter. Apparently, Lincoln was indeed "true as steel" to Mary Todd even though, according to Herndon, "I have seen women make advances and I have seen Lincoln reject or refuse them. Lincoln had terrible strong passions for women, could scarcely keep his hands off them, and yet he had honor and a strong will, and these enabled him to put out the fires of his terrible passion." But in his youth he was seriously burned by those fires. In the pre-penicillin era syphilis was epidemic—and, usually, incurable. According to Herndon: "About the year 1835–36 Mr. Lincoln went to Beardstown and during a devilish passion had connection with a girl and caught the disease. Lincoln told me this. . . ." Later, after a long siege, Lincoln was cured, if he was cured, by a Dr. Daniel Drake of Cincinnati.

Herndon suspected that Lincoln might have given Mary Todd syphilis. If he had, that would have explained the premature deaths of the three Lincoln children: "Poor boys, they are dead now and gone! I should like to *know* one thing and that is: What caused the death of these children? I have an opinion which I shall never state to anyone." So states to everyone Herndon. The autopsy on Mary Todd showed a physical deterioration of the brain consistent with paresis. If Lincoln had given his wife syphilis and if he had, inadvertently, caused the death of his children, the fits of melancholy are now understandable—and unbearably tragic.

The public Lincoln has been as mythologized as the private Lincoln. As a congressman, he had opposed the 1846 war with Mexico—a nasty business, started by us in order to seize new territories. In a speech that was to haunt him thirteen years later, he declared, "Any people anywhere being inclined and having the power have the right to rise up and shake off the existing government, and form a new one that suits them better. . . . Any portion of such people that can may revolutionize and make their own so much of the territory as they inhabit." When the South chose to follow Congressman Lincoln's advice, President Lincoln said they could not go. When confronted with his 1848 declaration, he remarked, rather lamely, "You would hardly think much of a man who is not wiser today than he was yesterday."

Although a small part of the country in 1860 (and all of the Mount Rushmoreites since) took it for granted that the main issue of the Civil War was the abolition of slavery, the actual issue was the preservation of the Union. Lincoln took the position that the South could not leave the Union. When the southern states said that they had every right to go, Lincoln shifted the argument to a positively mystical level: the Union was an absolute, to be preserved at all costs. As for slavery: "If slavery is not wrong, then nothing is wrong," he said. But: "If I can save the Union without freeing any slaves, I will do that. If I can save the Union by freeing some and leaving others alone, I will do that."

As it was, in the third year of his administration, he freed all the slaves in the states that had rebelled but he maintained slavery in the border states that had remained loyal to the Union. This did not go down very well in the world. But Lincoln knew what he was doing: First, the Union; then abolition.

Early in Lincoln's administration he acquired land in Central America for the newly freed blacks. "Why," he said to a black delegation, "should the people of your race be colonized, and where? Why should they leave this country? This is, perhaps, the first question for proper consideration. You and we are different races. We have between us a broader difference than exists between almost any other two races. Whether it is right or wrong I need not discuss; but this physical difference is a great disadvantage to us both, as I think. Your race suffers very greatly, many of them, by living among us, while ours suffers from your presence. In a word, we suffer on each side. If this is admitted, it affords a reason, at least, why we should be separated." Although Lincoln was at his dialectical best, the blacks did not want to leave a country which, as slaves, they had helped to build. Lincoln had no further solution to the problem.

The real Lincoln was a superb politician. He knew when to wait; when to act. He had the gift of formulating, most memorably, ideas whose time had, precisely, on the hour, as it were, come. He could also balance opposites with exquisite justice. As the war was ending, he said, "Neither party expected for the war the magnitude or the duration which it has already attained. Neither anticipated that the cause of the conflict might cease with, or even before, the conflict itself should cease. Each looked for an easier triumph, and a result less fundamental and astounding. Both read the same Bible, and pray to the same God; and each invokes his aid against the other. It may seem strange that any man should dare to ask a just God's assistance in wringing their bread from the sweat of other men's faces; but let us judge not, that we be not judged. The prayers of both could not be answered—that of neither has been answered fully. . . ."

As for himself: "I feel a presentiment that I shall not outlast the rebellion. When it is over, my work is done." The work was done;

and so was he. But for a century Lincoln's invention, the American nation-state, flourished. Now, as things begin to fall apart, Lincoln's avatar will have his work cut out for him, repairing that memorial we have so fecklessly damaged, the Union—or finding something better to put in its place.

The Los Angeles Times
FEBRUARY 8, 1981

GORE VIDAL wrote his first novel, *Williwaw*, at the age of nineteen while overseas in World War II.

During three decades as a writer, Vidal has written with success and distinction novels, plays, short stories and essays. He has also been a political activist. As a Democratic candidate for Congress from upstate New York, he received the most votes of any Democrat there in half a century. From 1970 to 1972 he was co-chairman of the People's Party.

In 1948 Vidal wrote the highly praised, highly condemned novel *The City and the Pillar*, the first American work to deal sympathetically with homosexuality. In the next six years he produced *The Judgment of Paris* and the prophetic *Messiah*. In the fifties Vidal wrote plays for live television and films for Metro-Goldwyn-Mayer. One of the television plays became the successful Broadway play *Visit to a Small Planet*. Directly for the theatre he wrote the prizewinning *The Best Man*.

In 1964 Vidal returned to the novel. In succession, he created three remarkable works: *Julian*, *Washington, D.C.*, *Myra Breckinridge*. Each was a number-one best seller in the United States and England. In 1973 Vidal produced his most popular novel, *Burr*, as well as the volume of collected essays, *Homage to Daniel Shays*. In 1976, thirty years after the publication of *Williwaw*, Vidal wrote *1876*, which, along with *Burr* and *Washington, D.C.*, completed his American Trilogy.

In 1981 he published *Creation*, generally acclaimed as "his best novel." Vidal lives in Los Angeles.